**Dedicated to those
who seek freedom**

with
Special Thanks

To Frances Adams for her loving assistance to Lester in compiling and preserving the original material for this book. Without her this book would not have been possible.

To Terry Britt and Dee Sell for their long hours in helping to prepare the manuscript.

To the staff and instructors of the Sedona Institute for all they do in assisting others in discovering the value of releasing.

KEYS TO THE
ULTIMATE FREEDOM

**Thoughts and Talks On
Personal Transformation**

By Lester Levenson

*Edited with a foreword by
George Cappannelli*

Sedona Institute
P.O. Box 32685
Phoenix, Arizona 85064-2685

Library of Congress Catalog Card Number: 93-087498

ISBN 0-915721-03-1

First printing 1993

Suggested Retail Price $17.97

"You are an unlimited Being. You always were and you always will be, you have no choice in that. Your only choice is to identify with your unlimited Beingness, or to identify with your self imposed limitations."

Lester Levenson

Here's to your Freedom!
Love,
Lester

TABLE OF CONTENTS

"We are unlimited beings limited only by the concepts of limitation we hold in our minds." With these few words, Lester Levenson, the founder of the Sedona Institute and originator of the "Release®" Technique" has given us a very powerful key to assist us in letting go of that which prevents us from leading the kind of loving, successful, joyful lives we want. Just 16 words and yet they contain both a concise discription of the obstacle which stands between us and the realization of our dreams and a clear prescription for its removal as well.

This is no small accomplishment. In this complicated, mad paced world where we are constantly bombarded by information and deluged by an endless number of techniques which promise to eliminate everything from flat feet to dandruff, it is rare to find statements as clear, practical and effective as Lester's. Rare and effective are two words which also describe the powerful and practical wisdom Lester shares with us in these private talks; wisdom which helps us better understand ourselves and achieve happiness in our lives. Above all, this wisdom is given to us in the form of specific tools which have been hewn out of the direct, personal experiences of the man who shares them with us.

Indeed, of the many valuable things about this material, this thing stands out most prominently — what Lester Levenson talks about, he knows. And he knows it not just from years of study in traditional academic disciplines, although he has spent ample time there. Instead, Lester's words come from his heart and from a wisdom borne out of first-hand experience. Just a few moments spent with him will convince you of this. Lester Levenson has met and mastered his own dragons.

On the verge of dying in 1952, he was forced to go outside the boundaries of traditional medicine, religion and philosophy to examine and discover a way to sustain his life and to renew his health. On the way to doing this, Lester made a number of significant discoveries. As a result, in just two short months, he went from being an avowed cynic and a non-believer, to a committed advocate of the unlimited power of consciousness and a faithful servant of that deep and abiding sense of unity and oneness which connects all things in Beingness and Love.

Lester also uncovered what he believes is the dominant desire which drives us to seek for some elusive state or condition which we believe or sense exists beyond the cycles of pleasure and pain, satisfaction and dissatisfaction that seem our usual lot. Lester describes this "elusive state" as — **a state of happiness with no sorrow.**

Lester is of course not alone in this belief. Even a cursory review of the wisdom offered us by other sages and poets, mystics and teachers from both past and the present, uncovers ideas which resonate with this common theme:

T.S. Eliot in The Four Quartets, suggests that — "We shall not cease from exploration, And the end of all of our exploring, Will be to arrive where we started, And know the place for the first time... Quick now, here now," he says, "always... A condition of complete simplicity (costing not less than everything)."

In the writings of Depak Chopra, contemporary author, physician and healer, we find the following suggestion: "Every single human being has an aspect of himself which is a non-material field of higher intelligence — a window to a more universal field of infinite possibilities... and when we get in touch with this aspect, we find that it has a computing ability which is far more precise, far more accurate, far more orderly than that which exists in the realm of rational thought."

Loa Tzu begins the third phrase of Tao Te Ching by suggesting — "Hence always rid yourself of desires in order to observe its secrets; But always allow yourself to have desired in order to observe its manifestations. These two are the same but diverge as they issue forth. Being the same they are called mysteries, Mystery upon mystery — The gateway of the manifold secrets."

And the Persian Poet Rumi, who has said it beautifully in so many different ways, tells us this — "O, You my soul's comfort in this season of sorrow, O, You my spirit's treasure in the bitterness of loss! What can't be conceived nor understood, Enters my soul when I worship You."

If we return our attention to Lester's quote, we find that it has more to offer us. **"We are unlimited beings limited only by the concepts of limitation we hold in our mind. So stop being what you are not, a limited body and mind, and just be what you are — an infinite, totally free, grand and flowing being, whole and complete."**

So what is this "state of complete simplicity costing not less than everything"—this "window to a field of infinite possibilities" — this "grand and flowing being, whole and complete"? Even more relevant, "How do we get there?"

This is precisely what these private sessions by Lester are designed to assist us in doing. They speak to the part of us that is all too familiar with the restlessness and dissatisfaction of human existence. They speak to the part that understands that beyond the wounds of childhood confusions or abuses, the disappointments of failed relationships, unhappy marriages, or the loss of loved ones; beyond the pain of illnesses and physical limitations, and the disappointment of careers that do not fulfill our purpose, there is a "state of happiness with no sorrow."

Lester's words also address another primary dilemma. The dilemma of knowing or, at times, sensing what to do, but not being able or willing to do it. Although confronted daily by disappointments; although sensing and occasionally even experiencing the grace of relief, most of us continue to remain victimized by our thoughts and the illusions of mind and emotion which keep up prisoners in a world seemingly not of our making.

This is no small dilemma. It surfaces some of the most fundamental and critical questions of our lives and to answer them, we must get beyond the limitations that Lester speaks so eloquently and clearly of and discover our true nature. We must move outside of what Depak Chopra calls a "fear-based, time-bound reality" to find a state of balance, harmony and happiness.

Before sending you on to explore this rich territory with Lester, there are a few suggestions which may help you on your journey. Each of the talks you are about to read is designed to bring a key theme into your awareness. Each also represents not only thoughts for your mind to digest, but more importantly, energy for your whole being to absorb. Because of this, Lester recommends that you not hurdle your way through them. Instead, read them slowly, allowing enough time for reflection and integration. In short, approach this material as you would a private talk with a good friend. Approach it with an open heart and mind and allow it to deliver its gifts to you. Above all, by working slowly with this material you will give yourself the opportunity to practice many of the powerful and practical tools it contains. If you do this honestly and persistently, you will give yourself a gift of inestimable value. You will discover for yourself a direct link to the source of your own wisdom. You will, as Lester so often says, "come to know that you know." And this, after all, is the ultimate goal of any true teaching.

Finally, it is important for you to know that these sessions are designed to give you a great deal more than a different intellectual perspective on the human condition. For as our guide says repeatedly in the following pages, — "thinking will not get you there." Instead, this material, the questions and answers, the aphorisms, and the suggested exercises are all intended as an introduction to a remarkable, experiential process that is as simple, as clear and as powerful as the words themselves. This process is called the "Release Technique," and it is, quite simply put, a very direct, easy to use way to eliminate the boundaries of thoughts, feelings, emotions and wants which stand between you and self-realization.

So after you have spent time in these sessions, I encourage you to turn to the material in Appendix A and introduce yourself to this innovative, transformation technique which Lester discovered on his journey to personal realization. Through it I believe you will discover a key to achieving the quality of life and consciousness you seek. And I know that through a loving and committed practice of it you will experience that unlimited, joyous and powerful state of being that is our natural right and our natural state.

I wish you a remarkable and joyful adventure.

George Cappannelli
Executive Director
The Sedona Institute

About the Author

I've spent most of my adult life looking for the ultimate truth and happiness. I tried many things — both from the East and the West — but absolutely nothing comes close to the simple and powerful teachings of Lester Levenson.

I met Lester back in 1976 at a seminar I helped organize for a noted organization. I was immediately struck by Lester's presence. He was very different from anyone I had ever met on the spiritual path. He was peaceful and loving with an air of absolute humility and equality. From first hand experience, he had discovered the ultimate truth. He wasn't like all the others who were just a little ahead of me, still striving to get there.

It was a big relief, I felt like I had come home. I knew immediately that working with Lester and his teachings were the reason I had come to be borne in this life. I have never waivered from this realization, nor have I ever regretted it. My life and my own inner peace have continued to flower ever since then. The simple yet powerful truths and techniques that he expounds have left no part of me or my life unchanged for the better.

When I first met Lester, he told me a little about his life and his realizations. What follows is as close as I can come to reproducing his story the way he told it.

"I was born July 19, 1909 in Elizabeth, New Jersey, into a middle class family as a very shy person. I tried to do things the way they were supposed to be done — doing the right thing, getting a good education, and being the best in my field. My natural inclination was towards science, especially the science of the world, and of man himself. I graduated from Rutgers University in 1931 as a physicist, after which I worked 20 some years in physics and engineering. In physics, I worked in research and development on measuring instruments and automatic control, connected with Brown Instrument Co., which later became a subsidiary of Honeywell. And in the engineering field, I worked as a mechanical engineer, an electrical engineer, a construction engineer, a heating and venting engineer, and a marine engineer. Actually, 14 different fields.

I also went into various businesses, including restaurants, lumber, building and oil, intertwined with engineering, wanting to make money—wanting to make it in the world. At that time, I did not know what I now know — that what I was seeking was actually the answers to life itself. Nothing that I had worked at would give me that answer, and as the years went by, I became heavy with depression and with sickness. By 1952, I had been through constant illness — I even had jaundice three or so times a year. I had an enlarged liver, kidney stones, spleen trouble, hyper and hypos acidity, ulcers that perforated and formed lesions, and to top it off, I had at *least* 10 years of migraine headaches. This all culminated in 1952 when I had my second coronary thrombosis.

After the second coronary, I was told I would not live much longer — that I might die any day and shouldn't make the effort to take so much as a step unless I necessarily had to. I was extremely fearful of dying, but I said to myself, "You're still breathing, Lester — there is still a chance." So I sat down and began thinking on an "around the clock" basis. I had been considered a very smart boy. I always made the honor roll. I had been the recipient of a four year scholarship to Rutgers back in the days when not many scholarships were handed out. But then being told after my second heart attack that I wouldn't live, I said to myself, "Lester, you are stupid, stupid, stupid." Having lived 42 or so years, and having reached the end of the line without happiness, without health — therefore all this knowledge you have accumulated is of no avail. I had studied Watson's behaviorism in the 30's and Freud's in the late 30's and early 40's. I had studied the philosophies. I had studied logic. I studied economics. I studied *all* the major fields of man, and with all that knowledge there, I was at the end of the line. This made me realize that the accumulated knowledge of man was of no use.

So I decided to start from scratch. Forget all that knowledge. Begin from point zero and see what you can pick up. So, I posed the question, "What am I?" "What is this World?" "What is my relationship to it?" "What is Mind"? "What is Intelligence?" "What is Happiness?"

I began by asking myself, "What do I want out of life?"... and the answer was happiness. Investigating further, I went into the moment when I was feeling happiest. I discovered something which to me was startling at the time. It was when I was loving that I was happiest. That happiness equated to my capacity to *love* rather than to being loved. That was a starting point.

I began correcting all my thoughts and feelings in that direction from that of wanting to be loved, to that of loving. And in that process, I discovered another major thing that kind of shocked me. I saw that I wanted to change this entire world, and that was the cause of my ulcers — or one of the major causes. In realizing how much I wanted to change things in this world, I saw how it made me a slave of this world, I made the decision to reverse that. And in the process of following out these two directions — actually unloading all the subconscious concepts and pressures in those directions — I discovered I was getting happier, freer, lighter, and feeling better in general.

As I saw this direction was good, I made the decision that if a slice of pie tasted this good, I wanted the whole pie. And I decided not to let go of this direction until I got that entire pie of happiness, and with it the answer to "What am I? What is this life, and what is my relationship to it?" This decision allowed me, as I claim, to get the answer to life itself in a matter of only three months. I believe if I can do it, anyone can do it if they have that much "want to".

In that three month period, all the ailments I had in my physical body corrected. All my miseries dropped away. And I ended up in a place in which I was happy all the time, without sorrow. Not that the world stopped pushing against me — it continued — but I was at a place where I could resolve things almost immediately. Having cleared out the negative fears, all the negative "I can not's," I would focus right on the answer to every problem, and get it very quickly. And so, my whole life turned around from being depressed and sick, to being happy all the time, and being in perfect health all the time.

One of the things that happened in this process was my identification with others. I saw that we are all related, we are all inter-connected — each mind is like a radio broadcasting and receiving station; that we are all tuned into each other unconsciously — that we are just not aware of it. As a lot of the suppressed energies are allowed out, this becomes obvious to us and once we identify with everyone else, it is just natural that we want everyone else to discover what we have discovered. That life was meant to be beautiful... meant to be happy all the time with no sorrow. And to be with perfect health. And so after reaching that high point of understanding in 1952, I have wanted to help others to discover what I had discovered."

Hale Dwoskin
Director of Training
The Sedona Institute

"If we could only be, just be, we could see our infinity. We could see that we are the all."

Lester Levenson

Session 1

THE BASIC GOAL AND WAYS TO ATTAINMENT

THE SEARCH

Everyone is looking for the same thing. All beings, even the animals, are looking for it. And this thing that everyone is looking for is happiness with no sorrow. A continuous state of happiness with no taint whatsoever of sorrow. We can call this a state of "Beingness."

Why is this the Goal? Because imperturbable happiness is our basic nature! And what is imperturbable happiness? Complete and total freedom, the freedom to do or not to do anything and everything. This is our natural state, the state which exists before we encumber it with limitations.

If this is so, why then do most of us not have this continuous happiness with no sorrow? There is only one reason. We have done away with this happiness by thinking, "I am an individual, separate from the All," and in this way as infinite beings, we have assumed limitation.

To make ourselves separate from the All, we must have a means to accomplish this separation — and the means is the mind. And using the mind we create our bodies and the external world. We then get caught up in our own creation and begin searching for the All in the external world, and in the process, create more and more thoughts and more and more matter, until we are so involved in the thoughts and matter that we forget our real identity as the infinite Beingness.

This original thought that "I am separate from the All," necessarily creates a feeling of lack and loneliness, for I can only be satisfied when I am the All. Seeking fulfillment of desire in the world therefore cannot undo the lack since the lack is not in the world in the first place. Lack is a creation of the mind. And yet we go on and on trying to satisfy desire externally. But of course, we never, never succeed. For if we could succeed, we would be able to satisfy desire and therefore all desire would disappear!

The real purpose of being here on this earth then is to learn, or to remember, our original natural state of beingness — a state which allows imperturbable happiness, complete with complete freedom and no limitation. Once we are led to see that this is our natural state, then we can begin to let go of all the limitations.

The prime and the very first limitation is the feeling, "I am an individual separate from the All." Eliminate that and you eliminate all loneliness, all limitation.

To say this another way, "God is all! Let go and let God be. It is not I but the Father who worketh through me." We must let go of the ego sense, which is the original sense of our separation from the All, and allow our natural Being to just be, and then everything will fall perfectly into line.

However, even after this idea is accepted, we do not find it easy to accomplish. We do not find it easy because of habits that have been established since the beginning of time. And for some reason we like these habits, and so we continue them. We call them subconsciously directed behavior. And we go on and on and on behaving automatically, as though we are a victim of our subconscious mind.

Now the subconscious or unconscious mind is really that part of the mind that we have the most trouble looking at! But when our desire for freedom is strong enough, we will dig up these subconscious habits, look at them, and begin to let go of them.

NATURAL BEING

Many people in many spiritual and transformational disciplines believe they must work hard to achieve "beingness," but there is no growing into the natural Being that you are. That Being is whole and perfect, here and now. There is only letting go of the concepts of limitation. The belief that you have limitations — that you have troubles — is in your mind and only in your mind. That is the only place where trouble is, because you can not see or conceive of anything anywhere else but in your mind. Whatever you look at, whatever you hear, whatever you sense, is in and through your mind. That is where everything is. Therefore, if you change your thinkingness, you change your world. Do this and you will have the proof!

So the way to freedom, the path itself, is really quite simple. What is not so simple is the method of undoing the limitations and the reason it is not is because of the force of habit. To overcome this habit, we need a very strong desire. Without a strong desire, there is no growth. This desire, in fact, must be stronger than the desire to control the external world or to have its approval.

THE WORLD AS A DREAM

The world as you now see it is really a product of your imagination and when you see the Truth, the world turns out to be a dream, a fiction created in your mind. First, you will see it as a dream, then you will see it as a dream that never really was. In fact, you will experience it exactly as you do a night dream.

While you are in the night dream, you have a body, there are other bodies, there is action, interaction, there is good and there is bad. And so long as you remain in that night dream, everything there seems real to you. But when you awaken from the night dream, you say, "My gosh, it was just a dream! It never really happened! It was all a dream!" This is exactly the same manner in which you will awaken from this dream called the waking state. You will come to see that it was only a creation of your imagination, only a dream; and then you will let go of it lock, stock, and barrel, and what you will be left with is the infinite you! Then you will call yourself fully realized, totally free.

Actually, we are fully realized all the time. That is part of the irony. We are fully realized Beings saying that we are not. So all we have to do is let go of "we are not" and what is left over is the fully realized and free Being that we are.

THE BEST METHOD

Do you have any questions on what I have said so far? Stop a moment and reflect on what has been said. Perhaps you understand this intellectually, but are unable to use it. If this is the case, you may not be looking at yourself honestly, truthfully, or with a deep enough desire to let go of your limitations. You may have set up in your subconscious mind all the things you will not look at, and allowed them to culminate in inhibitive and compulsive feelings.

If this is so, it may be necessary that you release all the inhibitive and compulsive feelings. You are now run by them. You are now the victim of them. By releasing them, your mind quiets and you become free.

Therefore, undo these limiting feelings and thoughts, quiet the mind, and this infinite Being that you are becomes self-obvious to you. Then you will see that you never were subjected to that mind, that body, and from that moment on, the mind and body will have no influence upon you.

You then determine for the body as you would a puppet, and it has no more effect upon you, any more than a puppet would.

So, the very best method of all methods is to quiet the mind by releasing all subconscious feelings and thoughts, all feelings of wanting approval, wanting control and wanting security. And what is left is the Being that you are.

THE FINAL QUESTION

The final question that everyone must answer is also simple — "What am I?" So my question to you is, "Why not begin with the final question?" If you could, it would be all good, all wonderful. But there are very few of us who are capable of just holding on to "What am I?" We have gotten ourselves so habituated with subconscious thoughts and feelings that we cannot let go of them, and therefore, we need other methods, other aids.

Other major methods from the East are called Jnana Yoga, Raja or Kriya Yoga, Bhakti Yoga, Karma Yoga. The path that is best for you is the one that you like best.

Each path includes all the other paths. The only difference is the emphasis. If we are intellectual, we emphasize the Jnana path, the path of intellect and wisdom. If we are of devotional nature, we emphasize the Bhakti path of love and devotion to God. If we like to be of service to mankind, we use the Karma Yoga path. Each path leads to the quieting of the mind, enough so that we may see the infinite Being that we are.

Since all of the above paths aim to achieve the quieting of the mind, however, why not go directly to the mind itself? It is more direct and practical, and the most efficient of all methods.

In fact, if we go directly to the mind, we will discover that it is simply the totality of all our thoughts, conscious and subconscious, and that all of these past thoughts on particular things have culminated into feelings. These feelings, in turn, now motivate additional thoughts. So, if our thoughts are motivated by our feelings, all we need to do to remember our "infinite beingness" is to release our feelings, the motivators of the thoughts. Then our mind will be quiet and when the mind is quieted, the infinite Being that we are becomes self-obvious. Simple, isn't it?

THE WORLD WE CREATE

Let us now take a look at this apparency called the world. As we have discussed, the world is only our mental creation. It is not external, but is a reality within us, within our mind. Some day you will discover this. Creation begins by first creating what we call a mind, which is a composite of all our thoughts and feelings, conscious and subconscious. Then through this mind we create our world.

In fact, every little thing that happens to each and every one of us we create first in our minds. We mentally create this thing called time which makes it even more difficult to see the creation process because we think now, and the effect of that thought happens much later. But the only creator there is, is mind, your mind. Is God a creator? Yes, because you are. Thou are That! You set up a mind and through the mind create.

It is necessary and good to discover that everything happening to us is caused by our feeling and thinking. Everything that happens to us is created first in our thought, and when you discover this, you discover that you create your trouble as well. And then you realize that if this is so, then you can create anything you desire, and you will begin to create only good things.

Still, even when you discover that there is nothing that you cannot create, you are still not satisfied. The reason is that you have separated yourself from your Infinite Beingness, your oneness, and only on recognizing and being your Infinite Beingness are you perfectly satisfied.

So, if there are any problems that remain, they only remain because you are holding on to them in your thought. The moment you let go of them, they are gone! If you tell me that isn't so for you, I tell you it is. The truth is you are still holding on to the problem and telling me that it doesn't work.

You see, trying to get rid of a problem is holding on to it. Anything we try to get rid of, we are holding in mind and thereby sustaining. So the only way to correct a problem is to let go of it. Don't focus on the problem, focus only on what you want. From this moment on, if you would only see what you want, that is all that you would get. But you hold in mind the things you do not want. You struggle to eliminate these things you don't want, and thereby sustain them. This means that it is necessary to let go of the negative and focus on the positive if you want a positive, happy life.

THE RIDDLE

Although I have been talking about this subject in intellectual terms, this subject cannot be learned intellectually. Although you have been using your mind to understand it, it cannot be learned in the mind. Truth, you see, is perceived just behind the mind. We can use the mind to release what is occupying the mind so that by getting it quieter, we can see behind the mind. If it were possible to get this subject through the mind intellectually, all we would need to do is to read the books on it and we would have it. But it doesn't work that way. We have to very concentratedly seek our Self that is just behind the mind. Turn the mind back upon the mind to release the mind, and then you may go beyond the mind to your Self.

To understand this, each of us must experience it, realize it, make it our own by going to the place just behind the mind and perceiving it there, and then we will know. Then we will know that we know. Then we operate intuitively, from the realm of all-knowingness.

Now as I've said, the very highest state is simply Beingness, and if we could only be, just be, we could see our Infinity. We could see that we are the All. We could be in a perfectly satiated, permanent, changeless state. And this state is not a nothingness, it is not a boredom, it is an Allness, an Everythingness, a Total Satiation that is eternal.

And as you come to this experience, you will come to know that you will never, never lose your individuality. The feeling "I" as you use it to mean your individuality will never ever leave you. It expands. What happens as you discover what you are is that you begin to see that others are you, that you are them, that you and I are one, that there is only One, and that you are now and always have been that one and glorious Infinite Being.

* * *

"If we don't like what's happening to us in the world, all we have to do is change our consciousness — and the world out there changes for us!"

Lester Levenson

Session 2

PROBLEMS AND HOW THEY RESOLVE

THE ILLUSION

We seem to have greater, more intense problems than ever before. This applies to all in general, not anyone in particular. And this intensification of problems makes it appear as though we are going backwards — but this isn't the case. The fact is we have risen to the state where we can better express ourselves outwardly, and so we express our problems out in the world rather than holding them dormant in the subconscious mind. As a result, things may appear to be getting worse.

Conversely, when we are apathetic, it's difficult for us to express and it's difficult for us to outwardly act. So our problems may seem less, but the truth is they are only hidden. They swirl around in our subconscious mind and as a result, don't come out and materialize in the world. This makes these seem better, but in reality, it makes finding solutions impossible.

STAGES OF GROWTH

When we begin to move a step above this apathetic state, as we begin to acquire more capability of action in the world, then our problems begin to manifest outwardly in the world. As I have said, at first this makes it seem as though the world is falling in on us. But it's actually a sign of growth, a sign that we are moving up from the apathetic state into the beginnings of the doingness state. I call this the State of Apathetic-Doingness because when we come into this apathetic-doingness, we begin to do with apathetic, agitated tendencies. Of course when we are in this state, we become outwardly or expressively destructive to the world and to ourselves. But it is important to remember that apathetic-doingness is higher than apathetic non-doingness.

Now, the step above apathetic-doingness is one of doingness in which we are equally constructive and destructive. Move up another step, and we move into the doingness-beingness state where we are big doers and only constructive. When we step up from there, we go into the beingness state — we do not have to do, we just "be."

The foregoing stages of growth are set out in the following chart.

STAGES OF GROWTH

Stage 1.   Apathy: Inaction, due to apathy, with resentments
           and hostilities, and fear to express for fear of
           retaliation. A subjectively destructive state.

           INACTION

Stage 2.   Apathetic-doingness: Beginnings of action, having
           enough will to express outwardly. A beginning of an
           outwardly active but destructive state.

Stage 3.   Doingness: Action that moves us out of Stage 1
           toward the equilibrium of Stage 5. Here one is
           equally constructive and destructive to oneself and
           to the world.   **ACTION**

Stage 4.   Doingness-beingness: Energetic doingness with
           calmness; much outward action, all constructive to
           oneself, the world and the universe.

Stage 5.   Beingness: Inaction, due to serenity; the ability to
           just be; witnessing, watching, allowing and accepting
           the world and universe as it is.

           INACTION

The world today is in a low state of Apathetic Doingness (Stage 2). It's a materialistic age. About 1700 A.D., we came out of the lowest state, a period predominantly marked by physical, animal sensuality. This was a state wherein we lived principally to satisfy our appetites.

We are now in the second period where we can enjoy the finer, more cultural things. But we are still having the growing pains of getting out of the first into the second. The second is, however still not a highly spiritual state. It is the period where, in the world, we advance scientifically.

The third period begins The Era of Knowing. This is a mental world and in it, we are all related. We will be more loving to one another and we will stop fighting each other.

The fourth period is the state which will be one in which we will know fully our beingness in God — and everyone's beingness is God. We will know ourselves as free, unlimited beings. These four periods are the Iron, Bronze, Silver and Golden Ages the ancient Greeks spoke of. The fifth stage is really beyond this world although accomplished in this world.

However, at any time, whenever anyone chooses, he may move into the highest state. We do not have to stay at the level that the world is in, and those of us who are on the path are moving up out of this general level. This makes us very fortunate. We know the way out. No matter how much the world hurts us, we know there's a way out. We have hope and a direction.

THE WAY OUT

And what is the way out? Not looking to the world for happiness, but looking to the place where happiness is right within us, within our own consciousness. Unlimited joy and freedom is our natural, inherent state. We have, through ignorance, undone it by imposing concepts of limitations: I need this, I need him, I need her, and if I don't get what I want, I am hurt, I have trouble.

Growth, on the other hand, is letting go of these concepts of lack and limitation or, on the positive side, going within and seeing this unlimited Being that we are and choosing to remain as such.

Any time we have trouble, any time we have a problem, we are trying to express the Self through the limited ego, and it is too small, so we get squeezed and it hurts.

So, if there is a problem, the thing to do is to ask yourself, "What am I doing? Wherein am I demanding with ego motivation?" If the answer comes, if you see how egowise, you're causing this so-called problem; you will pull the causative thought up from the subconscious into the conscious, and once it is conscious, you will naturally let go of it.

If you don't let go of it, it is because the cause, the thought that initiated the difficulty, remains subconscious. So, we must make the thought conscious and let go of it or, and this is the higher and the better way, we must remember that we are the Self. Knowing that we are the perfect Self, that we are not this limited body and mind, all problems immediately resolve!

It probably sounds quite indicting when I say that all problems, all troubles, are ego motivated. But if you investigate this for yourself, you will find that is true. When you are just your Self, there are no problems; there is only that which is perfect, harmonious, without effort. The more ego motivated you are, the more difficult it is to accomplish something, the less harmony and more misery you have.

IT IS REALLY AS SIMPLE AS THAT

What is hard is letting go of the habits. What is hard is moving beyond the limits of the ego. Habits are very strong and have been deeply ingrained over thousands of years.

However, the moment we choose to let go of them, we can. If we say we can't let go, it's because we really don't want to. The desire to let go isn't strong enough.

Do I make this too simple? You have probably heard it presented in more complicated ways, with a lot of things added to it that make it more difficult to see. But once we see the simplicity of it, all we need to do is effect it.

And no one can do it for us. We have to do it ourselves.

I have a friend who has problems. She is religious and seems very pious. When things get blackest and she has no more hope and is at the bottom, at that very moment something happens so that everything turns out right.

Do you know why she must reach bottom?

Because she does not really have faith. She is not really pious. This is her trouble. You see, faith would cause her to let go and let God. Being pious, being humble and surrendering would cause the same thing.

Outwardly, she's the way she says, but inwardly she's the way I'm saying. You see, she tries to control everything, and that is not letting go and letting God.

She prays, but she wants it the way she wants it. She has found out that her praying for it does not help her. If you surrender, you do not have to pray.

She has got to let go and let God. When does she let go and let God? When she, herself, can not do anything any more, she lets go. She lets go in the extreme. And the moment she lets go, everything resolves itself. Can you see that? When things reach the extreme, she feels "Oh, there's nothing I can do," and that is when she lets go and lets God.

If she could see this point, she would be more consciously able to use it. For Conviction, which is stronger than faith, absolute conviction of God — that will do it! Let go and let God and then everything straightens out. But when we try to do it, we have trouble.

When I say, "Let go and let God," what does that mean? Should you work strictly on inspiration, or just sit back and let things happen?

Not exactly: We must have the feeling of "letting things happen." To accomplish this, we have to let the ego-sense go. The ego is the feeling "I am an individual, and I have a body and I do things." That is the illusion. You have to get my ego out of the way and let God or Self operate. When this is achieved, you'll sort of float through things, and there will be no effort. If there is effort, there is ego.

Of course, you are going to have to use some effort, because you are not starting off as the realized Self. You see, only when this friend of mine goes to the extreme, does she let go of the sense of doership and things happen effortlessly. That's letting go and letting God!

HAVING DOES IT

Professing faith, professing all these things does not do it. Having them does it. The fact that she has troubles is proof that she does not have the conviction of God because God is All, God is Perfect; and if God is All and God is Perfect, everything must be perfect, and that leaves no place for imperfection or troubles.

If you take that attitude, so be it!

It is the feeling that I am not the doer and that I let go and let it happen.

How can we tell when we're being the ego?

When there's no effort, there's no ego. The more the effort, the more the ego.

So, when the effort is extreme, you have to more or less go the other way anyway.

The more the effort, the greater the ego. However, you are going to use effort until you are fully realized. Now, there will be times when you will use no effort and everything will fall perfectly into line for you; at these times you will be your Self.

Of course, some people are afraid that this type of thing makes you indolent. But, indolence is an action, a negative action. It is the act of holding oneself from moving.

THE ACTIONLESS STATE

To achieve the actionless state, you begin by letting go of your ego more and more. You do this because under present conditions, you cannot do it totally. If you could, you would be fully realized. But if you keep letting go of the ego, you will eventually drop it, and then you will be the witness rather than the doer. Does this make sense?

Be not the doer. Let it happen. It's God's world, whatever is happening, let Him do it!

Still the question arises, "How do we get rid of problems?"

First, you must realize that the moment you say, "I have a problem," you are stuck; you are making it real! You cannot get rid of the problem, because you are making it real. You have got it. This does not mean that when you have problems you should say, "There is no problem at all," and the problem will vanish.

If you say, "There is no problem," they won't vanish because you're saying, "There is no problem." You are mentally holding the problem in mind and therefore sustaining it.

Instead, you must erase the problem from your mind. Let it go. Know that everything is perfect; then the problem becomes necessarily non-existent.

You see, life can be totally effortless. There is no effort in life whatsoever when we are being our natural Self. But we're trying to be a limited ego and that takes effort. It takes effort to be limited when your natural state is unlimited. The more you try to be limited, the more effort it takes.

To be your unlimited Self takes no effort. Just like the woman I talked about earlier. When she gets to the extreme, she lets go and everything straightens out —with no effort. When she tries and tries, things get worse and worse. But when she gives up and lets go, things resolve.

Still people ask, "Doesn't she have to go out and look for a job? Doesn't she have to go to an agent? She can't just sit down and wait."

And I say all she has to do is to let go and let God. Then, even if she has locked herself in a chamber somewhere, the things would have come to her.

LETTING GO OF DOERSHIP

You do not sit down and wait — you do not do anything. Just let go of the sense of doership. You just know that everything is perfect and then the slightest thought you have will come into being quickly. There's no limitation on God, on the Self. Whatever you think will come into being if you let go, because you are invoking your infinite power, God, your Self. Nothing can stop it!

You do not have to struggle to get some action.

In fact, it's just the opposite. Lock yourself in a chamber and padlock it and if you will do what I am saying, you will find that what you want will be effected.

It has to be. Nothing can stop it! Omnipotence is invoked!

If this is true, then what is prayer for? What does praying mean?

Praying is for those who need praying. When you know what you know — to whom are you praying? If you are That, why do you have to pray to It?

Praying admits duality. "I" pray to "God." Instead, maintain your Oneness!

However, when one does pray, it is best to pray for one thing only. Pray for more wisdom, so that you eliminate all need for any prayer, for any asking.

Most people in the world today need to pray. But prayer admits duality; God is out there. And we should know that God is within. Even though Jesus said, "The kingdom of God is within," we still look for God without, and He's not out there —He's only within. He turns out to be our very own Beingness.

The "I" of us, with nothing added to it, is the God we seek. When you say "I am something that isn't It", that isn't God. But just pure "I" and only "I", — that is God.

That is why it is said that God is closer than flesh. It is "I" and how close is "I?" It's closer than flesh. It is God, your very own Self!

Just hold on to the word "I" only. "I..." and you'll become more exhilarated. Try it when you're alone. Just "I..." and not "I am a body, I am a mind," but "I..." that is Being.

BEINGNESS

I think the word that describes God better than any other single word is "Beingness." God is all Beingness. We are all Beingness pretending we are a tiny part of It, a limited body-mind. When you look within, you will see that you are all Beingness.

Beingness is God! Beingness is also Awareness Consciousness. They are the same thing. Later on, you'll see them as identical: Beingess, Awareness Consciousness.

So be your Self and there never will be a problem. Seeing a problem in the world is trying to be a limited ego-body-mind. If you think you have a problem, you do. If you will just accept that God is All, God is Perfect, that that is all there is, and look at Perfection, that is all you will ever meet with!

You have to wipe out the words "problem," "can't," "don't," "won't," — all negative words. In the future when man is in a state of harmony, these words will disappear.

The higher you go, the more you see the Perfection and therefore the less you see problems. The more one sees problems, the lower one is.

What everyone talks about is problems. The people who see them want you to see the way they see, and will tell you that you are wrong. This is one thing you must be on guard against. As you grow, those who are not up to you will try to pull you down to where they are. Let them think you are wrong. You know you are right! Do not argue. It is fruitless.

It is not how much you recognize a problem that shows unselfishness. It is how much you see that there is no problem, and help others see that there is only Perfection that shows unselfishness. This way you offer help; you're very constructive and unselfish.

You just feel love — you do not necessarily have to do anything.

Love — and your thoughts are positive. Thought is far more powerful than action. It is the basis of and effects action. It is the initiator. It comes before and determines action.

A realized being sitting in a cave somewhere all by himself is doing more good for the world than organizations of action. He is aiding everyone, as his help is being subconsciously received by all.

Now we are back to what we were talking about before: the bottom state is inaction, the middle state is action, the top state is inaction. The bottom state is one of apathetic inertia. It's destructive. If just wants to stop everything, actually destroy everything.

The top state lets everything be just the way it is because everything is perfect and anyone in this state powerfully projects this mentally to everyone.

The middle state is the action state which moves you from the bottom toward the top state of equilibrium and tranquility.

As you move up, those who are not as far along as you are will try to pull you down to where they are.

It is sort of a proving ground, or a testing, to see how much those things bother you.

It tests your conviction. Where is your conviction if you go with them? If you go with them, your tendency is to believe more the way they do.

16

KEYS TO BEINGNESS

Desire for ego approval makes it seem easier to go along with the world. You will find out otherwise. You have been one of the mob, haven't you? You've been like them. It's not easy. No, the right way is easier. Do you see that? The right way is letting go and letting God and then everything falls into line perfectly — no effort. But when you have to do it, it is not God — it is you, the ego, wanting to do, to change things, correct this world, and so forth.

Some people ask if a mantram or something like that is the best thing to remember when these things come up that way?

Affirmations are always good. A mantram is an affirmation that's repeated again and again. It is even more effective, however, to let go of your ego reactions. So, do whatever will help you to do and be what you think you should do and be.

Seek who and what you are, know your Self. This is the very best thing to do and be. There have been moments when you have let go and felt your real Self. How does it feel?

You could have it all the time.

Stay that way that's all. Be what you are! You are infinite, omniscient, omnipotent, right here and now. Be That! Stop being this limited, miserable, little ego.

If you want to help the world the most, help yourself grow, and you will do far more than you could by being involved in the world. The more you are capable of loving, the more you are helping the world.

Parliaments cannot right the world, but enough people loving can. The President of the United States must necessarily represent the sum total consciousness, the sum total thinkingness, of all the people of the United States added together. The world out there is only our collective consciousness.

The principle is that divine law supersedes man-made law. Consciousness, thinkingness determine everything. So if we do not like what's happening to us in the world all we have to do is change our consciousness — and the world out there changes for us!

There's no end to problems in the world. If you try to find the end you go on and on forever and ever solving problems in the world and you will always find more and more. As long as you are conscious of problems, they exist. Only when you discover the real you, will you discover an end to problems.

It is as if you put your hand in a fire and say, "Ouch, it's hot! My hand is burning! Boy, do I have a problem!" And then put your hand back in the fire and so on and so on. Until one day you see that you are doing it and you stop. If you have a problem, you're putting your hand into a problem and yelling, "It hurts!" and acting as though you're not putting your hand into it. You act as though you are not doing it. But you are.

So that problem is in your consciousness. It is in your mind. Change your mind, change your consciousness and immediately that problem is gone. Try it and you'll see that it's so.

And when you are by yourself, stop being what you are not, a limited body and mind, and just be what you are — an infinite, totally free, grand and glorious being, whole and complete.

* * *

"Thou art that"
"You are"

"The only growth there is, is the elimination of the ego."

Lester Levenson

Session 3

SPIRITUAL GROWTH

Let us vary the pace a little. Here are some thoughts on spiritual growth. It is suggested that they be absorbed one at a time. Read them, allow yourself to let the impact of each statement in before going on to the next. Let them build one upon the next. It is a kind of meditation for the whole being.

* * *

The whole object on the path is to let go of the ego. What remains is your Self.

* * *

The only growth there is, is the elimination of the ego.

* * *

Ego is the sense of "I am an individual separate from the All." In the extreme, it is egotism.

* * *

Growth is transcending yourself, your habitual self, which is none other than ego.

* * *

Growth is the ego getting out of its misery.

* * *

Recognize that all joy is nothing but your Self, more or less.

* * *

There is no happiness except that of experiencing your Self. When you see that, it makes the path very direct. You stop chasing the rainbow and you go for the happiness where you know it is — right within you.

* * *

Everything you are seeking, you are, and you very foolishly keep saying you are not. That's part of the enigma: everything everyone is seeking with such intensity, one has, — and much more.

* * *

"It," is you — when you say, "I," that is the Infinite. Great big joke! Here you are infinite looking for your Self, which you are!

* * *

When anyone says he is not a master, he is lying.

* * *

Your effort should be for proper identity. Identify with your Self!

* * *

Spiritual advancement is determined by how much you identify with your real Self.

* * *

The ego is very tricky. It often talks us out of this path for shorter or longer periods of time. But once we've gotten onto the path, we usually come back to it. So be careful of the trickery of the ego-part of us. It takes us away from the path. So no matter how far we have advanced on the path, the ego is always a tempting companion who can take us off the path, sometimes for an entire lifetime.

* * *

This is something we should be on guard against. The ego-sense latches on and says, "I am God." It latches onto the progress and it feels good and it says, "I am It" and by doing so, it sabotages further growth. Spiritual pride is deadly!

* * *

When you recognize the opposition of the ego, you can let go of it. After practice, it is easy and after you let go of enough ego, you just naturally feel the peace and joy of your Self.

* * *

It's actually a path of taking on more and more of your natural state of being infinite. You give up limitation. You give up misery. But you never give up anything worthwhile. You never give up anything good.

* * *

On this path you constantly give up trouble.

* * *

The first teacher is misery. It is usually the thing that causes us to seek the way out.

* * *

First we start on the path to escape misery. Then we taste the Self and want It because It tastes so good.

* * *

On the path you never give up anything, you just take on more and more of what you really want until you have the All.

* * *

Take it for the sweetness that's in it, not to get out of the bitterness that's out of it.

* * *

We discover that we never give up anything on the spiritual path but our self-imposed bondages and miseries.

* * *

If you are weakly for the path, you are strongly for the sense-world.

* * *

It's only the thought "I can't do it," that stops you from doing it.

* * *

You think you can't, that's why you can't.

Those who can't, don't really want to.

* * *

Your growth depends only on you.

* * *

It will happen as fast as you can do it.

* * *

The only one who is going to change you — is you!

* * *

Wishing won't do it, nor will trying. You have got to do it!

* * *

Good intentions are no substitute for right action.

* * *

To change more rapidly — expect it!

* * *

You must have a very strong desire to change because you are such a victim of habit that you want the world as much as a drowning man wants air. To offset that, you must want to know your Self as much as a drowning man wants air.

* * *

Your success is determined by your desire for it. If you get discouraged, you are not really interested.

* * *

Your only real friend is you. Your only real enemy is you. You are an enemy to yourself to the degree you limit your Self. You are a friend to yourself to the degree you de-limit yourself.

* * *

What you do to yourself, only you can undo. You did it. You must undo it.

* * *

This entire path is a do-it-yourself path.

* * *

Do what is available to you to do. Do your best.

* * *

Every experience is to bless you, not to hurt you. If you stay in accord with principle, you will come out higher!

* * *

Every place and every situation in life presents an opportunity for growth.

* * *

The best place to grow is right where you are. The best time is now.

* * *

Be thankful for the opportunities to grow.

* * *

The greatest of all tests are those at home, with your immediate family. Therefore, home is an excellent place to grow.

* * *

A lot of spiritual growth can be had by practicing the real selfless love on your mate and family.

* * *

It is a good opportunity to grow when people are saying things about you, opposing you. It gives you a chance to practice the real Love. It gives you a chance to practice the real Peace. Because they are making sounds with their mouths is no reason why you should feel bad about it. Opposition is a very healthy thing. It provokes and firms growth.

* * *

It is necessary to remember that everyone can be our teacher. If we react to praise or pleasantries, that is developing ego. If we're depressed on criticism, that is ego. When we are our Self, there is no reacting.

* * *

There isn't anything that happens that can't be used. There's no incident that cannot be used as a teacher.

* * *

Every minute of every day should be used to grow by.

* * *

If we assume that we are there and we are not, circumstances soon awaken us to the fact that we are not.

* * *

If you tell others of your high experiences, of your gains, because of their jealously, they say, "Ah, who does she think she is?" And that works against you and tends to pull you down.

* * *

Anytime you brag about anything, you're inviting a test of it. So, I warn you, if you are growing into these things, when they start coming, unless you're so sure you know by experience you can't lose it, it's better not to tell anyone.

* * *

Be proud of your spiritual accomplishments. Be happy with them. Be proud of them to yourself.

* * *

When you have false spiritual pride, you invite a challenge of the thing that you are proud of.

* * *

It is necessary to do away with doubts.

* * *

It takes more than faith. It takes knowledge. You start with faith, but you must convert it to knowledge. You must test it out, and then you know it.

* * *

In order to really understand, we must experience the knowledge.

* * *

When you experience, it is no longer intellectual.

* * *

You can get understanding without being able to put it into words.

* * *

The only maturity there is, is spiritual understanding.

* * *

Stand out and be different and don't let the others trick you back into where you were. It's not easy. It takes fortitude.

* * *

We should try to go all the way. To us it is given to do that. We have the possibility of going all the way back home — right to the Absolute.

* * *

Expect infinity — no more. You cannot expect too much.

* * *

Toe the line to the very end. The more you toe the line, the sooner the end.

* * *

Every gain is an eternal gain. Every step forward you make now is forever.

* * *

We climb a ladder and each time we get up to another rung, we forget about the rungs below. Then, when we get to the top, we kick the ladder away.

* * *

The proof of this subject is the result you get.

* * *

The more you grow, the less you feel the need to grow

* * *

The higher you go, the less the incentive to go further.

* * *

You never learn anything by disproving; you learn only by proving.

* * *

Studying the illusion helps make it real. If you want to know the Truth, don't study the opposite.

* * *

The whole process of growth is letting go of thoughts. When our thoughts are totally eliminated, there is nothing left but the Self.

* * *

Don't try to complicate it; it's too simple.

* * *

We can only expand out of the ego. The Self is.

* * *

Growth is letting go of being what you are not.

* * *

Let go of your ego — and be your Self!

* * *

As you grow, the whole world opens wide for you — you experience so much more. However, even if you have this whole world, you've only got a dot. Take the whole cosmos!

* * *

Longing for liberation is the key. Once you get that, you'll be carried all the way.

* * *

In our desire to attain liberation or realization, we are helped to the degree that we help all others.

* * *

Grow to the point where your whole attention is off you and on others.

* * *

Why shouldn't we all be masters, all of us, here and now?

* * *

The moment we decide to be the Self — really decide — it is so!

The higher you go, the more non-difference comes. You accept the leaders of all religions alike.

* * *

Having peace under ideal conditions isn't indicative of spiritual growth — it is escape.

* * *

When people are not growing, they are going in the opposite direction.

* * *

You should thank those who oppose you because they give you an unusual opportunity for growth.

* * *

When we start concerning ourselves with what they are doing, we're turning away from what we are doing.

* * *

You need constant confirmation until you don't need it anymore.

* * *

Perseverance is necessary.

* * *

Adversity is a prod to growth.

* * *

The more intense the crises in this world, the more we have an opportunity to grow.

* * *

It would be so fast if people would, with constant, intense effort ask, " What am I?"

* * *

When you get the answer to "What am I", then you have control over your body and mind.

* * *

If there is anything you don't like out there, there is a need to change yourself.

* * *

You may see fully who you are and not be able to maintain it. What happens is that, being the infinite Self, we can get a glimpse of the infinite, hold it for a while, and then suddenly feel as though we've lost it. The reason for that is that the mind has not been eliminated. The subconscious thoughts of limitation are submerged for the moment. You may go completely into your Self and let go of the mind temporarily. You haven't eliminated the mind, you just momentarily let go of it. So there you are, for the moment, totally the infinite Self. However, the mind that has been submerged, re-emerges, and then the ego takes over and you just can't understand what happened to you; what brought you back into the heaviness of the world again. What is required is that we re-establish that state of the Self again and again until it becomes permanent. Each time we do it, we scorch more of the mind, until finally we have scorched the entire mind. Then we are permanently established in the Self. Then you sit back and the mind is out there, and the body is out there and you are not the mind, you are not the body. As long as you know you are not the mind and the body, both of them can go on to their heart's content, and you know that they cannot touch you.

* * *

"Some of us are seeking Happiness where it is and as a result are becoming happier. And others are seeking it blindly in the world where it is not and are becoming more frustrated."

Lester Levenson

Session 4

HAPPINESS

As I have said, when we analyze that which everyone is seeking, it turns out to be happiness. And when we find God, our true Self, that turns out to be the ultimate happiness. When we seek and find the full truth, the absolute truth, again that turns out to be the ultimate happiness, and also the greatest good. The greatest good turns out to be the ultimate happiness. Every being is seeking freedom and the complete freedom or liberation is also the ultimate happiness.

So in the end, the words God, good, truth, liberation, freedom, and Self turn out to be the ultimate happiness. And everyone is seeking this Good, Happiness, Liberation, Truth, God, and Self. There isn't anyone who is not seeking It. The only difference between some of us and others is that some of us are consciously seeking It in the direction where It is and are becoming happier. And others are seeking it blindly in the world and are becoming more frustrated.

Yet, only when we go within do we discover that all happiness is there. The only place where we can feel happiness is right within ourselves. That is exactly where it is. Every time we attribute this happiness to something external, to a person or a thing external, we get more pain with it than we do pleasure.

If you have experience enough, if you have lived long enough, and if you have examined it carefully enough, you have discovered this. The happiness that we are seeking and thinking is out there and external to us, is not there. The "happiness with no sorrow" can only be found by going within.

THE SELF AND THE MIND

The second point is that this great Happiness that we are seeking is nothing but our very own Self, our very own beingness. And looking within, we discover it to be our most basic inherent nature, our very own Self unencumbered with our self-imposed limitations. And it is ours, here and now.

And, there is not one of us who is not in direct touch with, in possession of, an infinite Beingness that is all perfect, all present, all joyous and eternal. And there is not one of us who is not in direct contact with it right now! But due to assumptions, concepts of limitation, looking outwardly, and wrong learning, we have covered over this infinite Being that we are with concepts of "I am this physical body," "I am this mind." So, in order to discover this truth, this unlimited Being that we are, we must quiet the mind, we must let go of the mind. Only in this way may we achieve the ultimate happiness we seek.

The mind, after all, is nothing but the sum-total of all thoughts and all thoughts are concepts of limitation. If any one of us could stop thinking right now and remain that way, he would be an unlimited Being from this moment on. It is really that simple, though not necessarily that easy to accomplish.

So our first job is to undo negative thinking in order to get positive enough so that we may go in the right direction. Then, we must drop all thinking, both negative and positive thinking. When that happens, we discover that we are in the realm of knowingness, of omniscience, we have no need to think as everything is known and we are all joyous and totally free. Knowing everything, there is nothing to think about!

Thinking is just our way of relating things to other things, connecting things together. But knowing everything, we know the unity, the oneness and there's no need to relate things by thought. Thereby, we are free, free of all concepts of separation and limitation. This leaves us free to use a mind should we want to communicate with the apparency of the world.

The process of going within is a process of looking within and discovering that the mind is nothing but thoughts, and the thoughts are nothing but concepts of limitation. When we quiet the mind by letting go of these thoughts, we see this infinite Being that we are. This takes away the clouds covering this infinite Being and leaves us totally free.

BEYOND THINKING

Seeing this infinite Being is not, however, the end of the job. We still have to do away with the remaining habits of thought. Then, when there's no more remaining thoughts, subconscious and conscious, (and the subconscious thoughts are the difficult ones to let go of,) that's the end of the road of playing limited. Then we are totally free — forever!

Actually since we are infinite Beings, we are choosing to be limited! And, we are choosing to be limited to such a degree that now we are blindly behaving as though we are extremely limited beings.

As I have said, as a result, we have all these apparent troubles.

And troubles are only an apparency because they are assumed as real through our mind. Since we now know that everything we see in the world we see only in our minds and there's nothing but our consciousness, we know that nothing can be seen except through our consciousness. Whatever we see is in our consciousness, in our mind. So then our job is to change our consciousness and by so, change our environment.

Changing one's environment is a step on the way. And doing so you have the proof that what I'm saying is true. Nothing should ever be accepted on hearsay. Never believe anything you hear. If you accept what I say to you just by listening to it, it is only hearsay. You must prove everything for yourself. Then, when you do, it is your knowledge and it is usable. To progress in the direction of wisdom and happiness, it's absolutely necessary that everyone prove it out for himself.

As has been said before, this Truth can never be found in the world. The world as we see it now is multiplex, dual. But when we go just behind the world, we discover the absolute Truth. We discover that there is a singular Oneness throughout the world and universe and it turns out to be our very own Self, our very own Beingness, which some call God. The world is, but not as people see it. The world is truly only our very own Self. The "I" that we use when we say "I am" is the exact same "I" falsely appearing separate and divided. When we see the Truth, we see that you are me, that there is only one Beingness, there is only one Consciousness, and that we are the sumtotal of all the Beingness or Consciousness that formerly appeared separate.

So, again, to find Truth or Happiness, you have to go within, you have to see the Oneness, you have to see the universe as it really is, as nothing but your consciousness, which is nothing but your Self. Now, this is difficult to describe, it is something that must be experienced. Only when someone experiences it, does one know. It cannot be picked up from listening to anyone. Books and teachers can only point the direction. It is up to us to take it. That's one of the nice things about the path. There's nothing to be believed, everything must be experienced and proved by each person to his own satisfaction before it's accepted.

To sum it up, I take two quotes from the Bible: I am that I am," and "Be still and know that I am God." Or, in other words, thou art That which thou art seeking, quiet the mind until you see It. OK? Now we may go into questions.

QUESTIONS AND ANSWERS

Q: I come upon a difference — these people, all of us in this room, each of us has a form and I see it.

Lester: You're seeing wrongly. You're seeing in error. When you look at me, you should see the Truth, you should see your Self. Strive until that day in which you will see this Truth.

Q: After one has a certain amount of inner experience and begins to believe, there still comes an important decision as to what to do with your self as you find your self at that point. And then you have to decide what to do with the rest of your life.

Lester: Yes. You must decide whether to pursue your welfare by seeking it in the world or by seeking it within you.

Q: You've had a certain amount of experience, but you will always be called back to a certain contact with the outer world unless...

Lester: Unless you make the outer world you. However, do not be attached to the world and it cannot disturb you. Then you can carry on with equanimity.

Q: In order to make the outer world me, I would think I have to self-purify myself.

Lester: Yes. Practicing serving the world will purify you.

Q: Would I have to go out and sacrifice what remains of myself in some kind of service?

Lester: The only thing you will ever sacrifice in this direction is your misery. Rendering service would give only happiness — to the degree your heart is in it. The more you willingly serve the world, the more you discover that you are related to everything and everyone. There is no isolation. It is serving and becoming the All that should be our direction. You don't cut out and let others be separate from you. You become them throughout the practice of serving them.

Q: The only reason I would make an effort in this direction is so I could better help other people.

Lester: Good, but you can't help other people any more than you can help yourself. So, the best way to help others is to help yourself. It's automatically so, that you'll help others to the degree that you'll help yourself. Do both.

Q: So, help yourself by helping others; isn't it a two-way action?

Lester: Yes, but it's the motive that counts. If I'm helping you with selfish motives, it doesn't help me or you. If I help only to help you, I grow. But there are many people in the world who help for their own ego-glorification and it doesn't help them any, nor does it help you, because they then help you ego-wise, i.e., they help validate your ego.

Q: That's a very subtle thing, a very difficult thing to get rid of, that ego.

Lester: Right. When there's no more ego, the only thing left is the infinite Being that you are. Ego is the sense of separation from the All. I am an individual, Lester, and I am separate from the All, and all you people are other than I — that is the sense of ego — separateness.

The moment I'm not the All, I lack something and then I try to get it back. I think I need the missing parts of the All and I start trying to get them. Thus, I assume I don't have the All, I am limited, and this starts a downward spiral and we continue until we get where we are. However, we're all on the way up now. And the big problem is to get rid of our ego — the sense that I am an individual separate from everything. We can do this by looking at our motivations. When our motivation is selfish, we change it, make it altruistic; we act for others rather than for ourselves, and in this way we grow.

Q: Is growth a constant becoming aware?

Lester: Yes. You must first want to. When you want to, then you do become aware of your thinking. Then you become aware of your non-thinking which shows up as periods of peace and well-being.

Q: Like trying to find out, for instance, why one feels things or why one is sick– like these past two years of illness for me. It's tremendous, Lester. Even this morning when I was talking to my sister on the telephone, after speaking to her I kept thinking, "Why? Why? Why?" and I tried to be still, as still as I could possibly be, and all of a sudden, a realization of the why I had been so negative came to me with such tremendous clarity. And I thought of you so intensely and I thought, "Well, this is what Lester possibly means." It's finding out the why, and when one sees it, one immediately turns it into something positive and one is released.

Lester: Good. Keep that up until there is no more.

Q: That's what you mean about making the subconscious thought conscious and then letting go of it?

Lester: Yes. Pulling the subconscious thought up into consciousness and when it's there, you'll see it and naturally let go of it because of its negativity. But as long as it remains unconscious, you don't see it and can't do anything about it, can you?

Q: No. And tremendous things come up when one begins. Wow! Alligators! It's not that easy.

Lester: Ego-wise, you don't like what comes up and you tend to fight it.

Q: Many times I go along on an even keel and then something comes up in personal relationships or from other directions, and all of a sudden, you feel pain, you're showing your own limitations, and you step back, look at it, and release yourself from the whole situation.

Lester: Yes, every situation can be used for growth by observing what's going on, the way you do. DO THIS ALL THE TIME, until there is no more needed to be let go of, until there is no more ego.

Q: Creative work, for instance, has the ego involved in that, too. It's very subtle. And the more one sees spiritually, the more one is able to paint a picture, or make music, or whatever one does — this is a point that has always bothered me, the ego-involvement in this. It has worried me, how can one channel it, commercialize it, sell something?

Lester: The answer is simple: Commercialize it but be not attached to this creativeness.

Q: Difficult. It is the ego saying, "I am the creator."

Lester: It doesn't matter what you do, do not be attached to it. Let go of the sense of "I am the creator." Let the creativeness flow through you.

Q: I would think that in almost any creative act there has to be a spiritual part, the stem of it is basically some pure motivation, but it's almost always mixed with ego.

Lester: Let me clear up one thing, everything you do is creative, it's impossible to do anything that is not creative. That's because the mind is only creative, but when we create things we don't like, we call it non-creative and destructive. When we create things we like, we call that creative and constructive. But the mind only creates. Everyone is a creator. What we hold in mind, we create.

Q: So all this ego of ours is our own creation?

Lester: Right. It's better to create constructive things like beauty, health, affluence. They do not demand as much attention from us as a sick body or a sick pocket-book. Consequently, we have more time and ease to look in the direction of Truth and to discover our Self.

Q: Sometimes I think that one thinks too much of the ego and therefore the ego grows, and you want to fight it more and you give it more importance.

Lester: Yes. But it's too well grown right now, far more than you can see, in the unconscious part of your mind. Mind is nothing but the sum-total collection of all thoughts. The unconscious part of the mind is holding all the thoughts that we are not looking at this moment. But those hundreds of thousands of thoughts are there, and they're active. Unconsciously, you're operating that body; you're operating every cell. You're working a chemical plant, a circulatory, a cooling and a heating system– all these thoughts are active and are actively operating your body. Also there are thousands of likes and dislikes, thousands of thoughts of wanting things and not wanting things. But even if they're unconscious, they're active, whether we look at them or not, they are sustained and motivated by our ego. This is the difficult part for us, to make these ego-motivated thoughts conscious so that we can let go of them. However, someday we reach a place where we will not be that ego-mind. When we see that "I am not that mind, I am not that body, I am not that ego," then we'll really see, and when we really see we are not that, it's possible to drop that ego-mind-body, once and for all.

Q: Because one has re-become what one is?

Lester: Not re-become, one has re-remembered, re-discovered, re-recognized what he always was.

Q: So the ego-thing falls off like a crust.

Lester: Right, gone forever. Now that's what we do eventually. At first, we work at dropping the ego until we get enough attention free so that we can seek who and what we are. Then, when we see who and what we are, we say, "This is ridiculous," and we don't identify with the ego-mind-body any more. Then we watch the body go through life like we now watch every other body.

You watch it and you know that the body is not you. You're really above that body, you're not limited nor bound by it. You know you are eternal, whole, perfect and free, and you let the body go its way, like a puppet.

Q: And then you use the body for whatever you like, if you want to, or if not, the show just goes on.

Lester: Yes. You let the show go on. It's a show that you wrote called "Bodies Playing Limited." However, you are free to choose to use the body to communicate with others, to help them grow.

Q: Isn't everything we see, a piece of wood, a potato chip, part of that eternal Truth?

Lester: Yes, but you have to see it as nothing but you, then you see the truth of it. The world doesn't disappear, our perception of it changes, completely. Instead of theworld being other than we, it becomes us, or we become it. When you see the world as you, it will look entirely different from what it looked like when it appeared separate. You will love and identify with it and everyone in it.

When you fully love someone, you identify with and you become one with that one. When you become the universe you love the universe, or, if you fully love the universe, you become the universe. Love is absolutely necessary. When we love totally, we totally identify with the grand and glorious infinite Being that we are!

* * *

"The original state for all Beings is Love. Our troubles are due only to our covering over this natural state."

Lester Levenson

LOVE

REAL LOVE

Human love is limited and yet it is that which most people define as love. Real love, however, is a constant, persistent acceptance of all beings in the universe—fully, wholly, totally. It is acceptance of another as they are. In fact, it is loving them because they are the way they are.

Human love is controlling and restrictive. Divine love is wanting and allowing another to be the way another one wants to be. Human love is judgmental and relative. Divine love is seeing and accepting everyone equally. In fact, this is the test of how divine our love is. Is it the same for every person we meet? Is our love for those who are opposing us as strong as for those who are supporting us?

Real, divine love is unconditional and is for everyone alike. One of the greatest examples of unconditional love was modeled by Christ and His teachings: turn the other cheek, love your enemy, and so forth are perfect examples. In fact, if we as a nation were to practice these teachings, we could make every enemy of ours completely impotent. All we would have to do is to love them. They would be powerless to do any harm to us. However, we would have to do it as a nation — at least the majority of the people would have to love the enemy.

LOVE WITHOUT LIMIT

Human love is reactive, object dependant and selective. Real love is, however, something we can not turn on and off. Either we have it or we do not have it. With it, it is impossible to love one person and hate another. In fact, to the degree that we hate anyone, to that degree we do not love the others. Our love is no greater than our hatred is for any one person.

In truth, what most of us call love is really a need. If we say that we love this one person, but not another person, what we are actually saying is that we need this person. Therefore, we will do whatever we have to do so we can get what we want from those we need. This is not real love. It is conditional, manipulative and exclusive.

So where human love is selfish — divine love is selfless. Where human love is limited — divine love gives unlimited joy beyond our greatest imagination. Try it and discover this for yourself.

What follows are some additional thoughts about love. Read them slowly. Pause after each and let them work their magic within you. You do not have to think about them as much as you let them in, allowing each to build upon the last. If you do this, this process becomes a kind of meditation.

* * *

Love is a feeling of givingness with no thought of receiving anything in return. When we strive for this, we see and feel nothing but the most enthralling love everywhere and in everyone. We taste the sweetness of Beingness and are effortlessly locked in harmony with that. We are intoxicated with the joy that defies description.

* * *

The real love is the love we feel for others. It is determined by how much we give ourselves to others.

* * *

Full love is identifying with every other being.

* * *

When we identify with everyone, we treat everyone as we would treat ourselves.

* * *

Love is the balm, the salve, that soothes and heals everything and all.

* * *

When you love, you lift others to love.

* * *

The most you can give is your love. It is greater than giving materiality.

* * *

When you understand people, you see that they are doing right in their own eyes. When you understand, you allow, you accept. If you understand, you love.

* * *

When we love, not only are we happy, but our whole life is in harmony.

* * *

Happiness is equal to one's capacity to love.

* * *

If we love completely, we are perfectly happy.

* * *

There is always either love or the lack of it.

* * *

When one is not loving, one is doing the opposite.

* * *

The highest love is when you become the other one. Identity is love in its highest form.

* * *

If you love your enemy, you have no more enemies!

* * *

The power and effect of love is self-obvious. Just try it!

* * *

If you will look at it from your very own center, the words love, acceptance, identification, understanding, communication, truth, God, Self are all the same.

43

The original state of man was all love. His troubles are due only to his covering over of his natural state of love.

* * *

Love and discover that selflessness turns out to be the greatest good for yourself.

* * *

Love is effortless and hate requires much effort.

* * *

Apply love and every problem resolves.

* * *

Human love is needing the other one. Divine love is giving to the other one.

* * *

Love equals happiness. When we are not happy, we are not loving.

* * *

The concept of possessiveness is just the opposite of the meaning of love. Love frees, possessiveness enslaves.

* * *

Love is a feeling of oneness with, of identity with, the other one. When there's a full love, you feel yourself as the other person. Then treating the other person is just like treating your very own self. You delight in the other one's joy.

* * *

Love is a tremendous power. One discovers that the power behind love, without question, is far more powerful than the hydrogen bomb.

* * *

One individual with nothing but love can stand up against the entire world because this love is so powerful. This love is nothing but the Self. This love is God.

* * *

Love will give not only all the power in the universe, it will give all the joy and all the knowledge.

* * *

The best way to increase our capacity to love is through understanding ourselves.

* * *

I think everyone knows the wonderful experience of loving one person, so you can imagine what it's like when you love three billion people. It would be three billion times more enjoyable.

* * *

Love is a constant attitude that evolves in us when we develop it. We should try practicing the love first on our family. Grant everyone in the family their own beingness. Then apply it to friends, then strangers, then everyone.

* * *

The more we practice love, the more we love, and the more we love, the more we can practice love. Love begets love.

* * *

The more we develop love, the more we come in touch with the harmony of the universe, the more delightful our life becomes, the more beautiful, the more everything. It starts a cycle going in which you spin upwards.

The only method of receiving love is to give love, because what we give out must come back.

* * *

The easiest thing in the universe to do is to love everyone. That is, once we learn what love is, it's the easiest thing to do. It takes tremendous effort not to love everyone and you see the effort being expended in everyday life. But when we love, we're at one with all. We're at peace and everything falls into line perfectly.

* * *

In the higher spiritual love, there's no self-deprivation. We don't have to hurt ourselves when we love everyone, and we don't.

* * *

With love there's a feeling of mutuality. That which is mutual is correct. If you love, you hold to that law.

* * *

Love is smothered by wrong attitudes. Love is our basic nature and a natural thing. That's why it is so easy. The opposite takes effort. We move away from our natural self, cover it, smother it with concepts of the opposite of love and then, because we're not loving, unloving comes back at us.

* * *

We feel the greatest when we love.

* * *

The real love wins the universe — not just one person, but everyone in the universe.

* * *

Behind the concepts of non-love, there is always the infinite love that we are. You can't increase it. All you can do is peel away the concepts of non-love and hatred so that this tremendous loving Being that we are is not hidden anymore.

* * *

Love is an absolutely necessary ingredient on the path. To get full Realization, we must increase our love until it is complete.

* * *

When you really love, you can never feel parting. There is no distance, because they're right in your heart.

* * *

Only through growth do we really understand what love is.

* * *

When you really love you understand the other one fully.

* * *

Love is an attitude that is constant. Love doesn't vary. Love cannot be chopped up.

* * *

All love, including human love, has its source in divine love.

* * *

Every human being is basically an extremely loving individual.

* * *

When you love, you think only the best for those you love.

The more you love, the more you understand.

* * *

There's one word that will distinguish the right love from the wrong love, and that is giving.

* * *

You could hug a tree the same way as a person when you are very high. Your love permeates everything.

* * *

Total self-abnegation is the most selfish thing we can do. When self-abnegation is total we think only of others and are automatically in the Self.

* * *

Love is the state of the Self. It is something you are.

* * *

Consideration is a necessary part of love.

* * *

Anything but full love is, to a degree, hate.

* * *

Can you see why you can't be against anything? The ant is God, the enemy is God. If you're limiting any part, you're holding God away. Love cannot be parceled. Love has to be for all.

* * *

The greatest of all progress is love.

* * *

Your capacity to love is determined by your understanding.

* * *

If you don't trust someone, you don't love him fully.

* * *

If we love this world we accept the world the way it is. We don't try to change it. We let it be. We grant the world its beingness. Trying to change others is injecting our own ego.

* * *

The more we love the less we have to think.

* * *

Being love is higher than loving. The real devotee of God has no choice to love– he is love.

* * *

Love is your Self. That is the highest love.

* * *

Love is an attitude that is constant. Love doesn't vary. We love our family as much as we love strangers. To the degree we're capable of loving strangers, to that degree we're capable of loving our family.

* * *

Love is togetherness.

* * *

Love is the Self. The Self doesn't love. The Self is love. (Only in duality can you love.)

* * *

It's not loving, it's being love that will get you to God.

* * *

Love: Each one glorifies himself by service rendered to others and must, therefore, necessarily receive from others. Thus God flows back and forth and we delight in His exoticism. There is nothing so delectable as the spirit of givingness. It is intoxicating beyond any other experience capable to man. Discover this.

Service is the secret to bathing in the ever-new joy of God. Service opens the doors to the greatest fields of beauty and charm, wherein is enjoyed the nectars of the infinite variety of tastes, all blended into one drink, that of superlative love.

Come into the garden of the most delicious and everlasting joy by an everlasting desire to love and serve. Let go of the emptiness of selfishness. Fill yourself to the full with selfless love.

* * *

"Our real nature, the infinite real self that we are, is simply us minus the mind."

Lester Levenson

Session 6

REALIZATION

A BETTER WAY

Most knowledge is intellectual. It is acquired from reading books and from traditional, cognitive forms of education. Most of us have a lot of this intellectual knowledge. And yet we are still not realized. It must follow then that to achieve "realization," we need a different kind of knowledge, a knowledge that can be experienced, felt, and integrated. We can call this knowledge "Experiential." Experiential Knowledge is the only useful kind for growth, for through it we can finally realize our inner sight. This kind of knowledge also fits with our feelings. It feels right, and integrates with our whole Beingness. Through Experiential Knowledge we know, and even more importantly, we know that we know.

Realization is seeing something, really seeing it for the first time. Realization is like an electric light bulb turning on in the mind, and it allows you to say, "Oh, now I see." It allows us to hear something that we might have heard a hundred times before, but this time, upon hearing it and seeing, we experience it as real. This is realization.

This "Experiential" Knowledge is the only knowledge that does us any good. But, this does not mean we do not use our mind. We do. The difference is that rather than using the mind to "make up" the answers, we direct the mind toward the place where the answer is. And when we do, we discover that the answer does not come from the mind. It comes from a place behind and beyond the mind. It comes from the realm of knowingness, the realm of omniscience. By quieting the mind through stilling our thoughts, each of us has access to this realm of Knowingness. Then and there we realize. We know and we know that we know. Are there any questions about what I just said?

QUESTIONS AND ANSWERS

Q: Are knowingness and feelingness the same thing?
Lester: No. The feeling comes just before the knowing.

Q: Is knowingness beyond feeling? Is knowledge that which feels true?

Lester: The answer to both your questions is "Yes." It's something you'll have to experience. There's a feel of things, and also there are times when you just know and you know you know, and there's no feeling to it. Knowing is really a higher level. We start with reasoning, thinking, in the realm of thinkingness. Then we move into the realm of feelingness. The top realm is the realm of Knowingness.

Q: Is ego implied in feeling?

Lester: Yes. The ego does the feeling. It is a higher ego state. Therefore, there's duality — "I" feel "emotion." Knowingness is awareness. When I said: "You know and you know that you know," you're aware and you're aware of the fact that you are aware. There's nothing conditioning it. The very top state is the state of All Awareness, of All Beingness. Beingness and Awareness turn out to be the same thing when we get there. Before, it seems as though they are two different things. But when we move to the top, Beingness, Awareness, and Consciousness are all the same thing, because the Awareness you are aware of is being All Beingness. We see that we are not only this body, but that we are every other body, every other thing, every atom in this universe. So, if we are very being and atom, we are all Beingness.

Q: You mean I am That?

Lester: Yes, definitely! It's "I!" The top state is "I." That's all, not even "am." Just below the top is "I am." A step below that is "I am that I am." A step below that is "I am unlimited." A step below that is "I am great."

Q: Or one with God?

Lester: Well, where is "One with God?" One with God is not a top state because it's in duality. If I am one with God, there is an "I" and there is a "God." In the ultimate state, we discover that "I" is God, there's only a singular Oneness in the universe, and we are, we must necessarily be, that Oneness. That's what we discover at the end of the line, or the beginning of the line, whichever way you look at it. We are unlimited Beings covering over this limitlessness-with concepts of limitation, the first of which is "I am an individual separate from the All," — that's a very first and a very big error we make. "I am separate, I am a personality, my name is Lester, I have a body," — and

I spiral right down. After we assume a mind and a body, then we assume all these troubles and problems but they're nothing but assumptions. They are only a fiction which we see after we go within, quiet the mind, and discover all the truth right there.

This whole world, as now seen, is nothing but a dream-illusion that never was. The Truth is just behind the outward world. So why make trouble? The growth is simply the elimination of all the concepts of limitation. That infinite perfect Being that we are must always be infinite and perfect and therefore is perfect right now. That's one thing we can never change — our unlimited Self. That is all the time. But I, the unlimited Self, can assume that I am limited and that I have a mind, I have a body, I have problems. However, it is only an assumption.

Q: What's the technique for cutting through all that, for getting right to that state where you have that total awareness?

Lester: Pose the question, "Who and what am I?" and await the answer to present itself. The thinking mind can never give the answer, because all thought is of limitation. So, in quietness and meditation, pose the questions: "Who am I?" "What am I?" When other thoughts come up, strike them down. If you can't, ask "To whom are these thoughts? Well, these thoughts are to me. Well then, who am I?" and you're right back on the track of "Who am I?" Continue this until you get the answer to the question "Who and what am I?" regardless of how long it takes.

The answer is the unlimited Self. The only way It becomes obvious is when the mind stills almost completely. The only obstacles to immediate full realization are the thoughts, every one of which is limited. Eliminate those thoughts and you'll see this infinite Being that you always were and are, and always will be.

The difficulty is the past habit-patterns of thought, the unconscious constant turning and churning of thought in a mechanism we have set up that we call the unconscious mind. The unconscious thoughts are simply our thoughts that we do not look at, and so we call them unconscious. This is the enemy we set up. To lessen these unconscious thoughts, we first make them conscious. When we make them conscious, we may let go of them and they are gone forever. This quiets the unconscious mind. The more we eliminate the thoughts, the more obvious our real Self becomes. The more obvious our real Self becomes, the more we are able to scorch the remaining thoughts, until the mind is totally quieted.

Q: You have to still the conscious thoughts before you can get to the unconscious thoughts?

Lester: The conscious thought is only the unconscious thought made conscious.

Q: They come through dreams too, at that state, the unconscious thoughts?

Lester: Yes, but it's only in the waking state that we can eliminate them and thereby grow.

Q: You still your conscious thoughts through meditation, other techniques, etc. Now, the "Who am I?" will go right through both, is that correct?

Lester: Yes. Also, you can use "Who am I?" to still or eliminate thoughts. Pose the question "Who am I?" and when a thought comes up, you say, "To whom is this thought?" The answer is "To me." "Well, who am I?" and you're back on the track. Thus, you eliminate the thoughts as they come up.

Q: But what keeps the unconscious thoughts from popping up at that time?

Lester: They will and should pop up. It they pop up, they're conscious. Then you can drop them. Eventually, you eliminate all of them.

Q: How many minds do we have?

Lester: There's only one mind. What we are looking at this moment is what the world calls the conscious mind. The part of the mind we're not looking at this moment the world calls the unconscious mind. It's the mode of mind which we give a different name to. What we are talking about now, what we are aware of now, is what we call the conscious mind, the conscious thought. The unconscious mind is all the thoughts we are not interested in at this moment.

What some call superconscious thought — there's really no such thing as superconscious thought. The superconscious, that which is above consciousness, is already out of the thinking realm — that's the omniscience, that's the realm of Knowingness. The superconscious real is All Awareness, All Knowingness. There is no thinking when you know.

Q: Is unconscious different from subconscious?

Lester: Subconscious and unconscious are the same.

Q: Do you agree with Jung's collective unconscious theory?

Lester: I only agree with Truth. And this is one thing I emphasize — **Truth is the only authority for truth.** Accept nothing until you can prove it out. Don't even accept what I say, no matter how much I speak as though I know. If it doesn't fit into your knowingness at present, you can accept it for checking. But only that which you can prove out for yourself, only that should you accept. This is basically important. **It is absolutely necessary to prove all this knowledge for yourself.** Otherwise, it's hearsay to you. You must make this knowledge your knowledge.

Now, there's only one Truth, one Absolute Truth. So putting names to it doesn't mean anything. Whether so-and-so said it or I said it, it doesn't mean anything. Is it true? Does it integrate into your understanding? That's the only thing that matters. That's the point wherein we are different. We try to make this very practical so that you can use this knowledge and move toward the total understanding as quickly as possible.

Q: Is it necessary to go through stages?

Lester: No. How long should it take Infinite Power, Infinite Knowledge to know that It is infinite?

Q: It wouldn't take any time.

Lester: Right. When man so wills with full intensity of will, it happens quickly. If you would want this more than anything else, you would have it in a matter of weeks or months.

Q: Is there any way of making yourself want it more and more?

Lester: Yes, make yourself want it by experiencing the wonderfulness of it.

Q: Or make yourself more and more miserable?

Lester: Well, there are two incentives; misery is one but not the best. The sweetness, the wonderfulness, the glory should make us want it more than the misery should.

Q: The glory in what sense?

Lester: The glory, of knowing what you are. It's a tremendous experience, it's an ecstasy, an euphoria. There are no real words to describe it because, well, we're in an age where these things are not experienced and therefore not understood, so how can there be words for things that are not understood? There are no words to describe these feelings, they're so beyond present understanding. So you pick the words you know best to describe it and that's it. Paramhansa Yogananda uses the words "ever-new joy welling up every second," and that's a practical way of describing it. At first, it's a joy that spills over every second, just keeps pouring out, pouring out — you feel as though you can't contain it. Later on, it resolves itself into a very profound peace, the most peaceful peace you could ever imagine. It's a delicious peace which is far more comfortable than ever-new joy. But please, get the ever-new joy!

Q: But don't stay there.

Lester: That's it. It's very easy to get stuck in the ever-new-joy state. That's what they call the ananda sheath. It's the last veil we have to remove. It is the last wall we must break through. When you start this ever-new joy, it's so good you just want to continue it. Also, you have no feeling of need to change, everything is so wonderful. But it isn't the final state. The final state is the peace that passeth all understanding. It's a deep, deep peace. You move in the world, the body moves, but you have absolute peace all the time. Bombs could be dropping all around you and you have that perfect peace, regardless of what's going on.

Q: How do you maintain that state?

Lester: If you get it, you don't have to maintain it, because you have it, you are it.

Q: Well, in that particular state then, you are really omniscient and all the other things, and there's no necessity for thinking.

Lester: Right. That's the top state. Now, it is possible to dip into this state to a certain depth that's very deep and not maintain it because the habits from the past, the habits of thoughts that have not been eliminated, re-emerge and take over. We can feel this infinite Being that we are and it's a wonderful experience — then, the next minute, "Oh, so-and-so wants me to do this and I don't want to do it," a thought comes in and there you are: identifying with unhappy limitedness. You, the Self, are trying to be this unlimited Being through a very narrow ego, a very limited ego, and it hurts. That's all it is.

Q: How do you bombard that ego and get rid of it?

Lester: First and foremost, an intense desire to let go of the ego. Second, listening to someone who knows the way and following through on the direction, especially if that one is a fully realized Being.

Q: That's hard to find.

Lester: No, they are available right where you are. Wherever you are, they're right there. I can name some of them: Jesus, Buddha, Yogananda have been in the physical body. But there is no need for a physical body when you can get the others wherever you are — because they're omnipresent. All you need to do is open your mind's eye and see them. They're omnipresent so they must be right where you are. Also, they, wanting to help you, must necessarily come to you if you open yourself to them. They have no choice. They have made a commitment. So all you need to do is to ask for their help and guidance and open yourself to it and it is there.

However, since we think we're physical bodies, sometimes we more readily accept a fully realized Being when He is in a physical body. Therefore, we will take more help, because in our physical sensing, He seems to be more real. Because of that, it's good to have a fully realized Being in the flesh. However, if we don't have one, it doesn't mean we can't take the guidance of those who are omnipresent.

Q: Some aspect of the Hindu thought says you don't do it without a live Guru, but I think they've evolved beyond that now, and you're confirming it.

Lester: Yes. However, a Guru is alive, whether in physical body or not.

Q: Do people need a live Guru?

Lester: People need a Guru, a Teacher. He doesn't necessarily have to be live in a physical body, but he has to be accepted as being alive. He doesn't have to be in a physical body.

The reason why we need a Guru is that we are in a very difficult age. It's an age of materialism where everything, everyone, is shouting at us: "This is a material world. This is it!" We have been in this world again and again and again. So we really need the assistance of a fully realized Being to offset that constant weight of the world that says we are physical, limited bodies.

We should want the Truth more than we want air. Then we would get full realization very quickly.

Q: Did you coin that, is that yours, an aphorism?

Lester: Nothing is mine. Anything I say will have always been said before. I might just twist the words around this way or that way, in my own style, but there's nothing new. Truth always was and always will be.

There's a story in the Eastern writings of a master and his disciple. They were bathing in the Ganges and the disciple asked: "Master, how can I know the Truth?" And the teacher took him by the hair and held him under the water until he was about ready to go unconscious, and then he let him up and said, "Now, when you want Truth as much as you wanted air, then you'll have it."

They have some great stories. That snake and the rope story is an excellent analogy of the physical world. I guess everyone knows that, don't they? A person walks along the road at dusk and sees a rope on the ground, mistakes it for a snake, goes into an intense fear and a complete involvement as to what to do about this awful snake. Well, the snake is only an illusion. The real thing is a rope. So he spends a lifetime of maybe sixty-five years struggling and fighting this snake-world, and then takes a rest on the astral side and comes back and fights it again and again and again until he wakes up to the fact that the snake was only the rope, and it really never was. And that's exactly what happens to this physical world. It's just like that snake, it's an illusion.

The example I like best is that what goes on in this world is exactly the same as what goes on in a night dream. While we're in the night dream, it's very real, we are there, there are other characters, it's either beautiful or ugly, and when it's a nightmare, we're being killed.

It's a real struggle. All the time we're in the dream, it is real to us. But when we awaken we say, "Oh, my gosh, it was only a dream, it never really was." And that's exactly what happens when we wake up out of this waking-state dream of the world.

* * *

"The more you quiet the mind, the more you feel the Self — and the better you feel. You feel as good as your mind is quiet."

Lester Levenson

Session 7

LOVE, GIVING AND THE CHRIST CONSCIOUSNESS

THE SECRET TO JOY

"Love" and "giving" in fact, are two words that are synonymous. It is in the spirit of givingness that the secret to joy lies. When we fully have, we want to give everything we have to everyone we meet — we have infinite joy. It is so important. It is in the spirit of givingness. This does not, of course, mean the givingness of things, which unfortunately, has become a lot of what Christmas is about.

Christmas is related to Christ. Christ is not the man Jesus. Christ is the title Jesus attained, the Christ Consciousness. If you separate the two, Jesus and Christ, you will better understand the meaning of His words and the meaning of the Bible. When He says, "I am the way," He is not referring to himself as Jesus, but to the Christ Consciousness. Before going further, let me explain what I mean by Christ and Jesus.

Jesus was obviously the man who was born on this earth approximately 2,000 years ago, who through righteousness or right-useness, rightly used the world to attain the Christ Consciousness. By so doing, He showed the way to immortality that each and every one of us must take. We must die to death, i.e., eliminate from our consciousness all thoughts of death and hold in its place only eternality and immortality. In order to show us, He allowed Himself to be crucified so that He could prove immortality by resurrecting Himself. He was a way-shower, and dedicated and gave His life to show us the way.

Christ Consciousness is the consciousness that saves us from this mess that we find ourselves in when we try to be worldly. It is the attaining of the Christ Consciousness that saves us from all the horrors and miseries of the world. It is the Christ Consciousness that gives us liberation from all difficulty and leads us into our immortality. If we were to try to be Jesus, we would have all the trials and tribulations that He went through. However, when we become the Christ, being Christ-like and thereby attaining the Christ Consciousness, we eliminate every misery and have nothing but infinite joy.

So Christhood is a state that was attained by the man Jesus. He attained His Christhood before He was born and He came back to show us the way by actual example. And if you will keep these two ideas, their meaning in mind as you read the Bible, I believe it will make much more sense.

As a result of Christ Consciousness, Christmas is known primarily by the spirit of givingness, good will toward all men. Locked up in that word "givingness" is the key to all happiness. It is in the spirit of givingness that we have and experience the greatest joy. In fact, if you reflect on your life for a moment, you will see that when you were giving, you were most joyous.

Of course, the spiritual feeling of givingness is felt more around Christmas time than any other time of the year. And that is a wonderful thing. But, we should make every day Christmas. And when we get to full realization, that is just what we do. There isn't a moment in which we're not giving everything we know to everyone.

QUESTIONS AND ANSWERS

Q: You mean giving things, or giving of yourself?

Lester: Well, if we give with strings attached, with reservations, with recriminations, it doesn't matter. There is little joy in it. But when we give freely, we have the greatest of feelings. And it's this constant spirit of givingness that is the secret of eternal joy.

Now, the greatest thing we can give, as the Bible says, is wisdom, because when you give one wisdom, you give not just one single thing, but you give one the method of attaining everything. So, the greatest of all givingness is giving wisdom, is giving understanding, is giving knowledge.

It has been explained in this way. If you give a man a meal when he's hungry, he's made happy for the moment and he's satisfied. But three hours later, he needs another meal, and probably thousands of meals after that. So, what is one meal that you give to him? Relatively little. However, if you give the man the understanding of how to produce a meal, he will never go hungry! You will give him the knowledge of how to always have all the food he wants. You will have given him sixty thousand meals! So, that's the greatest givingness — giving understanding and wisdom.

Practicing this would be an excellent method of growth. Give this understanding to everyone whom you meet who asks for it. It's excellent in that it takes you out of your "little" self into the greater self. It's an act of love. I'm suggesting that this givingness be taken on as a way of life from here on — help others to get this understanding. It will help you to rapidly attain mastership — and it will give you he greatest of all joys.

There is nothing wrong with giving other gifts. It is good to give, but they should be given from the heart. Still, I think we are all at the point where we can give much more than just things. We can give wisdom and understanding.

Q: Should we give only if we are asked?

Lester: It is sometimes a good idea, for if we try to help people who are not asking for it, we may be just expressing our own ego. "I know something you should know," see? "I," talking down to "you," trying to teach you something when you're not asking for it, it can be ego-expression on my part. So a good rule is to give it when it is asked for.

Q: Is there a time when you become sensitive enough so that you do say things to people which they need, even without them asking?

Lester: Yes, there is. As you let go of your ego, you automatically tune in more with others. You reach a state in which they don't even have to ask. You'll discover that some people who ask don't really want help. Likewise, some people who say "I don't want any help," are really wanting it. It takes a little experience to handle situations like that. But it's true that as we grow, as we let go of our ego, we become more attuned to others and we automatically help them. And we help at all times, no matter what or where the situation is. It could be the cashier in a market, or someone you meet of the street. There's always a certain givingness that should be going on all the time. And it doesn't have to be only words of wisdom, it could be a kind word, an expression of love.

It wouldn't hurt to try helping others. That would be the greatest of all givingness. Any more questions?

Q: What is the second coming of the Christ?

Lester: The second coming of the Christ is not the same as the second coming of Jesus. The second coming of the Christ is when we attain the Christ Consciousness.

As a group, we are very fortunate in that we are close to Jesus. Jesus is very interested in us, in trying to help us with all the power that He has. That power is never given unless we are receptive to it.

There's no forcing it. He can only use His power when we open ourselves to Him. If and when we do, He is right there, ready and very capable. Just try Him. We need this direct connection with a master if we want to go all the way this lifetime. As I've said, it's so difficult in these times to achieve mastership, that it is necessary to have this connection with a master, so that when we are ready to leave this plane, he will assist us in getting full realization. There isn't anyone in this room who cannot make it this lifetime, if he or she will just stay faithful to the path until the end. Everyone of us can make it this lifetime if we really want it.

Q: Will you define "making it?"

Lester: Christhood and full realization. "Making it" is becoming a master. What is a master? A master is one who is master over all matter in the universe, and who is master over his mind. A master is one who sees his own infinity right within him. A master is one who has undone all thoughts of limitation, who has ripped off all the sheaths of limitations and is free.

Q: And this we can do in this lifetime?

Lester: Yes, definitely! You must want it more than anything else. You must want it more than you want things of the world. And if you do, when you're ready to leave this place, you'll get the assist from the master that you look to and he will help you over. The way he will do it is this: if you don't make it before you die, you will make it at the time of your so-called death. When a person dies, all thoughts of this lifetime and all thoughts of prior lifetimes come up for review. The master identifies with us. He sees us as himself, and as these thoughts come up in our mind, it's like coming up in his mind, and he, identified with and as us, helps us undo them. When they are totally undone, we are totally free!

Q: This is what we are doing every day when we say, "We're not limited. I won't accept this. I'm not this limited being." Isn't this what we should be doing all day long?

Lester: Yes. We should continue it until the end of all thoughts. We should not be limited by any thing or any thought.

Q: But this is jumping so far. I'm interested in being able to walk down the street without getting mad at the fellow in front of me.

Lester: I'm trying to show you the entire way. What I'm trying to do is to give you a map that takes you all the way. I'm not saying, "Bob, be this today." But I think if you have a map that shows the entire route, you can take it all by yourself. You don't need to have people like me say this to you. Once you have the map, all you need to do is to follow it. I'm trying to give you a complete picture, a complete understanding of what full realization is and the way to accomplish it. And it's a very difficult thing to do because you'll never really know what it is until you attain it.

Q: And the ego is simply the feeling that I am not this.

Lester: Right. The ego is a feeling that I am a separated individual, separated from the All and I need a body and a mind to be separate.

Q: That's limited?

Lester: Well, if I have a body and I have a mind, I have thousands of limitations; I have to feed the body, take care of it. I have thoughts. My feelings are hurt. This goes on and on and on. Realize what you are. You'll see that you are not the body, you are not the ego. Discover what you are and be infinite.

Q: Can Jesus save us?

Lester: Jesus doesn't save, the Christ Consciousness saves. We should believe not in Jesus but believe as Jesus believed. When we make an effort to attain the Christ Consciousness, Jesus helps us to realize it. Jesus is always available to anyone who asks and is receptive to His help.

You can contact Jesus, to the degree you actually accept the fact that you can. Were you to accept that you could talk to Jesus in a physical body — then you would meet with Him in a physical body. If you can accept meeting with Him in a vision or in a dream, then you would meet with Him in that manner. If you can accept Him as a presence, then you will feel His presence and receive His support. It is all up to you.

* * *

"If, with intense interest, you want to know: What am I? What is this world? What is my relationship to it? — if there's a real burning desire to get the answer, — then all other thoughts drop away and the mind becomes extremely concentrated."

Lester Levenson

EGO

The ego concept is the root cause of all delusion and therefore, all trouble. It is the false identifying of "I" with a body rather than with the Self. What follows are some thoughts and reflections on ego and limitation. Again it is suggested that they be digested slowly. Read one, pause, let it work within you and then move on.

* * *

Ego is the concept of individuality, of separation from the "I," the All. Therefore, ego is a false assumption. We are really the "I," we are not separate from it.

* * *

The ego is the source of birth and death and when the ego is let go of, you die to death.

* * *

Everything that isn't good has its source in the ego sense and is therefore unreal. Our real nature is an ultimate goodness.

* * *

Everything of the ego is the opposite of everything of the Self.

* * *

Everything an ego sees is a distortion in the light of Truth. Everything an ego sees is in duality. An ego can't see Oneness. The ego has an eye of duality only. There's nothing true that an ego sees. And on the opposite side, the Self sees only the Truth, the Self.

* * *

The coloring agent of Truth is ego. The less the ego, the less the coloring of Truth.

* * *

The entire trouble is wrong identity. We say we are the limited ego.

* * *

Ego can't do anything but be limited.

* * *

There's only one single growth and that is letting go of the ego.

* * *

Whenever you are not growing spiritually, you are growing in the other direction.

* * *

Every time you express ego, you are growing downward.

* * *

The more you grow, the more you can face your ego.

* * *

When things bother us and we look for the source, we find our ego.

* * *

The whole object of the path is to let go of the ego. What remains is the Self.

* * *

The whole thing is simple. Any complexity in life is the ego trying to undo the simplicity of Reality.

* * *

It is the ego that makes life difficult.

* * *

The more you think you are a limited ego, the more effort you need to get along. It is the ego that requires effort.

* * *

There is only one basic trouble in this world. It is the common denominator of all problems. It is trying to be an ego.

* * *

Identify with the ego and you identify with trouble.

* * *

We should shift from a desire to get out of misery, to a desire to let go of the ego.

* * *

The ego dies hard. But once you know the ego is the source of all misery and the Self is the source of all happiness, then it shouldn't be so hard to work at letting go of the ego.

* * *

When we start moving into the Self, the ego starts putting blocks in the way: we get sick, we go to sleep, we have other things to do, etc., because we feel we will be destroyed if the ego is destroyed. We have convinced ourselves over the millenniums that we are these limited bodies, and we think it takes time to let go of these concepts of limitation.

* * *

Time is an ego-thought.

* * *

The ego will always try to keep us from letting go of the ego.

* * *

Getting involved in intellectual questions and discussions validates the ego and avails you nothing.

* * *

Pose a question and ego is necessitated. There are no questions when one is realized.

* * *

All enquiries about the non-Self are directing one's attention away from, and are delaying one's realization of Truth. Any question about the ego directs the attention to the ego. The ego is the unreal, the untruth. No matter how much you talk about illusion, it will not give you the perception of the Real — the Truth.

* * *

In the beginning, the ego is the only thing you know.

* * *

There is only one thing to do — let go of the ego! There is no other way to grow. You are fully realized now! Just let go of the ego! That's how simple it is.

* * *

The weaker the ego, the more you can put attention on the Self. However, if you spent all your time on the ego, you would never see the Self, not until you looked at the Self. It amounts to weakening the grip of the ego enough so that you can turn toward the Self.

* * *

The more you do away with the ego, the more unselfish you are.

* * *

When a person is ego-centered, almost all of his attention is centered on himself. Everything he sees or hears is colored because it has to filter through his self-attention.

* * *

When you have completely let go of your ego, you are not interested in yourself, you are interested only in others.

* * *

If you do things to win approval, then you are doing it for yourself. If you are doing anything for yourself, it isn't selfless.

* * *

A problem is created whenever you want to assert your ego.

* * *

Whenever we react, it is always because there is something we selfishly want.

* * *

When there is no ego involved, we see things exactly as they are.

* * *

We are blinded to the degree of our ego.

* * *

Wanting our ego to be accepted, we see things the way we think they will help us to be accepted.

* * *

If you have any emotion, it is ego motivated.

* * *

Any human need or desire is ego motivated. My ego thinks it needs things. My Self feels and knows that everything is mine.

* * *

We should have no wants. Then we are never in trouble.

* * *

Talking is asking for ego attention. It's wanting ego approval. If you will remain quiet, you may feel that happiness that you are seeking through making the noise.

* * *

Almost every time we talk, we are asking for ego acceptance.

* * *

Ego is only destructive to one.

* * *

Everyone who has ego is destructive to the degree he has ego.

* * *

73

Ego is the opposite of Love. Love is the Self.

* * *

Egos want to direct the universe.

* * *

If you want to be most creative, do away with ego.

* * *

Ego is the most expensive thing in the universe, dollar-and-sense wise.

* * *

Any sense of doership is of the little self.

* * *

Ego equals blindness. Blindness equals ignorance.

* * *

Seeking any ego fulfillment is seeking the letting go of the agony of the concept of lack.

* * *

Any lack is necessarily an ego concept for the ego is necessarily a sense of limitation or lack.

* * *

Ego is a mere notion that feels like the deluge of an ocean.

* * *

When you are unhappy, you are looking for ego approval and not getting it.

* * *

Another definition for trouble is trying to be an ego.

* * *

Any defending of oneself is asking for ego approval.

* * *

If you want to be good at anything, the less the ego, the better you are. The ego is a limiting adjunct on the Self. Since the ego is a limiting adjunct of the Self, the less the ego, the more capable you are in everything (except one thing — misery.)

* * *

It took you millions of years to develop this ego. Keep letting go of the ego until you begin to see the Self. When you see your Self, you quickly drop your ego in short time.

* * *

After having eliminated much of the ego, when one is acting ego-wise, at that moment the ego seems like all. However, what has been eliminated, has been eliminated.

* * *

It's the ego sense of being an individual separate from the All that is the source of all trouble.

* * *

It doesn't matter what you do, it does matter with what you identify. If you identify with the limited ego, then you are unhappy.

* * *

After dropping enough ego, it gets weak and the Self takes us the rest of the way.

* * *

All growth is letting go of ego.

* * *

The ego is a false imposition of the "I." When you say, "I," that is the eternal you.

* * *

The ego cannot be subjugated by one.

* * *

Seek the source of the ego and it turns out to be your Self.

* * *

Humility is letting go of ego.

* * *

If you are hurt, look for the ego motivation and let go of it. You'll feel happier.

* * *

Unless you are eliminating ego, you're not growing. You see, you can't grow into the Self because that's what you are. You just lift off the cover, which is ego.

* * *

The ego creates and maintains the subconscious.

* * *

All subconscious thought is originated by the ego and hidden away in the subconscious by the ego.

* * *

The ego-principle is the cause of the seeming separation of you from the All.

* * *

The high states should be used to scorch the ego. The higher we go, the more we are capable of scorching the ego. When you are high, you can say, "All this silly reaction and ego, I'm through with it!" — and be through with it.

* * *

The real you, your Self, is infinitely grand and glorious, whole, perfect and in total peace, and you are blinding yourself to this by assuming that you are a limited ego. Drop the blinder, the ego, and be forever in perfect peace and joy!

* * *

Be your self!

* * *

"If you want to know what your sum total thinkingness is, look around you. What you now have is a result of what you have thought."

Lester Levenson

MASTERING MIND AND MATTER

THE ULTIMATE HAPPINESS

Our subject is happiness. We can say that when it is understood, Happiness as well as — God, Realization, Wisdom, and Understanding — become the same. We can also say that we are seeking is the real infinite Being that each one is. And when we recognize this, we then attempt to discover this inner Being that we are — until we see it completely, totally and do only it. When we do, the ultimate Happiness is established permanently, and forever. And with it's establishment comes immortality, unlimitedness, imperturbable peace, total freedom and everything else that everyone is seeking.

We get to this inner Being by directing our attention inward. First we focus the mind back upon the mind until we discover what mind is. Then we focus our attention on our Self to discover our real nature. And it turns out that our real nature, the infinite real Self that we are, is simply us minus the mind. We discover that the mind was a limiting adjunct covering our Beingness; that all thoughts have limitation which prevent us from seeing this infinite Being that we are. By turning our attention inward we discover all this. When we do, we let go of all these limitations easily and naturally and see that we have always been, are now, and always will be, this unlimited Being.

The prime obstacle we meet in seeking this unlimited being is the subconscious mind. It is full of thoughts of limitations which propel us every day and they do so automatically. We have made these habits of subconscious thoughts so strong that even when we recognize the direction we would like to go in, the subconscious thoughts keep directing us for quite sometime (sometimes lifetimes) until we finally succeed in overcoming them. We overcome them with thoughts of what we really want to do in life, and in that way we become master over the mind, — controlling and eliminating the thoughts until only the thoughts we want determine our behavior. Then we're in a position where we can do something about the mind. We can start to transcend the mind, rising above it and dropping it. In short we let it go! And when we do we find ourselves this pure, infinite, limitless, totally free Being that we naturally are. Then happiness is complete.

As I said the direction to go in is within, seeking and meditating to quiet the mind enough so that we can see the infinite Being that we are. The first step involves becoming aware of the fact that we are master over matter (and matter includes the body).

The second step involves becoming master over mind. And when we become really masterful over mind we are able to let go of mind and operate in the realm of omniscience, in the realm of knowingness. Then we are fully aware of the infinite Being that we are, and we discover the ultimate Happiness.

CONSCIOUSLY CONTROLLING MATTER

Let's look more closely at the first step, — consciously controlling matter. Whether we are aware of it or not, we are controlling matter all the time. Whether one wants to be a creator or not, one is. In fact, it is impossible to not be a creator all the time. We are creating every day. We are not aware of it because we just do not look at it. We have demonstrated or created everything we have! Every thought, every single thought, materializes in the physical world. It is impossible to have a thought that will not materialize (except that we reverse it). If we think the opposite right after we have a thought, with equal strength, we neutralize it. But any thought not reversed or neutralized will materialize in the future, if not immediately.

So this "demonstration" that we are all trying so hard to accomplish, we are doing all the time and are unconscious of the fact that we are doing it. All we need to do is to consciously direct it, and that we call demonstration. Everything that everyone has in life is a demonstration. It could not come into our experience if we had not had a thought of it at some prior time.

If you want to know what your sum total thinkingness is, just look around you. What you now have is a result of what you have thought. It is your demonstration! If you like it, you may hold it. If you do not, and want to change some part of it, start changing your thinking subconscious to the contrary. Concentrate it in the direction that you really want, allowing the thoughts to come up and let them go until the conscious thoughts become dominant over the subconscious thoughts. And when you begin to consciously demonstrate small things, you may then realize that the only reason why they are small is because you don't dare to think big. The exact same rule, or principle, that applies to demonstrating a penny, applies to demonstrating a million dollars. The mind sets the size. Anyone who can demonstrate a dollar, can demonstrate a million dollars! Become aware of the way you are demonstrating a one dollar bill and just increase it next time to a much larger amount. Take on the consciousness of the million, rather than the one dollar bill.

The material world is just an outward projection of our mind into what we call the world. And when we realize that it is just an outward projection of our minds, just a picture out there that we have created, we begin to understand how easily we can change it, even instantly, by changing our thought!

So, to repeat, everyone is demonstrating, creating, every moment what he or she is thinking. We have no choice. We are creator, so long as we have a mind and we think, we are a creator.

BEYOND CREATION

Now, to get beyond creation, and there is a higher state than creation, — it's the state of beingness sometimes called awareness or consciousness. We must go beyond the mind, and just beyond the mind there is a realm of perfection where there is no need for creating.

The mind finds it very difficult to imagine what it is like beyond creation, because the mind is involved constantly in creating. It is the creating instrument of the universe and everything that happens in the world. So if we take this thing called mind, the instrument which is only a creator, and try to imagine what it is like beyond creation, it is impossible. The mind will never know God or your Self, because you have to go just above the mind to know God, your Self.

To know the infinite Being that you are, to know what it is like beyond creation, we must transcend the mind. Here we find the final state, the changeless state. In creation everything is constantly changing, and therefore the ultimate Truth cannot be there.

So, to demonstrate what one wants, one needs to become aware of the fact that all we need to do is to think only of the things that we do want and that is all that we would get — if we would do just that. Only think of the things we want and that's what we'll be getting all the time. Simple, isn't it?

Also, take credit for creating all the things that you do not like. Just say, "Look what I did." Because when you become aware that you have created things that you do not like, you are in the position of creator, and if you do not like it, all you have to do is to reverse it and then you will like it.

After you can master matter by consciously creating that which you want, then master your mind and get beyond it.

Any questions?

QUESTIONS AND ANSWERS

Q: Am I to assume that everything that I see and meet during the day has been created by subconscious thoughts?

Lester: Yes. The difficult thing is the unconscious thinking. Every unconscious thought is active whether we are aware of it or not.

Q: So, if I have a habit of having someone who doesn't pay rent, this is a subconscious thought that was put there by parents or someone before.

Lester: No, put there before by you — it's your thought.

Q: So it's best to look at it and say, "Where did this habitual thought come from, and by looking at it, I can see where it came from and erase it from my consciousness and erase that particular habit or thought?

Lester: Yes. Putting it a little better, rather than seeing where it came from, seeing that it's been in you. Then you see how silly it is to have this thought working against you and you automatically drop it.

Q: I wish I could. I just don't automatically drop it.

Lester: No, you don't. There isn't just one thought on each subject, there are millions. I don't like to say this, but there are millions that you've acquired over many millions of years.

Q: If I have a habit of having something reoccur in my life, let us say a delay in getting things done, which is quite common in my business, is this purely my consciousness?

Lester: Yes.

Q: And it's nonsense to say this is the way real estate people operate, isn't it? I've got to look at my consciousness and if I say this is nonsense because it's my thinking, I can eliminate this type of delay.

Lester: Yes. It's possible.

Q: How does one eliminate re-occurring conditions in one's life?

Lester: By constantly working to undo it. Looking for the subconscious thoughts that are causing it and dropping them.

Q: It's my thoughts; I don't look at anything but my own thinking.

Lester: Yes. Now there is another way, a better way. If you can't pull up the subconscious thoughts, you can now put in a conscious thought with strong will — so strongly that it overrides all the prior unconscious thoughts. This is possible. This is called using will power. You can will it. And if you will it strong enough, it'll override all the subconscious thoughts. When you're feeling high, that's when you have your greatest will. Just will it to be the way you want it to be. The mechanism is: You put in a thought with so much power behind it that it's more powerful than all the former subconscious thoughts put together.

Q: A man died last night and he left $25,000,000! And the man next door had nothing. He died and went to heaven.

Lester: It's easier to get to heaven when you don't have $25,000,000 holding you here.

Q: It's easier to go, if you don't have $25,000,000?

Lester: That's right. He's attached to that twenty-five. He's trying to hold onto it right now, even though he is dead. And when he tries to pick it up, his astral hands go right through it and he's in trouble. It holds him back, whereas a man who didn't have anything will just go off into higher, freer realms.

Q: You mean now that he has so-called "died," he can still be attached to his money?

Lester: Oh sure! What he was the moment before he died, he is the moment after, except for the fact that he has let go of the dense body. The physical body is an exact copy of the astral body. And when you step out of the physical body, it feels the same to you and you try to do the things that you were doing just before in the physical body — if you have attachments to the physical world. If you don't have attachments, you adapt much easier to the freer way of life, in the astral body.

Q: I like your explanation of creation.

Lester: For the intellectuals, there are schools that argue this way: Is creation gradual or is it instantaneous?

Q: It's gradual because...

Lester: The mind toys it's gradual. And if you keep thinking about it, you'll discover that creation is instantaneous. And the instantaneity also has the concept of time in it. That's just something I'm throwing out for you to work on, if you want to.

Q: An instant — you're confining it to a certain amount of time; you are limiting it.

Lester: I'll give you a clue. You went to sleep and you dreamt that you were borne into a little infant body and you went through one year, two years, three years, into youth, middle age and old age, all the way up to ninety years. It took ninety years to get up to that old body. It was a long, long time — right? ninety years? — until you woke up and then realized it was a dream and it might have taken a second or two. The dream lasted a few seconds and in that time you went through a ninety-year period! And it seemed like ninety years while you were in the dream. It wasn't until you woke up that you realized it was only a few seconds. Some day you'll see that creation is instantaneous, with the mental concept of time in it.

Q: How do you equate our effort in trying to create that which we might desire with the statements, "Seek ye first the kingdom of God and all good things will be added unto you," and "Think not of what you shall eat and where you shall sleep"?

Lester: Well, it fits in. "Seek ye first the kingdom of God," — God is the essence of our very beingness. If we seek and discover it, we find the secret of everything. So, seek ye first the kingdom of God, go within, discover who and what you are, then you have the secret to everything, not only to creating but to everything. But you see, that's been part of several years of what we have been going through as a group: how to go within and discover this infinite Being that we are, which is the God-part of us. And when this infinite Being is discovered, everything is known — how to create, and more than that — how to uncreate. And still more important, how to get beyond creating and uncreating — which is the ultimate state. Then you will not think of what you shall eat and where you shall sleep. Did I connect it for you?

Q: Until you reach the higher state, I wonder if it isn't possible to get caught up in still trying to create before you become aware of the higher state?

Lester: Yes, I say that you are caught up in trying to create. You now have no choice whether to be a creator, you are that all the time. You should now consciously create only the things you want and stop creating the things you don't want. One of the grossest errors we make is trying to create in the future: I will have this, I will get that, and when we do that, it keeps it in the future, thereby giving it distance from us. This is the greatest stumbling block for most people. When you create something, it has to be seen in present time, in its is-ness — now. It is mine, now!

Q: Well, even if I can't believe that I may be going to have something, at least I can believe that the thought is mine, so, if I build on "The thought is mine," this gives me more foundation.

Lester: Yes. Discover who the thinker is.

Q: What happens when you reach the desireless state?

Lester: Well, what is desire? Desire comes from thinking we are not the All. When you reach the desireless state, you see yourself as the All, as the sum total, and there's no more need, there's no more lack — everything is you. It's not yours — you are it!

Q: So, it's a state of seek ye first the kingdom of God and all this shall be added unto you.

Lester: Everything, every last atom in the universe.

Please note that most of your questions have been on havingness, the havingness of things. This indicates what you think happiness is. However, you will discover that should you obtain all the things you desire, you would still find yourself not happy.

You must go beyond the havingness state and reach the beingness realm where you only are. There you know you lack nothing and that you are the infinite All. There lies the ultimate joy which is a deep and a most profound, Peace — the ultimate Satiation!

"The more you quiet the mind, the more you feel the Self — and the better you feel. You feel as good as your mind is quiet."

Lester Levenson

Session 10

THE MIND

The mind is an instrument created by you to image the Oneness separated into many interrelated parts. Here are some thoughts on the mind for your reflection. Trust them as you have the other reflections. Allow them to serve you. Let them build one upon another.

* * *

The mind is simply the sum total composite of all thoughts.

* * *

The mind becomes habitual.

* * *

The subconscious mind is merely the thoughts that we are not looking at now.

* * *

The subconscious mind is running us — making us the victims of habit.

* * *

The thing that keeps us from recognizing and expressing our infinity is simply the mind, conscious and subconscious. If we are to express this infinite nature, we can do it only by getting behind this mind. When we reach the realm behind the mind we operate without thoughts, intuitively, and are in harmony with the whole universe.

* * *

The direction is to still the mind. Quiet the mind and you'll see your infinity right there.

Just let go of the mind completely and what's left over is your infinite beingness, all knowing, all powerful, everywhere present.

* * *

Were we to direct all our energies to stilling our mind, we would soon be realized.

* * *

The mind quiets spontaneously in the company of a great soul.

* * *

The more you quiet the mind, the more you feel the Self — and the better you feel. You feel as good as your mind is quiet.

* * *

When the mind vanishes, there the Self is. Where the Self is, there is no mind.

* * *

The mind is reflected consciousness, reflected from its source, the Self, just like the light from the moon is reflected from the sun. While the moonlight may be used to reveal objects, it is no more needed when the sun rises. Although the moon may remain in the sky while the sun shines, it is dim and useless. Likewise, the mind is useless when we let the Self shine.

* * *

Your mind is an instrument used to identify your real Self with your body and world.

* * *

If you do not identify with your body or mind, neither your body

nor your thoughts will affect you. So it is when you sleep. Not identifying with your body or mind you have no problems nor suffering.

* * *

In meditation one subdues the mind and feels the wonderful peace
of the Self. This is the start. The finish is the total dissolution of the
mind. This is accomplished by recognizing the mind as not being
apart from the Self, by seeing it as a phantom product of the Self.

* * *

In this dream-illusion there's a thing called thought. And thought
determines and is the cause of all matter.

* * *

In your imagination you have written and projected a cinema show
of acts, actors and audiences on a screen and have lost sight of the
fact that it is all in your imagination, your mind. Discover this and
you discover the absolute Truth.

* * *

The world and universe are a mental concoction.

* * *

Mind subsidence is Realization. There are two ways to obtain it.
On recognizing what the mind really is, it is seen as an illusion and
therefore subsides. By concentrating on your Self and discovering You,
mind also subsides. Complete subsidence is full Realization.

* * *

The reason thoughts wander back into the world is because we
believe the world is real. But for this belief, Realization would be!

* * *

Mind distraction is wanting more the things of the world than the

Self. Wanting more to hold your Self, the world is not looked at!

* * *

A thought is an assumption of lack causing a wish to fulfill it.

* * *

All thoughts are of non-truth. It's so simple. You just stop the thoughts and the infinity that you are is self-obvious.

* * *

You've got to use the mind to quiet the mind. You need to use determination to still it.

* * *

When you begin concentrating on the mind, you begin rising above it.

* * *

Once you see what the mind is, you won't be subject to it any more.

* * *

Strength of mind is the ability to concentrate undistractedly on a single thought.

* * *

Without concentrated mind, progress is relatively small.

* * *

A wandering, waivering mind is one that dissipates one's energy in the form of many thoughts. Hold one thought and the energy is less dissipated and more conserved. Direct this conserved energy toward the Self and your Self will be revealed. The more you do this, the stronger becomes your direction and the easier it becomes to abide in your Self.

* * *

In the beginning, the mind pursues the Self intermittently between long intervals. As one continues, the intervals shorten. Toward the end, the mind is constant in the pursuit and does not wander from it.

* * *

The power of the mind is almost infinite. When there is only one thought all that power is right there.

* * *

Restless thoughts keep the Great Ones away. A quiet mind keeps the door open to them.

* * *

The more you eliminate mind, the more peace you feel.

* * *

The mind will never discover the Self because the mind is the cover-up over the Self. It's only by letting go of the mind that the Self is seen. You get the mind quiet enough to allow your Self to be obvious to you so that you may use It to let go of the mind.

* * *

Eliminating what you are not is growth.

* * *

The biggest difficulty is the subconscious mind. We have relegated things to the subconscious, stored them there, and thrown away the key.

* * *

If we could make our subconscious fully conscious, we would be fully realized.

* * *

Every mind uses the very same unlimited intelligence. Everyone uses it as much as he believes he can use it to fulfill his desires. When he learns that his mental limitations are self imposed, he lets go of them. Then his intelligence (I.Q.) can be raised to the degree of no limitation.

* * *

We are all in the same mind and the only thing that keeps us from reading the other one is that our attention is too centered on our own little self.

* * *

Everyone unconsciously reads everyone else and thinks that it is their own thoughts.

* * *

All minds are influencing each other.

* * *

A high-level mind tunes in with other minds of high level. A low-level mind tunes in with other minds of low level.

* * *

Mind is catchy. It's immediately infectious.

* * *

Thought is a mechanism of limitation.

* * *

The only intelligence the mind has is what you give to it.

* * *

Thoughts smother the capacity to be happy.

* * *

Every thought causes a demonstration.

* * *

There's no limit to the number of new ideas that man can have.

* * *

Anything man can think, can be.

* * *

You use your mind to still your mind. When you are meditating, holding one thought, other thoughts drop away.

* * *

Mind is always seeking external knowledge. Direct it internally.

* * *

Introvert the mind and realize to full realization.

* * *

The ego-mind struggles for survival and tries to subvert your direction.

* * *

The mind cannot give the ultimate answer because it's part of the ego, part of our limitation.

* * *

Real knowledge lies just behind thought, which is relative knowledge, and relative knowledge is ignorance.

* * *

When the Self, which is just behind the mind, is discovered, you see that the mind is limited and let go of it.

* * *

There is a mind that runs this planet. There is a mind that runs the solar system and a mind that runs the universe. All these minds are in the illusion.

* * *

Where is the world without your mind? Is there such a thing as world when you submerge the mind? The thought of the world creates it. This whole solid universe that you mentally say is a solid universe is just your thought that it is a solid universe.

* * *

Anything your mind is absolutely convinced of, materializes instantly.

* * *

Mind can do anything with the body.

* * *

The utmost that the intellect and reasoning can do for us is first, recognize its limitations and secondly, do that which helps the quest for the Self.

* * *

Every thought is an affliction. When the thought waves are completely stilled there are no more afflictions.

* * *

Every thought is motivated by a desire for pleasure or an aversion to pain.

* * *

Letting go of all attachments and aversions is letting go of all your thoughts.

* * *

Thought and desire are the same.

* * *

The only thing we are aware of is our own thoughts.

* * *

What we're seeing out there is our own mind.

* * *

That which you really want you never forget — it's always on your mind. Really want to discover your Self.

* * *

The mind is the brain of the astral and causal bodies..

* * *

The mind can be made quiet wherever you are. The place to do it is right where you are.

* * *

Don't mind the mind and the mind won't need minding!

* * *

The mind is not made noisier — it's just that you get quiet enough to notice how noisy it is.

* * *

Everything falls perfectly into line effortlessly and harmoniously without thoughts.

* * *

As mind gets quiet, first the sense of havingness decreases until a measure of security is felt. It becomes less necessary to have in order to be. Then the sense of doership decreases until a further security is felt in that one is not the real doer, that the real doer is a higher power, that one can actually be with much less doing and it becomes less necessary to do in order to be. Finally your real Self that has always been in the background steps in and takes over and you feel that there is nothing necessary any more that you must have or do, that there is no choice but to only be!

* * *

Use omniscience, don't use the mind! The goal is to eliminate the mind.

* * *

If there are no thoughts then there is no mind. Mind is only thoughts.

* * *

If you take away your mind what's left over is Omniscience. You are that omniscient Being that you are seeking, clouded over by mind.

* * *

Mind detached from world and centered only on Self is Liberation.

* * *

Depth of meditation is the degree of quietude of mind.

* * *

Unless we're eliminating mind, unless we're eliminating ego, we're not progressing.

* * *

The more we keep looking into the mind, the quieter we become.

* * *

Where the mind is all quiet — there is all knowledge.

* * *

Knowing the mind is full Realization.

* * *

The first thought of all thoughts is "I am an individual — separate." In order for there to be a he, she or it, first there has to be an I. So we create I, and then there are others. Without the first thought or I there can't be any other thoughts of anyone else. That's the first basic error — I am a separate individual. If I am separate then there has to be others, he, she and it. And you start dividing up the One by first becoming an individual separate from it. Thought first divides and separates you from the One Beingness, and then creates a multitude of beings and things and all the relationships. It's all your thought

— that's all it is. Let go of thought and what's left over is you, infinite, eternal, glorious, all joyous, serene!

METHODS OF MIND REVELATION

1. See the source of the mind and you will find your Self.

2. Turn the mind back upon the mind and it will reveal its secrets.

3. Concentrate the mind on one thought and all other thoughts will drop away.   Then drop this one thought.

4. Learn to control the breath, and you will automatically control the mind.

5. Eliminate the ego. The ego thinks and causes all thought. The ego is the identifier of the Self as the body.

6. Surrender the mind to God.

7. Eliminate all objectivity and the mind resolves. Then there is only subjectivity.

8. The mind must be eliminated permanently by realizing that it is not real but only an apparency, an illusion that has its source in your Self.

9. Where there is only subject and no object, there the Self is.

* * *

"You become everything instead of nothing. Become everything and you need nothing. Desire is lack and the consciousness of separation, the source of all trouble."

Lester Levenson

Session 11

MEDITATION AND THE QUEST

QUIETING THE MIND

The prime purpose of meditation is to quiet the mind. When we hold one thought with interest, other thoughts keep dropping away. Thoughts of the day, "What he did to me, what she did, what I should have done." All these thoughts are active on a subconscious level. As we hold to one thought, these subconscious thoughts quiet; they become still. They drop into the background, and that quiets the mind.

Now, the most important thing in quieting the mind is interest. When you are very interested in something, you will override all other thoughts. Likewise, if, with intense interest, you want to know, "What am I? What is this world?" What is my relationship to it? — if there is a real burning desire to get the answer — then all other thoughts drop away and the mind becomes extremely concentrated. Then the answer shows itself. It comes from within. The answer is there all the time. The quieting of the thoughts allows us to see it, to see the answer that was there all the time, there in the realm of Knowingness — the Self.

THE STARTING POINT

The starting point should be a strong desire for the answer. When that desire is strong we get the answer. That is why man's extremity is God's opportunity. Extreme adversity causes in us a desire to get out of it with such intensity that we concentrate our mind and discover the answer.

When I started my quest I thought "thinking" would give me the answers. I had a mind that was as active as any mind could be. But I was at the end of the line. I had had a second heart attack and they told me I was finished, that I had only a short time to live, so I had to have the answers. And even though my mind was far more active than the great majority of minds, the intensity of the desire for the answers caused me to hold to one question at a time, obliterating all else. This kind of concentration did it!

I started seeking with no knowledge of metaphysics, no knowledge of the way. In fact I was anti-religion and anti-metaphysics. I thought it was nonsense, a diversion for the weak-minded, for people who believed in fairy tales.

But it was only because of the intensity of the desire to get the answers — I had to have the answers — that they began to come, and they came relatively quickly. Over a period of three month's time I went from an extreme materialist to the opposite extreme: the material is nothingness and the spiritual is the All.

The wish to get the answer was so strong, that in spite of my mind being one of the noisiest of minds, the answers began to come. I automatically fell into things (I knew no words for them) like samadhi. I would concentrate on a question with such intensity that I would lose awareness of the world, lose awareness of this body, and then I would be aware of just a pure thought — the thought itself would be the only thing existing in this universe. That's absorption when the thinker and the thought become one. One loses consciousness of everything but that one thought. That's a very concentrated state of mind and the answer is always discovered right there.

I started with "What is happiness? What is life? What do I want? How do I get happiness?" I discovered that happiness depended upon my capacity to love. At first I thought it was in being loved. I reviewed my life and saw that I was very much loved by my family and friends and yet I was not happy. I saw that was not it. Continuing, I realized that it was my capacity to love that gave me happiness.

The next question was "What is intelligence?" I persisted until Ah! I saw it! There's only one intelligence in the universe and we all can obtain it.

I, then, worked on responsibility and discovered that I was responsible for everything that happens or happened to me. Creation was something I created!

A SINGLE QUESTION

Finally, I held the question "What am I?" until the answer presented itself.

And this went on and in a matter of three month's time I believe I saw the entire picture, I went all the way — only because of the concentrated approach. I knew nothing about the subject; I knew nothing about the direction, the way, the path, but I wanted to know: "What am I? What is this world? What's my relationship to it?"

You discover that the whole world is nothing but you, that there never was anything but you all alone, because there's only One and you are It! But that is not the final state. You come out of it and there's still a certain amount of mind left. So you go back into the meditative quest until there is no more mind controlling you. When you have eliminated all the habits of thought, all the tendencies of mind, you are free; then you can use your mind and you are the master and director of it. It no longer determines you, you determine it.

At present we are over 90% of the time controlled by the unconscious mind.

Do you have any questions?

QUESTIONS AND ANSWERS

Q: When you say 90%, do you mean the conscious and unconscious mind both?

Lester: Well, the conscious mind is easily controlled. The subconscious is not because it is not easily seen. It's a mechanism we set up to not look at our thoughts, of making them operate automatically. We did it to our entire body; it's all automatic now. And then we did it to all thoughts but the thought we're interested in at the moment.

Q: Why is it that we did it to all thoughts except the one we're interested in at the moment?

Lester: Because we don't want the thoughts in the first place, so we push them away to the background. We are happiest when there are no thoughts. Sometimes, when you work with your hands, you're very happy, right? Why? The thoughts are quiet.

Q: Then your mind is quieted at that time, or is it operating on the subconscious level?

Lester: Well, consciously and even subconsciously it's quieter. We really don't want thoughts. Thoughts are the things that make us unhappy; even the happy thoughts make us unhappy because while we are enjoying something, we're concerned about the possibility of maintaining this pleasure which we know is not going to last. The thought of the pleasure at the same time evokes the thought that it's not going to last. Even thoughts of happiness are limited. The really happy state is the no-thought state; it's the state of Knowingness and is beyond thought.

102

We started with the subject of meditation. Meditation does seem to be a question in many people's minds who have meditated for years and years. The best type of meditation is with question. When you just drop into a nice quiet state without question, you get a good feeling but no progress of getting the Knowledge.

Q: There isn't any progress when you're just quiet?

Lester: There is in that you're moving toward the quiet state. And the quiet state is a better state than the noisy state. In that sense it's a step forward. But the major problem we have now is called ignorance. We are ignorant of the fact that we are infinite. To get rid of ignorance we need the Knowledge of our infinity. To get the Knowledge we have to enquire. So when we go into meditation and just get peacefully quiet, that's good — but don't stop there. Go beyond that and get the answers. And it's necessary to get quiet to get the answers. Only the answer to "What am I?" gets us to the top. That is easy to see, isn't it? So if we want to take the quickest way, we start with the question that we finally have to answer, "What am I?"

So for more rapid growth meditation should be with question. Here's where the jnanis get the advantage over the bhaktas. Surrender and devotion throw us into nice feelings and they're good. But a jnani goes further; he says, "All right, don't stop there, get the answer." It's only when we fully know who and what we are that we're at the end of the road. So the fastest and best way to meditate is to pose a question, get quiet and stay quiet until the answer shows itself. Then go to the next one until all the answers are there.

Q: If we find we aren't making much progress, could we pose the question "What's holding me up?"

Lester: Sure — you could. That is a good one.

Q: You know I think you had it easier because you didn't have a lot of preconceived ideas.

Lester: You're right. I was very lucky that I knew nothing because intellectual knowledge about the subject is an obstacle. The ego substitutes intellectual knowledge for real experience. I was very, very fortunate not to have had any knowledge of it.

Q: You also didn't realize that it's as difficult as most people think it is.

Lester: Yes. However, knowing what you're telling me helps one let go of the obstacle of intellectual knowledge. I prod you in this direction, don't I? I say, "Don't believe anything. Start from scratch. Build up your knowledge on the solid foundation of proof, step by step." Everyone must do this.

Q: You can't take someone else's experience?

Lester: Right, you would be working on hearsay, on what they have said, and the only useful thing is that which you experience. I relate it to driving a car. If I say I know how to drive a car after reading a book that directs you to turn the key on, start the motor, shift into drive and step on the gas — do I know how to drive a car? No, not until I experience it can I drive a car. It's the same thing on the path; we must experience everything.

We must, of course, adopt the attitude that what the Great Ones say is so, that they have experienced it. However, you must check it out and prove it for yourself. And the basic Truth is that there's only one Reality; there's only one absolute Truth — and that is this whole world or universe is nothing but God, but better than that, is nothing but my very own Self. God could be far away; He could be miles and miles away in cosmic space, but my very own Self is right here, this is something I know about, this is something I can perceive — it is my very own Self! So, using Self as God is far more practical than putting Him out there, putting Him apart from us. But each one must start from the bottom and prove this whole thing for himself. As the proofs come, the more they come the more we accept until we experience the whole thing.

You still want to hear more on meditation?

Q: Yes.

Lester: Every aid should be a means of quieting the mind. If meditation is difficult we can prepare the way by chanting. Chanting puts our minds on the meaning of the chant itself and the thoughts of the day drop away and that quiets the mind. Exercising the body, doing certain asanas, etc., does the same thing. Anything that helps is good whatever it is. The basic thing is to quiet the mind. Being loving and good makes the mind quieter.

The mind is the only thing that keeps us from seeing our Infinity.

The mind is nothing but a collection of thoughts of limitation. And in meditation we try to quiet that mind so we can see this infinite Being that we are.

Meditation should never be passive. We should never try to force the mind to go blank. Meditation should always be with question for the best results.

The more we practice meditation the easier it is to do. To get the real deep insights requires a momentum. When meditation gets to be more enjoyable that things of the world, then we go at it with enthusiasm and desire for it. And then we just can't wait until we get back to it. When we get that momentum going, the mind gets quieter and quieter until this infinite Self is self obvious and just glares at us and we laugh. Now maybe with all this talk on meditation, we ought to try it, O.K.?

Q: Does concentrating on your hands help to get your mind quiet? It seems to for me.

Lester: If it helps, it's good.

Q: It's not harmful then?

Lester: No. There are several centers one may concentrate on. A good place is up here, between the eyebrows. Concentrating here takes your mind off other parts of the body. It is the center for the third eye, the astral eye, the spiritual eye. It pulls us away from the lower centers of the body when we come up here. Some prefer the heart center. But anything that helps — helps!

Q: I used to concentrate between the eyes but now when I do inquiry, I let the "I" sink down to the heart.

Lester: The heart is a good place because it is the center of feeling, and feeling is closer to the Self than thought. It depends on your background. If you're a vichara jnani, it'll be the heart, but not on the left side, on the right side. If you're a raja yogi it'll be between the eyes. When I did my concentrating it wasn't on any location; it was on wanting to have the answer. Concentrate on seeking the answer.

Q: I haven't thought in terms of answers, I just thought in terms of getting there, that's all.

Lester: You see, anything in life that you wanted with intensity you already have. This goes for everyone and everything. It's the same with the path. But it's the unconscious conviction that our joys lie in the world that keeps us away from getting the answer.

Q: It sounds so easy the way you say it.

Lester: The ease is determined by the intensity of your desire for the answer. That's the crux of the whole thing.

* * *

"There is an easy way to realization. Just get rid of all desires."

Lester Levenson

Session 12

DESIRE

A desire is a disturbance of one's natural, inherent peace and joy. Desires keep one involved in trying to satiate the desires, consequently detracting one from his constant, natural, inherent happiness. In short, desire is the enemy of happiness and the source of misery.

So here are some things about desire to reflect on. As usual, let each one speak to you. Let it in and see what occurs.

* * *

The more one lets go of desire, the less disturbed the mind becomes allowing it to become concentrated. The more concentrated the mind, the more capable one becomes of discerning or realizing his Self.

* * *

Silence quiets the noisy demands of ego desires and allows your Self to be seen.

* * *

Solitude is the absence of desire.

* * *

The absence of desire is serenity.

* * *

Every time one tries to satisfy a desire, he creates a greater intensity of that desire. This comes about because the momentary pleasure, which is inhering more in the Self due to momentary stilling of thoughts, is attributed to the object of the desire and therefore, one wants the object more and more, vainly attempting to satiate the desire, which is satiable only in being constantly quiet from thoughts, i.e., constantly inhering in the Self.

* * *

The simultaneous fulfillment of all desires is in the finding of your real Self.

* * *

Desire is a bottomless pit that can never be filled up.

* * *

Desire constitutes the world and desirelessness constitutes the Self, God.

* * *

Desire is seeking the joy of being our Self through objects and people. The mind originally creates the thought of need or lack, which agitates the mind and covers the Self. When the object is attained, the mind stills, the joy of your Self shines forth and this joy is attributed to the object, and the mind then goes on seeking the object as the source of the joy. But the joy being not obtainable from the object, the mind seeks it more and more from the object and is never satisfied.

* * *

Desire is the mother of all motion, the disturber of all peace.

* * *

The basic mechanism of desire is, first, we create a lack and then desire whatever is necessary to fill that lack. The desire creates thoughts. The thoughts cover the Self and this makes us unhappy. Then we look to relieve that unhappiness by fulfilling the desire which momentarily stills the thoughts. The stilling of thoughts removes a bit of the cover of the Self and it's the feeling of a bit more of the Self that we call pleasure. We wrongly attribute that joy or pleasure to the thing or person that was used to fulfill the desire to relieve the agony of the thoughts of desire that were covering the Self. Because of this wrong attributing of the joy to the person or thing, the desire will never be satiated because the joy is not in the person or thing. The only possibility of satiety is to remain in your Self!

* * *

Fulfilling desire is momentarily letting go of the agony of the feelings of being limited by lack. This understanding should help you let go of the frustrating drive of seeking happiness where it isn't — in the world!

* * *

Desire is mind disquieted.

* * *

Recognizing who and what you are instantly satisfies all desires.

* * *

We should desire only God.

* * *

Desire leads only to misery and death.

* * *

Any desire upsets and disturbs the natural, inherent tranquillity and peace.

* * *

If one will stop thinking of something, his desire for it will disappear.

* * *

After you discover that desires are undesirable, you discover that there's a joy and peace that's ever-constant and more profound than any joy you have experienced before.

* * *

Desire is the start of all agitation.

* * *

A desire is an artificially created lack.

* * *

Ignorance creates the universe, desire sustains it, and enlightenment dissolves it!

* * *

If there were no desire there would be no world or universe of limitation.

* * *

Desire is the source of all trouble.

* * *

If desire overwhelms us it is because we want it to. Who turns on the desire? If it's in your power to turn it on, it's in your power to turn it off. The more it is turned off, the weaker it becomes.

* * *

Desire only growth. Everyone makes the Goal eventually, but the intensity of the desire determines when and how soon. If your desire is strong, you think only of that. The doubts then drop away.

* * *

Don't suppress desire, actually let go of it. If you create the desire in you, you can uncreate it.

* * *

The worst thing to do is to suppress a desire, any desire. When it is suppressed, from that moment on, it will try to express itself. Recognizing it does not mean we must try to satisfy it, but does prevent suppressing it.

* * *

Nervousness is caused by wanting two opposing things at the same time, one consciously and the other subconsciously. The battle is resolved when you make the subconscious desire conscious. On the other hand, if you know what you are, there will be no conflicts. You can do that through seeking. It is not necessary to understand the negative. It is far better to be the positive. Be your Self.

* * *

Seeking any ego fulfillment is seeking the letting go of the agony of the concept of lack. Any lack is necessarily an ego concept.

* * *

In order to be infinite beings, we must have no desires because any desire is a limiting action upon ourselves. If we think we need something, we think of ourselves as being limited. If you have everything, if you are everything, how could you want something? You know you don't need anything and you go through life knowing all the time that you need nothing. Your attitude is different. With this attitude, should there be a need of the body, it's immediately fulfilled. You don't have to think about it, it is taken care of immediately.

* * *

The only thing that creates thought is desire. As long as there is one single desire, there will be disturbance and lack of complete contentedness.

* * *

Any desire satisfied disappears forever.

* * *

There is an easy way to realization — just get rid of all desires.

* * *

One way to overcome desire is to have a very strong desire for God. And, in the end, you have to get rid of your desire for God. Then you are It!

* * *

Every little ego wish is a clamp down on your freedom which is tantamount to saying every desire is a clamp down on your freedom.

* * *

Desire creates thoughts, desire to have or not to have. Before desire is ego. So ego is the starting point. I'm an individual separate from the All, so I've got to desire to get the All.

* * *

The only thing that disturbs peace is desire.

* * *

When things are approached with pure love, there is no more desire.

* * *

Desire plants seeds for the future.

* * *

Decrease desire for the world; increase desire for the Self.

* * *

You must get rid of all desire. You can enjoy without desire. In fact, if you really want to enjoy things, you can enjoy far more without desire.

* * *

Desire is the cause of everything. Any time you have any problem, there's desire behind it.

* * *

Any desire except desire for liberation is causing misery.

* * *

The odd thing about desire is that the more you try to satisfy it, the stronger it becomes. The more people try to satisfy their desire by having things, the stronger that desire becomes. People have more things today than they have ever had and they are unhappier than they have ever been.

* * *

Desire just cuts off happiness.

* * *

You should have only one desire — a desire for complete liberation, complete realization. Any other desire will keep you in trouble. We should try to let go of all desires. We should not try to fulfill desires. Every time we fulfill a desire, we strengthen that desire, rather than weaken it. I believe that is obvious to all of us —that we never satiate desires. The more we try to satisfy them, the more we want of them. So, it is better to not satisfy desires and by doing so, the mind gets quieter. When the mind is quieter, we have a better chance to see the Truth. When we see the Truth, we scorch the desire, and this is the better way — actually the only real effectual way of getting rid of desire.

When you see the Truth, desires are scorched because a desire is really trying to be your own real Self through some indirect means, through some thing, through some person. When you see this, you let go of these silly desires because why struggle through an indirect means to be that which you are? The indirect means cannot make you what you are, so it is fruitless and extremely frustrating. Consequently, we have this frustrated world. We are all trying to satisfy desire; it is absolutely impossibly to do it, and we go on and on, lifetime in, lifetime out, until we recognize that desires are our enemy.

Desire is an admission of lack. If I am the infinite One, I desire nothing; I am the All. We must get back to that state by behaving as one would in that state. The greatest behavior, the greatest ritual, that we can perform is living as a fully realized Being would live. Try to attain the state of dispassion — no attachments, no aversions. Try to attain a state of equanimity, a feeling of equalmindedness toward every thing, every one. Try to attain the desireless state. Then, you will see that you are the All, that you are That!

* * *

"No one can do anything to us. No one can do anything for us. Someday you'll see this."

Lester Levenson

Session 13

WHAT AM I?

WHERE HAVE WE BEEN

Let us pause a moment to take a look at what we have been talking about, and where we are going.

As I have said, I describe the ultimate goal of every being as total and complete happiness with no taint of sorrow whatsoever. We are all striving for this in our every act, but somehow most of us keep missing the goal. In my opinion, the reason we miss our goal is simply that we do not have a clear vision of the goal and we, therefore, aim blindly. And, so long as we aim blindly, we remain blinded, and, can never attain the goal of perfect happiness.

Then, someone comes along and says, "Attention! You have spent many lifetimes looking in the wrong direction! Stop looking without and look within! Only there will you find that which you have spent lifetime after lifetime seeking!" You meet someone like Lester who tells you, "Seek your very own Self. Therein lies your complete happiness. Stop looking for happiness in people and things. When you look for happiness outside yourself, you merely eliminate the pain of the desire for one thing by substituting the relief of another and you call this substitution pleasure. But the pleasure is short lived because the desire is not eliminated. It has only been transferred to another object, and therefore as soon as the person seems to turn away or they change, or the circumstance allows the pain of the desire to re-emerge, it continues to gnaw at you."

However, the starting point is you. You can take the way that leads toward discovering you. And of course, only you can do it. Accept nothing unless you can prove it yourself. Prove it and it is yours. Prove it and then you can use it.

THE SCIENCE OF ALL SCIENCES

The uniqueness of this science, and someday you will see it, it's the science of all sciences. It is a subjective science. We have to seek it within; we can't put it out on a table in front of us and examine it. We can only examine it within our own mind, or better, within our own being. Also, the intellect does not avail it to us. The intellect can get us in the right direction to find it. The right direction is turning within, stilling the mind and experiencing this truth, this knowledge. And only by experience can we get to know it.

Methods are many, but the very highest is the method that everyone uses in the final end, and that method is finding the answer to "What am I?" This quest should be kept up all the time, not only in meditation, but during the day. While we are working, no matter what we are doing, in the back of our mind we can always keep that question posed, "What am I?" until the answer makes itself obvious to us.

The answer cannot, however, come from the mind. For any answer the mind can give us must necessarily not be it because the mind is an instrument of limitation. All thoughts are qualified; all thoughts are limited. So any answer the mind gives cannot be right. The way the answer comes is simply by our getting out of the way. By letting the blindness that we have imposed upon ourselves by assuming thoughts fall away. When the thoughts are quiet, the limitless Being is obvious. It's self-effulgent. It's there all the time. It's just covered over by thought concepts, every one of which is limited.

So, the way to uncover it is to pose the question, "What am I?" and quietly await the answer. Other thoughts will come in, and the biggest difficulty is quieting these thoughts. When other thoughts come in, if we pose the question, "To whom are these thoughts?" The answer naturally is, "To me." Then, "What am I?" puts us right back on the track again. That way we can continuously keep our attention on "What am I?"

BE NOT THE DOER

In addition to posing this question until we get the answer, it is good practice in our daily life to not be the doer, to not be the agent. Just be the witness! Acquire the, "It is not I but the Father who worketh through me," attitude. This is the main conduct of life that we should strive for. The more we become the witness in life, the more we become non-attached to the body, the more we are our real Self.

So, there are two things I am suggesting, one is the quest, "What am I?" and the second is, in living life, "Do not be the doer; be the witness. Let things happen; allow life to be." That's the way we are in the top state, and the best behavior in life is that which is characteristic of the top state.

There are many other things which I am sure you are aware of:

118

humbleness, goodness, kindness, honesty, etc. All these things help, but the greatest aid is — be not the doer. Be the witness.

THE APPEARANCE OF THE SELF

Now, when the Self of us presents Itself to us, it is a tremendous experience! It is a very difficult one to contain. We feel as though we are going to burst because we recognize our omnipotence, omniscience, and omnipresence! But just seeing it once does not establish us in that state. However, once we experience it, we will never let go until we reestablish it. We will continue to try, and we should continue to try, to get back into that state. The next time, it will last a bit longer, the third time, still longer, until finally we are in it twenty-four hours a day.

When we attain this top state, we are not zombies, but we are all-knowing and everywhere present. Everything falls perfectly into line. We move in the world just like anyone else moves, but the difference is that we see the world entirely different from the way everyone else sees it. We watch our body moving through life like an automation. We let it go its way. And since we are not really that body, nothing that happens to that body can effect us. Even if it were crushed, it would not mean much to us because we fully know that we are not that body. We know our eternal Beingness and we remain That!

So, one who has attained the top state is difficult to distinguish from anyone else. He or she will go through the same motions of life and whatever they were doing before, they might continue to do. But their outlook on life is entirely different. They are completely egoless with no concern for their own bodies. They are interested in others and not in themselves — they are interested in all humanity. Whatever they do has absolutely no ego motivation. Their body will continue to live its normal span and usually goes out, in the eyes of the unknowing, the same way most bodies go out, via so-called death and coffin. But the one who was originally connected with that body never sees any of this death. They see this entire world and body as an illusion that was created mentally just as we create scenes, cities and worlds in our night dreams. When we awaken, we realize there never was such a thing. And in the same way, when we awaken from this waking state, we see that the whole thing was a dream and never really was. That the only thing that ever was, was my Being, the absolute Reality, being all beingness, infinite, all perfect, all knowing, all powerful, omnipresent.

So, to reiterate, the main two points that I want to bring out are that the very highest method is the quest, "What am I?" As we pose this question in quietness, when other thoughts come in, ask. "To whom are these thoughts?" The answer is "To me." "Well, what am I?" and we're right back on the track again — until we get the total answer. The second point is to be the witness, not the doer. I believe that sums up what I have been trying to get across up until now. And questions on this?

QUESTIONS AND ANSWERS

Q: To not be the doer, do you plan? Do you do everything normally?

Lester: No, the right way is not to plan. Let it happen. Let go and you'll be guided intuitively. Instead of planning with thought, you'll do exactly the right thing, perfectly at the right moment, from moment to moment.

Q: There is a situation where someone might take a position of that kind when he hasn't really felt it; for example, he will say, "I'll just stay in bed until I'm moved." Meantime his rent isn't paid.

Lester: So, he'll have to move! If we assume that we are there and are not, we are soon awakened to the fact that we are not there, see. I'm talking from a higher level now, the perfect state, where everything is in absolute harmony every moment. There you never think, and at every moment you know from within just the right thing to do. You're guided intuitively each and every moment and everything falls perfectly into line.

Now, if you're not there, of course you have to think; you have to plan.

Q: Well, in practice then, in the beginning, it's probably a combination of the two where things go very easily, and then there's a hump in which you have to plan.

Lester: Definitely yes! In the top state, you do by knowing; you just know from moment to moment. One feels "I know it!" That's just the way it feels and there's no thinking to it — only "I know it!"

Q: I know from my own experience, I slip back and lay out a

plan, but sometimes that plan comes very easily and quickly to me and sometimes I have to struggle like the devil to work it out, step by step, and I don't know what's going to happen. Other times, I just lay out a plan and I know what's going to happen and I have no difficulty with it.

Lester: The word "know" as you use it, is the key. You know how that word feels when you say, "I know it!" There's no doubt, not one iota of doubt there. And it happens. That's the key. That's the realm of knowingness. Make that all the time. Keep working for it until it comes and stays. The quickness with which we attain this is determined by the intensity of the desire for it. The more we desire this top state, the sooner it comes. Everyone makes it eventually. I'm convinced that the majority of people on Earth today will probably take millions of years to make it. But any one of us who is consciously seeking the way out can do it this lifetime.

This so-called grace of God is always there. All those who have made the top grade before us are radiating the consciousness of perfection to us. We have tremendous grace being actually pushed our way all the time. However, they have no right to impose themselves and don't. We have to open ourselves to it in order to receive it.

We need this grace. Because of the state of affairs today, man is relatively low. We are very strongly convinced that we are a limited body and by long habit we are trying to hold onto it. So it's not easy to let go of this body, and because of that, we need the grace of the Great Ones who in our eyes have passed on, but in their eyes, they're still here. When we recognize that they are still here, we can see them and talk to them the way we talk to each other. If we accept them partially, we can talk to them in a dream or a vision. The way we meet with them is determined by our acceptance of them. If any one of us believed that he could go down to a restaurant and have a snack with Jesus, the way you believe you could do it with me — if you had that much acceptance — then you would do it.

Now, some of us know that if He were suddenly to appear in a physical body in the room, it would be too much for most of us to accept and therefore He doesn't. But the way He comes to us is determined by our acceptance of Him. He gave signs to some here and some did not recognize that He did. However, most of us did!

The point I'm trying to make now is that we should open ourselves to the help of the great masters. Jesus and the Great Ones want each and every one of us to know our perfection. They can't force it upon us. But their hand is always extended. It's good to keep this in mind. Then we open ourselves more to the help.

Q: How do you request and receive this help?

Lester: You have to be accepting of Jesus as being alive, just as much as we are, and capable of meeting with you, the way we meet with you — then it can happen. You have to be open to it. The help is always being sent to you.

Q: Are there words to say, thoughts to carry?

Lester: Yes. But I can't give them to you; that's up to you. See, I give you the general principle — acceptance of Him, the way He is. Don't expect Him to be not Christly because He won't be that. However, He can appear as a very humble human being in form. Being omnipresent, at any moment, He can appear to anyone and speak with him.

Q: Lester, He will be as Christ, He won't be in disguise, will He? The beggar at the door?

Lester: No. The only disguise is the one we put on Him. He would never disguise Himself. He wants to be recognized as Christ. That's not His name. The man Jesus had the Christ Consciousness. And we have to accept Him and His consciousness which is extreme humility, simplicity — no Hollywood glamour.

Q: Would you define humility?

Lester: Yes. The greatest humility is through surrender. It is surrender of the ego, the ego being a sense of separate individuality. Not I but thou; not I, but the Father who worketh through me. Everything I do is God's work, I am not the doer.

Q: If you surrender yourself as an individual, how about the other person? I think we mentioned before that we recognize the other person as ourselves and we treat them as though we are the same. Who is this other person?

Lester: From where you stand now, the other person should not concern you. The only thing that should concern us is what we do. For me, it matters not what your attitude is toward me. You could hate me with every cell in your body. But it's of extreme importance what my attitude is toward you. While you're hating me, I should love you fully and completely. Then you'll understand the answer to your question and you will see only the One. When you separate and then ask what's up here in the One, it just doesn't fit.

When we love, and only love, we are using the most formidable power in the Universe. No one and no thing can harm us. We can never ever be hurt or unhappy — if we would only just love without any hate. You can never be hurt when you love in the sense that the love is full, complete — divine love. It's just love with no, not one bit of, hate in it. It requires turning the other cheek, loving your enemy– that's the kind of love it takes.

Q: Love is understanding?

Lester: When you love fully, you understand the other one fully. Love is understanding. It's identifying with the other one, being the other one. Coming down a step, it's wanting the other one to have what the other one wants, loving the other one, the way the other one is.

Q: Then who is our enemy?

Lester: In reality, we have only one enemy and that's ourself. No one can do anything to us; no one can do anything for us. Someday you'll see this — that we in our consciousness determine everything that happens to us.

Q: Then it is our idea of ourselves which is incorrect?

Lester: Right. And that could be made better!

Q: When you say understanding, do you mean understanding in a logical sense, or do you mean acceptance of them without questioning the reason why they're doing things, good or bad; just acceptance of whatever they are in entirety?

Lester: It's acceptance in entirety. But the real understanding requires knowledge of what the Universe and the World are. When we see someone doing wrong, we have to know that this is a god-being, misguided. He's looking for God in the wrong place. Am I making sense? That's the understanding.

Q: Which in his mind would be happiness, right?

Lester: Yes. He's looking for happiness the way he sees it. Even a Hitler, in his mind, is doing right, and therefore should not be hated, but should be loved —wanting him to be what his real basic nature is. Now this doesn't mean approving of his program — it doesn't. But whether we approve or not of his program, loving and hating are two different things. So we love everyone, see them as misguided beings, forgive them for they do not know. They're like children — misguided. Attain the highest state of loving everyone equally as Christ did!

* * *

"Become everything instead of noth-ing. Become everything and you need noth-ing. Desire is lack and the consciousness of separation. The feeling of lack is the source of all trouble."

Lester Levenson

Session 14

THE KEY TO CONSTANT HAPPINESS

YOUR FREEDOM

I would like to give you the key to maintaining constant happiness. I did not do so earlier because we had to lay some groundwork, and you had to have some experience with the material. Also, if you just take my word for it and you receive a lift, you might say that I did it. This develops a dependency relationship, which isn't good. You, and you alone, can do anything and everything that you want. You can have, be, or do whatever you will or desire. It is much, much better when you do it and do not think you need someone to lean upon.

I know that what most people would like to know is how to maintain this new found happiness. And so here is the key to the understanding. It will help you develop happiness that remains.

THE KEY

This is the key: When you really know what happiness is, then you are able to establish it. Then you do it more and more until it's all the time. But the key is knowing what happiness is. When you do know what it is, you look for it where it is rather than where it isn't. Looking for it where it isn't is causing you to drop down from beingness. Is there any question on what I've said so far?

The key is knowing what happiness is, so that you can go directly for it. Not recognizing what happiness is makes it difficult to establish permanently. So when you get to see what this happiness really is, then when you become miserable you'll move in the right direction and establish that happiness.

HAPPINESS

All right, what is happiness? Most people call it pleasure but for most people pleasure is only escape from pain! Most people call themselves happy when they get away from their pain through socializing and entertainment, but this is really only an escape! Unable to be by themselves, with their own thoughts, they run to a movie, a nightclub, visit someone, or just get some action going so they are not facing their own thoughts. When their mind is taken away from their own thoughts, they feel better, and they call this pleasure and happiness. In many ways all entertainment is escape! A happy man needs no entertainment and no socializing. He is content.

However, when you become free, if you choose, you can enjoy entertainment far more than before because you are free from the hunger-need for it.

The happiness that I am talking about now is not the escape-from-misery kind. It is really the only happiness. It is the joy that results from being your own real Self. The more we are our real Self, the more we feel joyous. Sense-joy of the world is accomplished not because of the thing or the person out there with whom we associate it. It is accomplished by satisfying and stilling the thoughts of wanting to acquire or control or seek the approval of that person or thing. When we quiet those thoughts, we feel our Self and are happier. The quieter the mind is, the more we can just be. The more we abide our real Self, the more joyous we feel!

This is something you have got to experience for yourself — that the quieter you get your mind, the happier you are. It is good to play with this. Experiment with it until you see it. Whatever that joy was, it always resulted in quieting of the mind, and then you felt happy. Seeing this, you will begin to let go of attaching happiness to people and things. You will begin to see that the joy is only in you abiding as your very own Self. Then, when you discover this, you are not going to look for joy where it is not. You will immediately let go and just be. And finally, you reach the place where you need no one and no thing to be happy — you just are happy — all the time!

Are there any questions on this? I guess intellectually it is seen by everyone? Whether you see it through your own mind's eye or not, you should have it intellectually at first, then experiment with it, test it out, and you will discover that this is   so — that every time you feel happy, your mind is quiet and at ease, and that what you attributed to the person or thing outside of you is something going on within you. Quieting of your mind, you abide more as your Self. Then, when you see this, you will not bog down anymore. Because the moment you become unhappy, you will know where to look to re-establish the happiness!

QUESTIONS AND ANSWERS

Q: That would be within yourself, wouldn't it?

Lester: Yes, but one must first recognize that the happiness is not the external person or the thing, but the quieting of the thoughts of desire for the person or thing, which allows you to go within and just be your Self, i.e., just be. When your mind is on things out there, you're not just being, you're being involved with externals. But I say the key is seeing just that point — that your happiness is the quieting of your mind through the satisfying of the desire, which stills the hunger thoughts for the thing and allows you to just be. When you actually see that in your own mind, you can do it directly. (You can let go of those thoughts without achieving the person or the thing and immediately you're happy!)

It is important that you move toward happiness in the direction of where it really is — in you, not in the externals. In that way you establish a state of happiness that is continuous.

Q: I have heard this before and did not receive it.

Lester: All right, before it was just an intellectual thing or you did not understand and so it's as though it were new now. But, I always feel as though I'm saying the same thing over and over again, from this side, from that side, from another side — but it's always the same thing. However, until you see it in your own mind's eye, until you recognize it, until you realize it, it isn't meaningful to you.

Q: It sounds as though you're saying we should not desire automobiles, we should not desire homes, we should not desire wives or sweethearts, we should not desire anything, but become nothing.

Lester: Everything was right but the last part of your sentence. You become everything instead of nothing. Become everything and you need nothing. Desire is lack and the consciousness of separation, the source of all trouble. If you are everything, the All, you need nothing. See, everything was right down to that last part of your sentence — just reverse that and you've got it. O.K.?

Q: If we become everything, then we become the wife, then we become the World, we become everything. Instead of separating ourselves, we become the other one.

128

Lester: Yes. And that is the greatest of all feelings! That's the highest —when you become the other one. When you let go of your feeling of separation, that identity is love in its highest form. In other words, you think that she didn't break the dish, we broke the dish; she didn't spend money on a dress, we spent the money. This is the highest love.

Q: I become the automobile, therefore I don't desire the automobile. Or, you become everything, you become...

Lester: Now, you're going to have to work this out for yourself. You are going to have to realize that when you become everything and feel that you need nothing, then the slightest thought for something will bring it to you immediately.

Q: Desire is, "I haven't got it!"?

Lester: Yes! You create an artificial lack, you create a lie when you say, "I haven't got it." Desire, causes you to feel "I have not." And this will cause you to have not! Let go of desire and you feel "I have." This causes things to come to you.

Q: If I look at the world as though I'm writing a novel and say I am the characters, I'm all these creatures that I create in my story. And yet this is what I'm living today, aren't I? I create my difficulties; I'm writing this story. Instead of doing that, I should say I am the power, and why bother creating limitations? I don't need to. So, I stop it. But what do I have when I don't create?

Lester: What do you have when you don't create? Everything that you really want — your pure Beingness.

Q: I have peace.

Lester: Yes. You are the All — everything is in you. Feeling that way puts you completely at peace.

Q: Until the phone rings; then I'm right back in my habits.

Lester: Don't allow a little bell to push you around that way.

Again, I say each one has to realize this for himself or herself, but when he or she does, then happiness can be made permanent, because then you look for happiness where it is and you stop looking for it where it isn't. There's no happiness in people or things. Happiness is our basic nature. Happiness is our very own beingness. And when we are only being, we are infinitely happy. Yes, when we are only being, and nothing else, we are infinitely happy!

Q: In other words, when you have these various things, like you have an automobile, you utilize that automobile but you have no attachment to it, in order to attain the feeling of joy. Because if you become attached to that automobile, then that attachment has some sort of hold on you wherein you have a responsibility to it.

Lester: Yes. The greater the attachment the greater the unhappiness. (Likewise, the greater the aversion, the greater the unhappiness.) It's unfree to be attached to anything. You can have things and not be attached to them. Be attached to them and you are necessarily putting yourself through unhappiness.

Q: So when you're in a state of beingness, that does not mean that you're an ethereal being who floats from spot to spot. That means that you are in that state where you know the Truth and thereby don't have to go through all the habits that have been piled upon you by your ego.

Lester: Yes. It's knowing your infinite Beingness that is eternal and never changes. Then this world cannot touch you. You see it as a fiction, a dream. You witness it. You move through life with no attachments and no aversions. Then no one and no thing can disturb you, and you have the infinite peace and joy that is constant.

Q: When I try to explain this to people they think that I become a shadow or substance which vanishes from sight of everybody, or something like that.

Lester: The only difference between a fully realized individual living in the world and one who is not is his point of view of everything. An unrealized person identifies with a single limited bodymind. A realized person identifies with everything, every being, every atom and sees them as his Self. He sees the beingness in everything as his beingness.

Q: Therefore getting joy out of everything that happens?

Lester: No, your very nature is joy. You don't get it out of everything that happens — your basic nature is unlimited joy. That is your natural state! No need to get it!

Q: Therefore being in a state of joy perpetually?

Lester: Yes. As long as you don't lock it onto a person or thing, it's there all the time. But if you say you can't have joy unless you do or have something, you limit your joy. The natural state is unlimited joy. This is the real natural state. The natural state is being infinite, but we superimpose over that all these ideas of limitation, of needs, attachments and aversions that block out this infinite joy that is natural. If a being would do absolutely nothing, he would be this infinite Being. He would then be only a witness.

Q: But you can still put in a hard day's work?

Lester: Oh, yes. You go through life like everyone else.

Q: But it's your attitude.

Lester: Right — you see things differently. You see yourself as a witness rather than a doer.

Q: It's there but you're detached somewhat from it. It's an eerie feeling sometimes.

Lester: It's a nice feeling, isn't it? It's eerie because you're not used to it. When you get used to it, it's dearie rather than eerie!

Q: Lester, is this thing really easy, and we're making it hard?

Lester: Yes. You are so right! All your difficulty is keeping yourself limited. You have compounded limitations on top of limitations and are holding on to them in your thoughts. Therein lies your difficulty.

You must let go of all your thoughts. Every thought has limitation in it. Drop all your thoughts and what is left over is you in your infinite happiness — your Beingness. Then you will realize that it is as easy for you to discover that you are an infinite Being with infinite happiness as it is for you to discover that you are a male or a female!

"If you have a car, you do not say you are the car. Why then, if you have a body, do you say you are the body?"

Lester Levenson

THE BODY

Why should we have need for this body? If we are infinite beings, why do we need a body? Is it possible that being born into a body shows that we are ignorant of our infinite Being? Is it an indictment right in its own de facto situation? These and other things are worth considering as you reflect on some of the following thoughts. As in the previous sections, do not analyze, simply allow.

* * *

The body is the greatest shackle, imprisonment that we have — the greatest obstacle we have placed in our way.

* * *

The only way out of all difficulties is to know that you are not the body.

* * *

We came into this world to be a body in order to learn that we are not a body.

* * *

The worst habit we have gotten into over the millenniums is that we believe we are this body.

* * *

The body is a slow action machine — that's all it is.

* * *

The desire to survive as a body is the basis for all our present aberrated behavior. Everyone wants approval (love), struggles hard for it, spends almost all his effort in life to attain it. As an infant, as a child, in our formative years we believed our parents would not take care of us if they did not approve of us and we would therefore die! So we developed perverted aberrated behavior patterns through suppressing our own wishes and desires in order to get that approval from our parents, which meant survival. The patterns are so deeply subconscious because of being formed in the very first days and years of our life and with so much suppression, that it is extremely difficult to reopen and consciously examine them now. However, once we know that we are not the body, all this behavior is gone.

* * *

You fear that if the body isn't you are not.

* * *

All fear is either directly or indirectly the fear of the body dying.

* * *

You're infinite and there's nothing complicated about that, but the habit of being a body is so strong it complicates and overwhelms your abiding as your Self.

* * *

The entire body of misery relates to the physical body. The entire body of happiness is being what you are, the Self. Happiness is exactly what you are. Misery is exactly what you are not. The natural state is happiness. The artificially self-imposed state is misery. That is the choice — to say that the body is real or the Self is real.

* * *

How attached are you to the body? That's how attached you are to misery.

* * *

This body is nothing but a dying mechanism — from birth till death.

* * *

If you have a car you do not say that you are the car. Why then, if you have a body, do you say you are the body?

Sleep is the pleasure of non-bodily existence.

* * *

You actually drop your body when you are in deep sleep and recreate it in the morning when you wake up. There's no difference between sleep and death except that after death you pick up a different body while after sleep you pick up the same body. The time between sleep-bodies is short and the time between death-bodies is long.

* * *

Wrong belief that one is a body is the basic cause of desire and aversion.

* * *

We shouldn't pay too much attention to the body. Give it what it needs and no more. Do it without attachment.

* * *

Because of the extreme limitation of the human body, the incentive to be free is great. It affords the greatest prod for growth.

* * *

To make your body perfect and to live in a consciousness of the body is not as high as to live with an imperfect body in a consciousness of your Self.

* * *

It's a higher state to have a sick body and not identify with it. And that's why certain Masters do that. They will go through life with a weak or sick body, all the time maintaining their peace and equanimity. And they welcome it because it is an opportunity to be constantly reminded that they are not the body.

* * *

The body is the disease — not the sickness of it.

A perfect body can keep one in bondage as well as an imperfect one can.

* * *

If you know that you are not the body, you are not the mind — so what if they hurt?

* * *

The body is just a thought. Everything about the body is a thought.

* * *

All functions of the body at one time had to be done consciously before they became unconscious.

* * *

People are not aware that they run their bodies entirely. Subconsciously, we know more chemistry than all chemists today know consciously.

* * *

The mind is the switchboard for the nervous system of the body.

* * *

The body is nothing but a robot, controlled by us. We create it and then say, "That's I."

* * *

It makes just as much sense to identify with this body as it does to identify with a body on a movie screen.

* * *

"Me" and "mine" are binders to this body and to possessions.

Some people who take no care of the body are very attached to the body. It is our attitude toward the body that counts.

* * *

When you think of the body as God that is conceit.

* * *

If you think you are the body, then make it perfect. If you think you are the Self, then it doesn't matter.

* * *

Body equals pain and Self equals infinite joy.

* * *

The basic motivational force in body that operates the physical body.

* * *

"I am the body," is Ignorance. "The body is not apart from the Self," is Knowledge.

* * *

The body is one of the least things that we can have.

* * *

All trouble starts with wanting to be a body.

* * *

The body operates on the law of cause and effect, and is an effect of the mind.

* * *

There is always a decision to leave the body when we do.

body that operates the physical body.

* * *

"I am the body," is Ignorance. "The body is not apart from the Self," is Knowledge.

* * *

The body is one of the least things that we can have.

* * *

All trouble starts with wanting to be a body.

* * *

The body operates on the law of cause and effect, and is an effect of the mind.

* * *

There is always a decision to leave the body when we do.

* * *

Misery is caused only by identifying with the body.

* * *

Give the body its due. Keep the body healthy etc., and then forget it.

* * *

The healthiest foods are fruits and vegetables from the flower of the plant. The unhealthiest foods are flesh.

* * *

Cooking kills the vitality. We should eat fruits and vegetables un-cooked.

Exercise is good if one believes it is good.

* * *

The best method of exercise is seeing cosmic energy flowing in and out of the muscles and body as they are tensed and relaxed.

* * *

We should see every body as our body.

* * *

You are so convinced you are the body that you don't want to look away from it, and therefore you look away from your Self.

* * *

You feel yourself as you no matter what body you have on you.

* * *

You're only free when you know that you're not the body.

* * *

If you want immortality, stop holding onto the body.

* * *

Once you know you are not the body, it doesn't matter what happens to the body.

* * *

Be a body and be forever submerged in misery. Be your Self and be forever at peace.

* * *

The body is like a strait-jacket when you see the Truth.

139

You have the concept that you are only that body and only through that body can you be somewhere. That's not true. If you would see the Truth you would see everything going on anywhere right now.

* * *

When you see you are not a separate individual, you transcend the physical, astral and causal bodies. Separate individuality is the cause of body form. You should see your individuality as the one Being.

* * *

In the process of realizing what you are you will see all bodies as your bodies.

* * *

An unusual thing happens — you become all beings. You give up being one body and become all bodies. But the bodies appear different from the way they look to you now. They become a flimsy, dream-like substance.

* * *

Nothing that the body does should shake you from abiding as your Self.

* * *

We should live our way of life so that we are not identifying with this extremely limited, garbage producing vehicle called the body. It only cuts off joy, because we attach joy to it when really the joy is nothing but the experiencing of our real Self. Our way of life should be to be not the body, but be the witness of it.

* * *

It's impossible to find God if we're accepting the body and the world as real. When you are the Infinite Self you don't see bodies, you see only the Beingness in them.

To be not the body is a beginning step. As long as you are trying to be the body you haven't got a chance of seeing the Truth because the Truth is you're infinite and the body is at the opposite end of infinity — it's the most limited thing you can be unless you want to be a stone.

* * *

Saying "I am a body," is tantamount to saying, "I'm not the limitless Self, I am a limited body."

* * *

Identify with your body and the extreme limitations of a body are yours. Identify with your Self and you are all bodies, all things, all knowledge and power, with no limits, and totally free!

* * *

Be not the body and the world is a dream, a beautiful and perfect dream.

* * *

There is a physical, astral and causal body. When you know what you are, you let go of all bodies. When you let go of the concept of being a body, you go all the way to the top. This physical plane is the greatest because in it we can transcend all planes and be Free!

* * *

We have free will to identify with the body or to identify with our unlimited Self.

* * *

If you think the body is so great, after realizing your Self you can make a thousand of them, all alike, all perfect!

* * *

Die to the body and you die to death!

141

"Develop the habit of honest intro-spection by asking yourself, 'Whenever did I cause this to happen to me?'"

Lester Levenson

RESPONSIBILITY

OUR MASTERSHIP

If you want one practical key for quickly reaching the Goal, I would recommend that you take full responsibility for everything that happens to you. We have lost sight of our mastership and have deluded ourselves into thinking we are victims in a World that controls us, that pushes us around. It isn't so! We are causing what is happening to us by giving power, our power, to the external World. If you want to regain your control, you must take full responsibility.

How to regain your control? Examine your thinking and correct it. Develop the habit of honest introspection by asking yourself, "Wherein did I cause this to happen to me?" Then hold it until the thought that caused the happening comes out of the subconscious into the conscious plane. Then you recognize your mastership, that you caused that pleasant or unpleasant experience to happen to you. The more you do this, the easier it becomes and the more able you become, until finally—you recognize that you were always the master.

QUESTIONS AND ANSWERS

Q: So I myself am my own block, and other people do not influence me?

Lester: Yes. It's not what other people say; if you follow their thinking, it's because you want to.

Q: Because I think they know more than I do?

Lester: You know everything. You've got to accept this as a premise at least, if you want to grow.

Q: Well, I can accept that a part of me knows everything, but that part of me does not appear to be operating, because my World out there is not in good shape?

Lester: It does not appear to be operating? You don't operate that part of you? That is the way you're talking! No, you operate it. You choose not to use your omniscience, your basic nature. You choose to be ignorant of your omniscience, by saying, "I am a limited mind-body." That's your choice. When you choose to identify with your real Self, then you'll see that you always were omniscient, are right now, and always will be; and you'll stop saying you're not.

Q: You mean I can actually make that choice?

Lester: Yes, not only can you, someday you will. When you get tired enough of all this limitation you have set up for yourself, then you'll make that choice.

Who thinks all your thoughts? You do! It's all your doing. What we accept is what we choose to accept. It's always our choice. It is now our choice to be extremely limited bodies. And when you don't accept your responsibility for that, you have no possibility of getting out of that extreme limitation.

Q: I say I want to get out of that limitation and think I want to get out of that limitation, and then when certain things happen, I just don't get out; I'm right there in that limitation.

Lester: What you need to do is not to say it, but want it so strongly that you override the contrary unconscious habits and do it!

Q: Overriding the unconscious habits is hard to do because they keep sneaking up on you and you don't realize you've got them.

Lester: It depends on how strong your desire is for the thing that you want as to whether the unconscious habits override it.

We have infinite power, infinite will — and when man so wills, he's immediately set free.

Q: Gee, that sounds so easy.

Lester: That's the easiest way to do it. Just will it! And it's possible for everyone of us, because we are infinite and therefore have infinite will power. And the reason we don't do it is that we don't have enough desire for it. We still have more desire to be limited bodies.

Q: I believe that anyone would take the other choice, if he really had a choice.

Lester: Oh, if you had a choice, pardon me! (Laughter) You see what's happened? You're convinced we don't have the choice.

Q: No, speaking from experience, sometimes when you really want something, it seems like the opposite happens.

Lester: Everything you really wanted strongly in your life you got, because the mind is only creative. These are things you have got to dig out and recognize for yourself. You're getting exactly what you want, as is every one. Because you don't look at your thoughts and you call them unconscious does not mean you don't have them.

Q: I'm afraid of my unconscious, did you know that?

Lester: How does that help you see your unconscious thoughts?

Q: Consciously, I tell them to go away.

Lester: So, they stay operative all the time. Thoughts have no will of their own. You have the will. Unless you pull them up into consciousness and look at them, you can't let go of them. When you see them consciously, you'll automatically let go of them.

Q: How can you become conscious of your unconscious thoughts?

Lester: By practice. Just the way you're doing it now; anything you want to think of comes to your mind. What you are going to say to me five minutes from now is not conscious right now, it's unconscious. Five minutes from now you'll pull up what you want. Now if we make it a habit of pulling up thoughts, we can do it easily. The more we practice it, the easier it is to do. It's a good habit and saves a lot of unnecessary living out karma. Honest introspection works quickly and beautifully like a surgeon with a knife.

We control the unconscious; we keep back there all that we want to keep back there, and then when we want it up in the conscious, we pull it up.

Q: You really believe that we control it?

Lester: Do I control your unconscious?

Q: No, I don't think you do.

Lester: Then who does?

Q: Well, I don't know. I think it's unconscious control.

Lester: It's your unconscious. Can you remember things that happened yesterday that you're not conscious of? What did you have for breakfast yesterday!

Q: Ham and eggs!

Lester: All right, a minute ago that was unconscious, and now it is up in your consciousness, right? Do you have control of your unconscious? Can you pull things up from it? You did just then!

Q: But, you see that does not have any emotional impact, what I had for breakfast.

Lester: It had a good emotional impact. You showed you liked it. However, it does not matter whether there is an emotional impact. What matters is the desire to pull up something from your unconscious.

Q: But you triggered her bringing it up. She wouldn't have brought that up otherwise.

Lester: Yes, but so can she. She wanted to. If she had not wanted to she wouldn't have remembered. Pleasant things are easy to bring up and unpleasant things are difficult because we have little desire to bring up the unpleasant.

Q: Do you have to go through this phase of clearing up the unconscious before you can accept the theory that you are unlimited?

Lester: It is necessary in the beginning and it also makes for rapid progress. Later, after much progress, you can will it out. There are basically two ways of growing: one is eliminating the mind, the subconscious; the other is putting in the positive, by seeing who and what you are.

Q: When you put in the positive doesn't the opposite seem to take effect?

Lester: Sometimes. However, when you see your real Beingness you'll scorch the opposite. You'll say, "That's ridiculous to remain miserable, sick, unhappy, etc." and you'll begin to scorch it. There is a tendency in the direction you're asking. If I say "hot" you think of "cold", right? If I say "up" it implies "down." That is in the nature of thought itself. But I wouldn't use that to imply that we can't wipe out the negative by seeing the positive that we are, because we can.

Q: Well, I don't know. You see, at the hospital I went around trying to use light, love and peace because I thought that these were the things that were essential. And it seemed like the more I tried to dwell on light, love and peace the worse things got.

Lester: Love is something that can't be turned on and off. Either you've got it or you haven't. If you have love you may say horrible things to people and they don't mind it. So this thing called love isn't something we can turn on and off like a faucet. We can only express it to the degree that we have it. Now, if you have love for these people you would want them to have what they want.

Q: So what I'm doing is playing an ego game?

Lester: Yes, Can you see it? When you see it, that's good. Then you will, I hope, let go of it.

Q: By the way, you mentioned before that by bringing up the subconscious you could eliminate karma. How?

Lester: Karma is in the thought, not in the act. When you do something, it's the thought that's carried over in the subconscious that instigates the act next time. Eliminate subconscious thought and you eliminate future karma. It's the thought that carries over from lifetime to lifetime. So if you bring the thought up and you reverse it, karmically it's gone.

Q: I want to know how to control what I think. I do not feel I can control how I think.

Lester: You do it by first accepting the idea that you can. Then you try it and when you succeed once; when you succeed once then you know you can try it again. When you succeed twice, the second time is easier. The third time is yet easier than the first two, etc. The more you do it the easier it gets. This leads to complete control and freedom.

Q: By control you mean changing your thinking?

Lester: Yes. We control all our thinking. If I do something wrong it's because I decide to carry out something wrong, that's all. And if I make it unconscious, I do it.

Did I hear you say, "Take full responsibility?" — that's it! If you want to grow you must take full responsibility for everything you do, for everything that happens to you. Trace all happenings to their originating thought in your mind.

Q: I still feel I can hurt people.

Lester: You can't. People hurt themselves; you don't hurt them.

Q: I wish I could finally see that.

Lester: I call you "stupid." You've got a certain reaction there, right? It wasn't good, was it? Who made you feel sad? You thought, "Well, he called me stupid, well, I'm going to feel sad." All right, now I say, "You're brilliant." You thought, "He called me brilliant, I'm going to feel happy." But you do the up and down in your feeling; I don't do it. I come out with a sound — "stupid" "brilliant" —and you choose the way you feel about it. It's just a little bit of sound energy that went from me to you, to your ears, and you felt first sad, then happy. You did all the doing there. Can you see that?

Q: Well, if I can't hurt anyone, I can't help anyone either!

Lester: Yes, that's true.

Q: This business of trying to put in a positive thought and strengthening the negative — is it because while you're putting in the positive, you're holding onto what you're fighting?

Lester: Yes. When you want to do it enough, you'll just do it.

Q: When you do that, you just let go of it. You don't hold it in mind and it isn't anymore?

Lester: Right! When the conscious desire to let go is stronger than the unconscious wish to hold on, then you let go. These habits are very strong; the unconscious wish for them is very strong. The conscious wish has to be stronger to override it.

Q: Then if you have a conscious wish and you're trying to ac complish something and you can't do it, it's because you have a sub-conscious habit that is blocking you. So how do you get rid of that subconscious wish that's blocking you?

Lester: By making the conscious wish stronger. Or, by pulling up the unconscious wish to the contrary and looking at it. When you see it, you automatically let go of it; you won't hold it down any more.

Q: I want to meditate well and I can't seem to.

Lester: How many hours a day do you practice meditation?

Q: Three-quarters of an hour in the morning. When I'm working I can't do any more.

Lester: How many hours a day do you do the opposite?

Q: An awful lot of hours.

Lester: That's why it's difficult. Now, out of a sixteen hour day if you spent eight hours trying to meditate and eight hours in the world, you'd have an even push for and against it in your daily doing. Meditating is quieting the mind. Activity in the world is doing the opposite.

Q: But even during the day when I try to think of God, I can't.

Lester: Because your mental habit is so strongly on things of the world and every day you develop that habit further. So when you take some short time off and try to do the opposite, you don't find it easy. You've got to take more and more time off for meditating until you succeed.

Q: You mean by increasing the desire for meditation, the oppor-tunity will present itself?

Lester: Yes, and therefore you will succeed. If your desire for meditation were intense, you'd be meditating rather than doing other things. Then, you would become able to keep your mind on God while in the world.

Q: When you reach Oneness in meditation, do you have to re-gress back into your separateness?

Lester: Yes, when you first see it, it's a tremendous experience and you'll never forget. But the mind has not been undone and therefore

149

re-emerges. But seeing it scortches a good part of the mind each time you see it.

Q: The more you see it then...

Lester: The more you scorch the mind, until the mind is totally undone. Then you're in the steady state. You regress no more.

It's possible to see all the way, see the Oneness, by momentarily submerging the mind. But as long as that mind is not undone it will re-emerge. But you'll never let go once you drop into that state of Oneness. You'll go into it again and again until it becomes permanent.

Q: You can't will that?

Lester: Oh yes — by wanting it that much! The reason why it's so difficult to want it that much is that we have been wanting the illusory world for so long that we don't let go of the illusion very easily. Even though intellectually we know the illusion causes the misery, through long-time habit of thinking that the joy is in the external world, we just don't let go of it easily.

Q: That's why people say traveling is a fool's paradise.

Lester: Yes, it's chasing rainbows. The ultimate joy is closer than flesh. How far do you have to go to get it — that which is closer than flesh? It's the "I" of you. Find that "I" and you've got it. So the place to go is within.

Q: Is isolating running away?

Lester: It could be. If one is isolating just to get away from the world, that's escape. If one is isolating to dive into one's Self, that is not escape.

Q: How do you know which one you are doing?

Lester: By being honest with yourself.

Q: There's something about being next to nature.

Lester: The nice thing about nature is it gets one away from worldly restimulation.

Q: That's escaping though, isn't it?

Lester: Right, you go out into nature to enjoy nature; what you're really enjoying is the freedom obtained by the dropping away from all the unhappy thoughts and pulls of society. And that's escape.

Q: You mean you can't enjoy nature, and at the same time go within?

Lester: No, I don't mean that. All joys should be being what you are. We should never enjoy anything. In order to enjoy something we have to go into the illusion of separateness. The joy should be independent of things, independent of people. However, when one sees the Truth, one can choose to enjoy, and the closer one gets to Truth the more one is capable of enjoying. One becomes sensitized and everything becomes far more intense. But there's no need to go out and enjoy nature because your basic nature is joy. You are the ultimate joy. Looking for joy would be me looking for Lester. I am Lester. I don't have to go out there and look for him. If I am joy I don't have to look for it out there. There's no need to go out for joy when it's inside you.

Q: It's simpler to understand it in an isolated spot.

Lester: Yes. Even if you're escaping you'll reach a point where your thoughts will get unbearable; then you'll be forced to go within.

Q: You're helping us by throwing back some of the things we're saying, and giving other things to us — one needs that, doesn't one, in one's search?

Lester: Yes, it is an aid. The only thing anyone else can do for us is to point and support us in the direction. And when we are pointed in the wrong direction, it's very good to have someone point us in the right direction. Mirroring your thoughts back to you, helps you see your wrong direction, so that you may change it.

Q: How do you know if you're pointed in the right direction?

Lester: Intuitively, or by the results achieved. Unconsciously, everyone is seeking his infinite Self. We call it happiness. When we beat ourselves long enough and hard enough, we begin to open ourselves to the right direction. Then a Christ, a Yogananda, a Ramakrishna, a Budda comes into our experience. Becoming acquainted with these Great Ones is no accident. They point to the right direction.

Let me conclude with the following: You are responsible for everything that you feel. They are your feelings; they are your thoughts. You turn them on; you think them, and no one else but you does it — and you act as though you have no control! You turn a faucet that flows on your head and you say, "Oh, someone is getting me all wet." It's you who's turning on the faucet and getting yourself wet. So, your direction should be taking full responsibility for what's happening to you. Then you'll see by looking in the direction of "I am doing this," that you are! Then, when you see that you're torturing yourself, you'll say, "My gosh, how stupid can I be?" And you'll stop. Instead of torturing yourself, you'll make yourself happy.

No one is an effect of the unconscious mind, the unconscious habits and tendencies, unless he chooses to be. You are the cause over the unconscious mind; you set it up; you're choosing to follow it. The day you decide not to, that day you're through with it!

It's simple. When you don't look at what you are doing, it's a forever process of being miserable. You think miserable thoughts and you feel miserable, and you don't take responsibility for thinking these thoughts. So what chance have you got for getting out of it? Once you take responsibility for your thoughts, you've got control. You can turn them off, change them, put in good thoughts, until you overcome the bad thoughts. Then you'll drop thoughts. You'll see how stupid it is to think. All thoughts are things of limitation and you're happiest when there are absolutely no thoughts. And when there are absolutely no thoughts you are in the top state. So what's difficult about that?

Q: The unconscious mind.

Lester: No. It is you! It's not the unconscious mind. This is the point I've been trying to get across. It's not the unconscious mind. You would like to make it the unconscious mind. You would like to make it other than you. That's why you want the Masters, or you want Lester to pass a wand over you and do it for you, but you don't want to do what makes you happy. You're choosing to do what makes you unhappy. Can you see this? It's so simple. Whose thoughts do you think they are? Why all these unhappy thoughts? The moment you choose not to have them, you won't have them.

Q: We'll look to you and we'll look to us.

Lester: Look to you, look to you. Look to find out who and what you are. Only when you know who you are, will you know who I am. Only by discovering what you are will you understand what this universe is. Until you understand what you are, you cannot see this universe clearly. It's a hazy mist. When you discover who you are, you'll see that this whole universe is right within you. Like the universe in a night dream is within you.

You must take full responsibility. Otherwise you have no chance of ever getting out of the mess. If you attribute the cause to something other than you, not being true, you can never get out of the mess.

So the day you decide to do it, that's it! Because! Take full responsibility and have your Mastership!

* * *

"The greatest of all aids is a living teacher who has realized."

Lester Levenson

Session 17

GURUS AND MASTERS

THE TEACHER

A Master is a fully realized Being, someone who is awake and free and who knows that they know. A Guru (or Sat Guru) is a Master who has chosen to help others find their Freedom. God, Guru and Self are all one and the same. This becomes obvious when the illusion is gone and the Reality is known.

There is no greater aid than to have the guidance of Master or Guru. To quote one of the greatest accepted authorities on Monism of the East, Swami Shankara, "No known comparison exists in the three worlds (physical, astral and causal) for a true Guru. If the philosopher's stone be assumed as truly such, it can only turn iron into gold but not another philosopher's stone. The venerated Teacher, on the other hand, creates equality with Himself in the disciple who takes refuge at His feet. The Guru, therefore, is peerless, nay, transcendental!"

A Guru may be in a physical body, or an astral or causal body. The finer the body-form, the more readily He gets around.

Can everyone have a Guru in a physical body? No, because rare is the Guru who chooses the extremist of limited form, the physical body. There just aren't enough of them to go around.

Can everyone have a Guru? Yes, if he will accept a Guru who has transcended the physical body. Having transcended the physical, the Guru can use His omnipresence and actually help everyone calling on Him.

Can we sense a Guru who is not in a physical form? Yes, everyone can, to the degree of his acceptance. If we are up to it, He can appear and talk with us in a physical body. If our acceptance is less, He can appear in an astral body and talk with us. If we have less acceptance than this, He may appear in a vision. Least of all, we may feel Him as a presence. However, He may come to us and to our aid in any one of the foregoing manners. All we need to do is to demand it and then accept it when it comes.

IS A TEACHER NECESSARY?

Is it necessary to have a Guru? Theoretically, no. Practically, yes! Our present era is one in which we are so sunk in the apparency and delusion, that superhuman means are needed.

Should we have a Guru? Definitely yes. Can we find one? Definitely yes. When the pupil is ready, the Teacher appears! If you have not found your Guru, just expect and know that you have contacted Him and you cannot but experience Him!

How can we know a real Guru or Master? How can we tell the degree of one's realization? A fully-realized Being has an inner peace that cannot be disturbed. He is completely selfless and His every act is for others only. He is equal-minded toward all. He is desireless. He is fearless. He is Love that is all givingness. He expects nothing from anyone. His every moment is oneness with God. To the degree that one has all the above qualities, is the degree of one's realization.

Here are some other thoughts on Gurus and Masters for you to reflect on. As ususal, allow them.

* * *

Getting a Guru we garner the greatest good and get our godly goal.

* * *

Although we don't see it, the Great Ones work more and more with us as things get worse in the world. Don't lose your head. Keep yourself open to them and you will be safely led through.

* * *

On the stage of Earth a Realized One play-acts a character as a human and knows Himself as divine. He sees no contradiction between human and divine. He merely sees the world as in Him rather than external to Him. The unrealized one sees the world as external.

* * *

It is hard to judge a Master by His behavior because He is free to be any way He wants to be. He can even choose to be human. The top state doesn't exclude the limited states. It takes them in, too, without being touched by them.

* * *

To the degree we have reservations about the Master or Teacher, to that degree we cut off His help.

* * *

If one's ego feels it can dominate the teacher, the teacher has no chance of helping.

* * *

When the pupil is ready, the Teacher must necessarily appear.

* * *

When a Master in this world looks around, He sees His body and He sees all bodies around Him, but He knows that every body is His Self — that's the difference. He sees every body as much His body as His own.

* * *

Just point of view — that's the only difference between a Master and a non-master.

* * *

For a fully-realized Being, His outer activity does not disturb or effect His consciousness. Likewise thoughts do not disturb His consciousness.

* * *

I think the hard thing for disciples of a Master (in physical body) to see is that the Master is in the world and not of it, that His body is the least part of Him.

* * *

You are always pointed in the Direction when you are with the Wise.

* * *

You think a Master in a physical body is more effective because you are unable to see Him in His finer body and therefore think He is not with you.

* * *

The greatest of all aids is a living Teacher who has realized. Why? Because, although we all potentially have infinite power, the more we realize, the more we can exert this power. When a living Teacher, who has realized something, is trying to convey that to another one, He puts all His power behind what He is saying to help the other one realize it. He sees the other one as a limitless being, gives him and inward lift, points and sets him up to receive that which is being said, and uses the power emanated to effect the realization.

So, the greatest of all aids is a Teacher who has realized what He is saying. The next greatest aid would be reading His words. There's a definite import to His written words. That's why I say that we should read only fully-realized Masters. Everything that They have in writing is intended and calculated to give the reader a realization. The written word carries the original import of the One who said it.

* * *

As the behavior in life, the very best behavior is imitating that of a realized Being, because that is conducive to giving you His realization. When you're acting it out, it points you in the direction of seeing that which you're acting out.

* * *

Stay with your Master and be with your Master all the time by constant thought of Him and by constant reading of His words, as though He is talking directly to you.

The Masters are living to give us realization. But if you don't accept this, Their love does not allow Them to impose Themselves on you.

* * *

All the Masters are at every moment helping us to see who and what we are.

* * *

A savior is a servant who serves.

* * *

A Master's behavior is completely selfless. There is a total self-abnegation in a Master.

* * *

A Master feels like a servant.

* * *

A Master does not interfere with the lives and ways and wishes of others.

* * *

Masters seldom give advice. They give principle.

* * *

It's not that Masters mind the world — it's that the world minds them that causes them to withdraw.

* * *

There's no realized Teacher who wouldn't want you to listen to all other Masters. They want you to listen to any realized Being, because

159

They all see Themselves as the same. But They don't want you to listen to anyone less than a realized Being.

* * *

All Masters are exactly the same Self with different names.

* * *

When you can accept every Master as your Master, that's good. Then, when you can accept every person on the street as a master, you're almost there.

* * *

Every fully-realized Being that comes into the world, in order to come in, must assume some desire and karma. If you don't have some desire you cannot stay.

* * *

Masters will go through life with a weak or sick body, all the time maintaining their peace and equanimity. They welcome it because They use it as a constant reminder that They are not the body.

* * *

For one who's in a body, it's nigh onto impossible to look on a Master as not a body.

* * *

Christ is against nothing. Love is all-accepting.

* * *

Masters never reject — they only accept.

A Realized One doesn't enjoy bliss, He is bliss.

* * *

The Guru helps set the background for realizations — the peace.

* * *

A Master is a help in that He points us in the right direction and reminds us of the direction when we want to be reminded.

* * *

Reading Their words is association with the Sages.

* * *

A fully-realized Being is inactive in his own consciousness. To others, He appears active. He looks at His Self and others look at His body.

* * *

It takes a Master to understand the behavior of a Master. If you could understand His behavior, you would be like Him.

* * *

Any time you get totally absorbed in any saying of a Master, you make contact with that Master.

* * *

There are no limitations to a Master. He can be one body; He can be a thousand bodies. A Master can actually have a thousand bodies and talk through the thousand bodies at one time to a thousand people, a thousand different people. There are no limitations on a Master.

Masters are a 100% correct!

* * *

Masters, isolated, are doing far more good for the world than presidents and kings are.

* * *

A Realized One, being unlimited, may or may not use the mind.

* * *

When we start on the path, we start with much confusion. We don't recognize that what is out there is only that which we have set up. The Teacher we look up to is in our consciousness and only there. However, though, when we look up to a Teacher, we humble our ego, our ego being the only thing that prevents us from seeing the Truth. Looking up to a Master puts our ego into the background and we take our direction from someone who knows.

Now, the outside Master or Teacher will always point us inwardly to the Teacher of all teachers, our very own Self. This doesn't become apparent at first. When we allow the Teacher out there to become successful enough, He shows us that the Teacher has always been right within us, that the Teacher has always been our real Self. So that, in the end, there's only one Teacher, the Teacher within, your Self.

* * *

When you're moving in the Direction, every Guru and Master is supporting you, yes, every one of Them.

* * *

If your mind is on a fully-realized Master, He works to pull you over.

* * *

The place where saints are is right where "I am." So when you find out what you are, you'll see the "saints come marching in."

* * *

Read the words of a Master. Better, imagine His saying them to you. Best, hear Him saying them to you as you read them!

* * *

Truth is Truth and all Masters speak identically. It appears different because They tailor it to suit the hearer.

* * *

The Teacher is only as effective as is His conviction that the other one is a Master.

* * *

When you know your Self, you know everything. A Master knows far more about every field than the top world authority in that field.

* * *

When an individual becomes a Master, He operates by intuition. He doesn't need to think.

* * *

Just one Master could help every single one of the nearly four billion people on this earth at one and the same time because Masters are unlimited and omnipresent.

* * *

What is night to all humans is a day to the Realized. What is day to all humans is night to the Realized. What the human sees the Realized doesn't see.

* * *

To the Realized One the world may be likened to a moving picture on a screen. He sees the changeless screen as the substratum of the action. The unrealized man takes the moving pictures to be real, and if he would investigate by grabbing hold of the moving pictures, he would discover the truth — that it is just a changeless screen. Grab hold of your Self and discover the changeless substratum of the world!

* * *

A Master sees nothing but the one Self which others chop up into millions of parts.

* * *

Since Masters are Beingness They can never not be. But Their Beingness is other than what you attribute to Them. Beingness has no body or form. Beingness is unlimited. Form is limited to the form.

* * *

A Master has equal-mindedness toward all beings (even animals and insects).

* * *

When one is around a Guru, if one gets quiet and digs for Truth, whatever one is aiming for, he will get through the assist of the Guru. He gets it through the silent teachings, which are the very highest of all teachings. This can also be done from afar!

* * *

In the end the teaching has to be in silence because it's an experiencing thing; it's not a verbal thing.

* * *

A Master sees us as Himself, as His very own Self. There are no others to a Master. There's just one infinite Being. This helps us to see what He sees.

You can meet the Masters in body when you can accept meeting Them just as much as you can accept meeting me.

You cannot invoke a Master without His coming in.

"Your thought force either helps or hurts the world's spiritual progress and is consequently hurting or helping yourself."

Lester Levenson

Session 18

HELPING OTHERS

THE NATURAL WAY

Real love, divine love, is a feeling of givingness with no expectation of receiving something for it in return. When we attain to this, we see and feel nothing but the most enthralling love everywhere and in everyone. We taste the sweetness of God and are effortlessly locked in harmony with Him. We are intoxicated with a joy that defies description.

Loving God, loving All, loving everyone is the easiest and most natural way to attain full realization. It requires no giving up. It is an expansion of our inner feeling of love to encompass and embrace all, everyone, everything. Expand your love, for your family, for your friends, for those of your country, for those of the entire world. Expand it until there is no more room for expansion and then remain eternally intoxicated and one with God!

Love is basically an attitude. To express this attitude, give from the bottom of your heart and discover that it is the giver who is most blest.

QUESTIONS AND ANSWERS

Q: Can you say more about the giving?

Lester: We're moving toward a Goal that is unlimited. We must become totally free. We have been moving in ups and downs; and our lives have become much better and happier. Yet there is a distance to go, right?

To date, I would say that you have mastered many of the principles as applied to life. You've learned how to let go of a certain amount of limitation; you've learned to accept the positive; you've learned to accept the power of thought; you've learned that you are the creator in your life; and of course, the thing that goes along with this is that you have increased your capacity to love.

As we expand our consciousness, our love automatically increases. Likewise, as our love increases, so does our understanding and wisdom.

And yet these things which we have so far gained are not all-satisfying. Even though life has become happier, it still isn't full, complete. Anyone take any issue with me so far?

Q: Not a bit.

Lester: All right, the path we're on is from here on until we make it to the goal — total Freedom. That's the first point I'd like to make. Second, we can do this in this lifetime! Generally it takes many, many lifetimes for the great majority of those seeking to make it. However, we can do it this lifetime. First because we are ones who want this quickest, most direct way. Second, we have the right direction to make it this lifetime. So, if we ever come back to the earth in the future it will be by choice, not by necessity. Those of us who very much want to help others, might come back just to help others. But that's a matter of individual choice. The main thing is to achieve the ultimate state.

Now, becoming master over life is really a basic and necessary step through which we learn that rather than victims in life, we are the masters. Then after we master the ways of making our environment the way we want it, we look beyond. No matter how happy we make our life, so long as it's involved only in everyday living itself, it will never fully satisfy us because our real nature is that of being infinite.

Beyond this our direction in the future must become more universal. We will need to let go of our own livingness to the point where we can live outwardly more for others. For we must come to have the attitude that if we are universal beings, we must behave like universal beings.

I use the word "attitude." We can't help people much by giving them things; there's just too much needed and we do not have it. But we can give them that which is much more than things. We can begin to give them the wisdom that we are getting. Our attitude should be one of desiring to help everyone who desires help.

I want to stress this, for one of the important rules in this step from personal to universal love is never help those who don't want it. This would be imposing on them. We should try to help just those who cross our path and ask us. We don't have to extend ourselves looking for people as those who desire what we know will just fall into our experience. They'll ask us questions and as we give them the answers they will feel that we are giving them the right answers, that we are helping them and they will ask for more. And it's really our obligation to help those who come to us sincerely seeking the right direction. Remember, "You are me."

The irony is that as we begin to live more expansively, thinking less of our little self and more of the other one, we really help ourselves. By helping others, we help ourselves toward the Goal. We will never make it unless we have an attitude of love and a feeling of compassion, of oneness with everyone, with a wish that they, too, know what we know.

So to repeat, we have gotten to the point where we have learned how to better control life and make it happier. Now we must try to make it happier for others. This does not mean stopping our own growth; that we never do. We keep working for our own further growth — by helping others. Any questions on that?

Q: I feel that I have to work for a living and I've got to pile up so much money or so many goods, but if I give somebody else something, I won't have enough. Is that wrong?

Lester: Yes. We should feel that we could give away what we have and know that we will be fine. For what we will have left is not important and most essential. The world is in a state that many people think all they need are things. But it is not the things they need. It's understanding. One need only look at the amount of wealth and the accompanying unhappiness which exists in our country today.

Q: This seems to be a little different and very important. Do I understand that to give people things without giving them the power to be what they really want is not giving them anything.

Lester: Yes. Things are small when compared to wisdom and understanding.

Q: But I don't demonstrate this. I have come to the point where I have an easier life, a happier life — but certainly, at times I sure fall on my face.

Lester: Most of us do, but why?

Q: Because we think limited thoughts?

Lester: Yes and because we are trying to be happy only in the business of everyday livingness.

Q: Speaking for myself, I would have to say, "Yes." When a deal goes through I'm happier than when it doesn't.

Lester: Right. But try to not be the doer. Let go and let God. Be happy at making others happy.

Q: I put my fingers in it and mess it up?
Lester: But you don't have to.

Q: Just let go and let God?
Lester: Yes, why don't you do it? Why don't you let God?

Q: I would say habit is in my way.
Lester: It's habit, all right, but why allow the habit to run you?
You're living in a world of separation. You are there and people and deals are over here. But when you see the Oneness, when you begin to live for others; you see them as you.

Q: But the others, that I see, come to me because they want things. I never had anybody come to me and say, "I want peace."
Lester: That's your consciousness. Begin to live for others and expect to meet people who want peace. Live in and for "oneness" and peace-seekers will come into your experience.

Q: You spoke of love and compassion. Could you define what they mean?
Lester: Love is only understood when you love. Basically, it is the attitude of givingness with an understanding of and an identifying with others. Compassion is understanding what the others are experiencing without sharing their misery and with a wish to promote its alleviation.

Q: Love should be wanting for others the same as I would want for myself without feeling "I am limited."
Lester: Yes. Let me summarize. Once life has become happier the next step is to live more outwardly, more expansively, live for others, or, live more for others. This, in another way, is seeing God everywhere and in everyone. Feel that everyone is you because there is only one Beingness — you. There is only God and God is All. Therefore, that which I am, my Beingness, is God!

"Your thought force either helps or hurts the world's spiritual progress and is consequently hurting or helping yourself."

Lester Levenson

Session 19

MORE ON HELPING OTHERS

One who is not in some way helping others is injuring them. This "some way" is basically and generally in thought. Any thought other than one of good will or good wishes toward anyone, is injuring others and therefore injuring oneself.

The above is effected through the interconnection of all minds and by the fact that the law of compensation, i.e., karma, is effected in the thought, whether the thought is carried through into action or not. Here are some additional thoughts on helping others.

* * *

Your helping others is more by your attitude of how much you love them, than by your behavior.

* * *

When you love you are very constructive whether you are in action or not. Just feel love and your thoughts will be those of love.

Thought is far more powerful than action. Thought is the basis of action. It is the initiator. It comes before it. It determines action.

* * *

The degree of lack of recognition of woes of others is the degree of one's ego. The more one knows his Self, the more compassion and desire one has to help others.

* * *

The more you are capable of loving, the more you are helping the world.

* * *

All minds are interconnected, interactive and inter-react. The more an individual increases his love, the more everyone is helped.

* * *

Your thought force either helps or hurts the world's spiritual progress and is consequently hurting or helping yourself.

* * *

He who is not helping the world's upliftment is helping its degradation.

* * *

The greatest good is done by the person who best understands himself.

* * *

Everyone can be helped in every situation that involves more than one person, and no one has to be hurt when love determines.

* * *

When you let someone know you are doing something for them, they are obligated and return a "thank you ". When they don't know and don't return, then the Infinite returns — overflowing!

* * *

When I give and you give back, you stop me from receiving a blessing from the Infinite.

* * *

It's helpful to you to help others, provided there's no ego motivation behind it and that it's done without attachment.

* * *

A high being sitting in a cave somewhere all by himself is doing much good for the world by his sending out powerful thoughts of love and peace.

* * *

Charity is aiding and abetting the lie that God will take care of the sparrow but not man.

* * *

Charity is saying, "You can't help yourselves."

* * *

Charity is good and necessary for one who is at that level of givingness and havingness.

* * *

The greatest thing we can do for others is to help them to help themselves.

* * *

Blessed is the giver because he is the happier — if he gives from his heart.

* * *

To the degree you straighten out yourself you may help others. Again I say, you're not going to help others any more than you help yourself. But try to help others because that will help you help yourself.

* * *

You don't need any special training to help others. You do it naturally, from your own state of beingness.

* * *

Everyone is a teacher teaching at his level. He does it unconsciously in his daily relationship with others.

* * *

The greatest givingness is not in things. The greatest givingness is your attitude of love.

* * *

Giving out money is like giving out snake protection (the snake and the rope concept). The greatest giving is giving the understanding that there is no snake to protect yourself from.

* * *

Have an attitude of givingness. It's not how much you give; it's your attitude. Some people give to hospitals etc. to get their nameplates on them, and that is the extent of their reward.

* * *

Whatever we do we should do with a desire to serve.

* * *

Serve with the feeling that it is not you but the God in you who serves.

* * *

The giver should say "Thank You" and the receiver should say, "You are welcome." (The giver is the more blest.)

* * *

The less ego we have the more we know the perfection of others. And it's to the degree that you know they're perfect that you support them in their being perfect.

* * *

A completely giving person always has whatever he wants.

* * *

We help mostly by raising our own state of being.

* * *

The higher you go the more you lift everyone.

* * *

When you're holding good thoughts, you're sending out good thoughts to everyone.

* * *

When you're helping others, where's your attention?

* * *

Selflessness is an excellent yardstick to measure the state of beingness of an individual.

* * *

Givingness is also a good yardstick. One's state of beingness is proportional to one's feeling of givingness, one's wanting to give.

* * *

Does a Master ask things from the devotees, the disciples? A Master is all-givingness.

* * *

Our feeling of givingness should be equal toward everyone. Giving to someone who likes you is ego motivated. A Master has equal-mindedness toward all.

* * *

Anyone who has spiritual pride is only giving out words, and the other one picks it up as words with no import or authority.

* * *

To help another one you have to equate him to you, i.e., not think you are spiritually higher.

* * *

When one understands, one sees everyone equally a master.

* * *

If everyone lived only for others that would right the world. It would make it a utopia!

* * *

When we live only for others, then we're at the top.

* * *

Any and every relationship should be for the purpose of helping the other one attain Realization, or for your being helped in attaining Realization.

* * *

Service to mankind will get you full realization if you do it with no interest in the fruits thereof.

* * *

"We can't have a sick body without holding (consciously or unconsciously) a mental picture of sickness. It's impossible to hold anything in the body that's not in the mind."

Lester Levenson

Session 20

HEALING

I often work with doctors and I find that a doctor, who is already trained in the field of healing, becomes a better doctor when he seeks a deeper understanding of life, when he finds more of the basic causes behind life in a body.

In some ways what I often say to doctors is, "Gosh, you're in a sick business!" And seeing this sickness is unhealthy for you unless you, in your mind, reverse all this sickness that you apparently see.

QUESTIONS AND ANSWERS

Q: Well, that happens to be one question I had for you. I don't know how you knew that.

Lester: I wasn't conscious of that. When I let go and let God, the questions in the minds of the listeners usually get answered.

Q: I feel this very strongly. How do I reverse it?

Lester: You see, the mind is only creative, and it creates the pictures we hold in mind. Having a picture of sickness, we tend to create sickness — unless, as we see it, we mentally reverse what we are seeing.

Q: Would you define what you mean by "reverse"? I had a patient today, for example. I'd like to reverse the whole incident, or I'd like to see none of the imperfection, see only the perfection of God. But when I looked at the patient today, it was very difficult for me to see any perfection.

Lester: You're in a most difficult situation. It's easy for me because I have been doing it for 16 years. When people say, "Oh, this is bad, and this hurts, and the doctor said that..." I hardly hear it. I become aware that what they are telling me about is imperfection. I see that they are trying to convince me of what is in actuality an illusion. So I look at them and I know the perfect Being that they really are and I immediately reverse the apparent imperfection by seeing their perfection.

The Truth of our Beingness is absolute perfection. The more you experience the truth of Perfection, the more you will know it, the more you will see what they say as an apparency, and the more able you will be to reverse it. But it's going to take a knowingness of the Truth behind this world. That Truth is its beingness, its existence (which is the source of its apparency).

Q: Well, you say exactly what I read but I have not had the experience of it.

Lester: Because you are so much with the apparency, it makes it extremely difficult to see the absolute Perfection that actually is, here and now.

If you've read Goldsmith, I guess that what I'm saying is very familiar to you. However, you must discover the real You in order to discover the apparency of the world.

Q: Yes.

Lester: Let's take the snake and the rope idea. Have you heard that? We see a rope on the road at dusk; we think it's a snake. The moment we think it's a snake, we're very involved in fear and want protection from this snake. There's quite an involvement so long as we think it's a snake. Now the reality is the rope is an illusion. It can be compared to the way most people see the world. So long as we keep looking at the illusion of the world we do not see the reality of it. It requires getting quiet enough with oneself to see the Reality, the basic Reality being "I Am That I Am." We are that infinite Beingness of the world. And what is required is quieting the mind enough so that this infinite Beingness that we are is self-obvious.

When you discover that you are a perfect Being, then you will know it. When you see your real Self, then you see that the Perfection that you are is omnipresent. And this Perfection is the rope, wrongly seen as the snake. So what is necessary is to stick to this path, meditate, release, dive within, dig within until you see the Reality of you. When you see the Reality of you, you'll see the Reality and perfection of the World. And although it now looks like many bodies and much separation, when you see the Truth, you'll see an absolute Oneness wherever you look. You'll see nothing but you wherever you look. You'll see that this whole world is in your mind. You'll see it's your universe. You created it just as you create a world and people in your night dream-world.

So, to sum it up, you're in a very difficult situation because of your profession, but that doesn't make it impossible. If your wish to discover that Truth is strong enough, you'll see it.

Q: So when you see it and that so-called "ill" patient comes to you, you don't see that at all; you just see Perfection?

Lester: Yes. By your knowing that he is perfect, you help him drop the image of illness that he holds in his mind. If people come to me and tell me of body ailments, I don't see the ailments; I don't hear the ailments. As they're telling it to me I'm mentally saying, "You are perfect." You can do this as well.

Q: And you're speaking of the perfection of the spirit?

Lester: I'm speaking of the perfection of the person who I'm talking to. A sick body is an illusion. The perfection of the person is real.

Q: You mean the twisted...

Lester: The distorted body is an illusion. But until we see it, it doesn't seem that way. Take a mirage on a desert where we see water in the distance. If we never check it, it always seems to be water to us. If we go over to the spot and discover it is sand, from that point on we know that the water is a mirage. The next time we see the mirage, we still see the water, but with this great difference: we know the water to be an illusion. Until we discover the reality of the body and the world, we are accepting an illusion as being real. Discover the real you, your Beingness, and then you can know the reality of the body and world.

Q: In dealing with a patient, if I see the Perfection, that helps me. By seeing the Perfection, am I helping the patient?

Lester: To the degree that we know the Perfection of the other person, we support the other person in knowing his Perfection. The degree that he accepts it, is the degree of his healing. When these faith healings or instantaneous healings happen, it's because the one who had apparency of the sickness within him sees the perfection, and there's an instantaneous healing.

I can't have a sick body without having a mental picture of sickness. It's impossible to hold anything in the body that's not in the mind. The body is composed of carbohydrates, minerals, etc. It is only matter. It has no intelligence. We are the intelligence; we image and hold the life of the body. It's impossible to be sick without holding that sick picture in our minds — of course, unconsciously. If it were conscious, we would correct it immediately. Being unconscious, it's difficult, because we are not looking at it.

Have you seen spiritual healings? Have you seen so called "miracles"?

Q: Yes.

Lester: Well, then you know it is possible. It's done simply by the individual, who's running the body, mentally changing things, that's all. The instant we change the mind-picture, the body changes. But again, because the sick picture is most often unconscious, it's often difficult.

Q: How can we become aware of our unconsciousness and make it conscious, and secondly, how can we help the mind visualize more perfectly what we wish if we do not know Perfection ourselves?

Lester: To become aware of our subconscious we must engage ourselves in the practice of honest introspection which we call Releasing. The more we turn our attention within, the more we become aware of our subconscious thoughts and programs. When we become aware of any subconscious thoughts, we are able to let them go and the more we let them go or release them, the more conscious we become.

In short we get to know the Perfection by looking in the direction where the Perfection is. And Perfection is in here where we are, where the "I" of us is. So, first, we have to direct our attention inwardly; we have to pose the question, "What am I?" until the answer comes. When the answer comes, we know. And to get the answer to "What am I?" it's necessary to still the thoughts, for thoughts are a kind of noise which blankets the Truth. The thoughts are also concepts of limitation and there are many of them which are constantly bombarding us.

Q: Yes, I know. When I sit quietly I have this experience of the noise but how can I make the mind quiet?

Lester: Intense and persistent desire to discover what you are. When your interest in knowing what you are becomes stronger than our interest in this world and in the body, then your thoughts of the world and body are quieted and you discover that you are not the mind. You discover that the mind is an instrument you set up and this instrument is other than you. At that point you are in control of your mind. So, intense and persistent desire is the key.

Q: The reason I asked this is because I've come to a point in my life where I've made it real that nothing that happens bad or good is outside myself. In other words, I know that I created this. I'm responsible for my life. I'm creating my life from moment to moment. Now I've come to this. I accept it. I take full responsibility, but I'm stuck. I've seen this but now I want to go beyond this. I want to break the barrier, do you understand?

Lester: Yes, you want to go further. Taking full responsibility is an excellent means of growing because you will get to see your mastership; you will get to see that whatever is happening to you, you created.

Q: Yes, I see that.
Lester: All right, you first become master over matter, and body is part of matter, then you become master over mind — now this is the part you want.

Q: Right.
Lester: When we are master over mind, then we are a full Master. So you continue until you gain that mastership. In the Eastern teachings they call this "tapas", or discipline. Mastering the mind is consciously changing your likes and your dislikes; walking out into the cold and not minding it; walking into a high temperature and humidity and feeling comfortable; having pain in the body and not being bothered by it.

Q: That's conscious suffering?
Lester: No, you don't have to suffer when you do this. When you know you're not the body and the body pains, you know the body is in pain, but it just doesn't bother you. When someone else's body hurts, you do not feel it because you do not identify with it. If you would identify with that other body, you would feel the pain of it.

Q: Yes, I've glimpsed that. I had tremendous disorder this past week; I misplaced a few things, and I went through such a mess and I was observing myself constantly, but behind everything there was something that was always — you know O.K.

Lester: Always O.K. Yes. There's a well-beingness behind every thing.

Q: Right, now the question is how do I get to it and hold it?

Lester: By continuing to do it, you develop it more and more until someday it remains permanently. You'll have complete mastery over the mind, and then you're a Master.

Are you your mind?

Q: Am I my mind? My answer to that is partly intellectual and partly emotional. When I am most aware I think that no, I am not my mind, but I am the life behind it.

Lester: Yes, that is the right attitude to take. The mind is a composite of thoughts. Who thinks the thoughts? You do. So it must be that you are other than the thoughts if you are thinking the thoughts. Continue what you're doing; continue working to master the mind. The more you do it, the more you will see that you are not the mind, the more you will see what you really are.

You've got a wonderful method. Take full responsibility, then work to master the mind. If you can have pain in the body and say, "I am not the body," then pain gets to be dull. What you are actually doing is moving out of that body. You're moving your center of consciousness out of the body. Most of us put our center of consciousness right within the body and so we remain imprisoned by it. But it is possible to operate the body from outside the body and this is what we should do.

We should see the body as being other than we. Then, as a puppet, move it around. Practice will get you to the full knowingness that the body and mind are external to you and are at your command. And when you see this clearly enough you'll throw the mind out and you'll work in the realm of omniscience, which is just behind the mind. In fact you won't need to think any more. Everything will be known and perfectly in tune. Every action will be a right action because you'll be initiating it from omniscience, which is perfect. The mind is imperfect because it takes tiny bits of omniscience and lets them filter through it.

Am I answering your question?

Q: Yes you are. I guess, the thing that has stopped me so far is my desire to experience some of the psychic phenomena that supposedly come with development. In my studying and reading I became interested in astral projection, or the ability to see the aura, and because I was a doubting Thomas, I've been looking for some sign and although something in me has grown and needs no proof, still I would love to experience just one of these things.

Lester: Getting interested in psychic powers is a wrong approach. Being interested in the powers, one might develop the powers. Using the powers without having your understanding of them, you will misuse them. You can use them too selfishly and they'll turn around and hurt you, causing you to lose the powers. This happens to all psychic people who develop beyond their level of understanding. So I suggest that you develop your understanding until all the powers naturally open up to you, and then if you choose to use them, you'll use them rightly and you won't be therefore, hurt.

Someday, we'll go back to recognizing that we are all powerful, that all the powers are ours, and they happen with no effort. When you try to develop these powers it's extremely difficult because you need to use effort, right?

Q: Right.

Lester: The state in which all powers exist is the effortless state. Whereas the ego with its concept of limitation, requires effort. In omniscience, omnipotence no effort is needed. If we are the all-powerful Self, then no effort is needed. This is also true in the idea of letting go and letting God. When we let go of our little ego-self, then we can let any miracle be, and it is instantly effected without effort — by just letting go and letting it be. Does that make sense?

Q: Yes, very much so.

Lester: So developing powers isn't something we should strive for. And when they do come we should be interested in whether am I doing a wrong thing by using my desire? If you do that, it works, doesn't it?

Q: It does work. So I am not imposing my will on anyone when I do that?

Lester: No, not when you let go and let God.

Q: I don't want to impose my desires on these people.

Lester: You are not imposing your will when you let go and let God. If you can do that, you're a great, great doctor.

Q: How do I find out if I am doing that?

Lester: You know by experience. That man could survive even if he lost all his blood — if you let God take care of it. Everything is possible to God.

Q: I don't know how to pray. I don't know how to say the prayer for this patient.

Lester: Yes you do, your prayer is, "Whatever is best for him should be." The prayer is there all the time; you don't have to voice it.

Q: That's what I've said but haven't known if it was sufficient.

Lester: It is sufficient. The prayer is there whether you voice it or not. He's alive, isn't he?

Q: Yes.

Lester: When a person decides to die, no one is going to keep him alive. We can't keep anyone here who has really decided to leave. And you've seen the opposite where the body has had very little chance of surviving yet the person lived. See, it's the individual who's running the body who really makes the decision. We can only guide and support that.

Q: Is there a subconscious desire to leave?

Lester: Yes. Often we all have preset the time when we're going to leave.

Q: Oh, we've already preset it! Can we change that presetting?

Lester: No, but you can transcend it. When you transcend it, you do not die. You consciously and by choice leave the body in a manner hat you choose.

You can't change the karma of the body. That's a law we set up and it goes on and on. In trying to work out karma, we are creating karma. The only thing we can do is rise above it. When we get above it, if we want a body, we can make a hundred bodies. But when you get above it, you're not that foolish to limit yourself into a little physical body. The most extreme limitation that you can impose upon yourself is the state we call physical. And when you get above it, there's no need for it. You've had your lesson. If you want a body, you'll use an astral body which moves around instantaneously and if it is damaged, you will instantly straighten it out.

When you get above the physical body, unless there's a reason, and there could be, for you to maintain one, you won't maintain a physical body. So, to answer your question, you can't change a preset course. But you can get above it where the body becomes like a puppet to you.

Everything in the physical is cause and effect, action and reaction, and this is called karma, the law of compensation. When we know this it makes life easy because we do not fight it. Now this can help you in your profession. Everything is going to be exactly as it has been predetermined by us. We can't change anything in this life. We can just change our attitude toward it.

However, there is a free choice. It is to identify with this physical body or to identify with our real Self; that's the free choice. When you identify with your real Self, everything is perfect. When you identify with the body, you necessarily subject yourself to untold body misery. Worldly life necessitates pounds of misery for every ounce of pleasure. But we're so steeped in the misery we don't know really how much misery we're in. We reach a tolerance point at which we can tolerate very much. I guess you know that from your experience.

So the thing to do is to properly identify with the infinite Beingness that you are. Try to accept the physical state as an illusion until you actually see it that way. When you see it that way, you see it as a game, and you play that game knowing that it's only a game.

Now all these things cannot be done intellectually; you have to experience this knowledge. If you accept anything I say just because I say it, you're just harming yourself; you're working on hearsay. You must experience this yourself; you must prove it out yourself. Then it becomes your knowledge and is useable. The only thing I can do is to point out the direction, the way, to get this knowledge.

Q: Other than what you've told us tonight, how can you heal yourself except with realization?

Lester: To relate things relatively, if a person can spiritually heal himself, he should; it's instantaneous. If he can't, he should do it mentally; it's goes from instantaneous to quick. If he can't do it mentally, he must do it physically; he must go to a doctor. So we use that which is available to us. I suggest to people that they see a doctor because that's the level of healing that they need and it will help them. Doctors are necessary, as necessary as they are today. You wouldn't have this large medical field if it weren't necessary to help those whom the field is helping.

Q: I've read in so many writings that the state of celibacy is necessary for realization. Is this true?

Lester: This thing we call happiness is merely the infinite Beingness that we are experiencing to more or less of a degree. The real Self brings infinite joy. And if we would take it only directly from where it is, that's all we would have. But we miserly take it in tiny amounts through external means by assuming that we need something; we are not whole; we are not complete; we need something out there to make ourselves complete; and we create a want, a lack, which, when we fulfill it, the thoughts for it drop away, and when our thoughts drop away we remain at that moment more in our real Self. And that's what is called happiness, joy.

So, any time we are seeking joy in the world we are fooling ourselves into thinking it's out there, creating a need for it, satisfying it and feeling a bit of pleasure, which is only a relief from the agony of a desire. But we are trapping ourselves if we think that the thing out there gave it to us. What we did was to still the thoughts for it, create enough mental quietude to allow the Self to be a little more, and that's what happiness is. Now we have to give up all that seeking for joy externally. So it is not only sex, but it is everything out there that we credit with giving us happiness. Point one.

Point two. Giving it up and intensely wanting it can be as mentally disturbing as having it. What we have to do is let go of the desire for it, which seems impossible for most of us. So the best thing to do is, rather than fight it, be moderate and keep digging for the Truth until someday we get the understanding of what that joy was that we were having in sex. And then we see that we are always in a state of joy that's higher than anything that sex ever gave us and it's no problem to let go of it. Then, if you try to enjoy through sex, instead of it giving you joy, it takes a bit of it away, because you're limiting it through the sex act. Be moderate as much as you can; stay away from it when you can, and as you get your realizations you'll get to a place where you'll let the whole thing go because you've got the joy all the time that you were trying to get through sex.

Now the pleasure we get from sex is merely being more aware of our Self by the stilling of the thoughts. There are more suppressed desires and thoughts over the many lifetimes on sex than any other thing in life, so that when we satisfy ourselves sexually, we still the greatest number of subconscious thoughts.

Q: You mean we have brought thoughts into this life from past lives too? And we have to quiet all of them?

Lester: Eventually you get to the place where you can drop the whole remainder of the mind.

To sum it up, celibacy does not give realization. However, you won't get realization without it, nor will you get it without the dropping of all desire. But as you grow it gets easier and you reach a point where it's very easy to let go of sex and of other desires.

You see it's silly to tell someone to let go of sex who's so involved in it. People have to be lifted to the point where they are able to let go of it.

I guess there's another reason why people are down on sex. Originally we created bodies mentally. In the Garden of Eden we decided to do it the way the animals were doing it. And we got caught up in that. And it's a mess.

We are now on the way up. We'll reach a state where again we'll let go of the animal way of procreation and two physical beings will get together with one astral being and create a third physical body into a family. And when we do it that way we don't lose our memory of the past. And someday we'll return to that, here on earth.

And so, a desire for sex runs us down lower than anything else. And unconsciously the race knows it and makes it evil. It's a stupid approach we have to sex; "it's evil," — and yet we all come in that way. But people don't see the overall reason why, and therefore distort it. For that matter eating food is evil if having sex is evil. You see the evil thing is creating lack and then having a desire for that thing, and keeping ourselves bogged down in this delusion. So I see food as evil as sex, if either one of them be evil. The thing to do is to attain the desirelessness state. No desire, no needs, and then you are in the happiest state.

"Life in the world should consist of only two things — that which helps us grow — and that which helps others grow."

Lester Levenson

ATTITUDE AND ACTION

Attitude and action in our daily life should be consciously used for growth all the time. When so used there is no time when you are not growing. It is an excellent way of constant and continual growth. Remember, when you are not growing, you are regressing. Consider this as you reflect on some of these additional thoughts on attitude and action.

* * *

All attitude and action should be in the direction of helping yourself and others toward Realization.

* * *

Have an attitude of harmlessness toward all beings and do not want them to behave as you would like. The same thing said positively would be: have an attitude of love toward all beings and allow them to be the way they are.

* * *

To every action there is an opp1osite and equal reaction. This is the law of compensation, also called karma.

* * *

Daily toil is a waste of time unless you continuously use it to learn what you need to know from the resistances of it. Square it with love, take full responsibility and the resistance melts. The less toil and more quest and realization of Self, the righter the direction and the easier becomes living.

* * *

Every act and every attitude is a step forward or a step backward.

Everything that we do that is not in the direction of the Self forestalls the continuous bliss and sustains the misery.

* * *

Determine the goal of your life and then find the shortest road to it.

* * *

Everyone is doing exactly what he or she wants to.

* * *

It isn't right for us to tell anyone anything unless they want us to.

* * *

Don't waste your time socializing; use it realizing.

* * *

If you can't do it yourself, how can you tell someone else how to do it?

* * *

Nothing happens to us that isn't caused by us.

* * *

"I can't" means, "I won't." Everything is possible.

* * *

Hurriers are worriers and worriers are hurriers.

* * *

Everyone is right as far as he goes.

* * *

The more you act out the law of mutuality, the more capable you are of carrying it out naturally.

* * *

Praise is destructive. It encourages and develops ego.

* * *

Every act and thought that is not for the good of others creates a bondage, a limitation, that must necessarily materialize.

* * *

Attitudes are far more important than actions.

* * *

No matter what happens to a human being, no matter what it is, the heaviness is caused by his attitude toward it.

* * *

When anything bad happens to you, know that only you are causing it. Then you can change it.

* * *

Trying is an excuse for not doing.

* * *

If two people want to fight, should we stop them? If it is mutual, it's right for them.

* * *

Economize your time. Minister only to your needs. Don't waste time creating things beyond your needs.

Spend your time in search of ever-new joy or bliss. Then rest in the eternal serenity of bliss, night and day.

* * *

Dependency is deadly for growth.

* * *

A dependency relationship does not allow you to think for yourself, admits you are dependent on another human being, and prevents you from seeing your infinity. Conformity is dependency, is having to do what others do, wanting their approval. An independent person is always an oddball, not understood by society.

* * *

Everything you do is with your inner motivation and is motivated from your inner state of beingness that you have attained.

* * *

All action is ritual.

* * *

You've got to read behind people's words.

* * *

Life in the world should consist of only two things — that which helps us grow, and that which will help others grow.

* * *

Crying is motivated by a feeling that we cannot do. If we feel that we can do something about it we have no grief. Our thought goes to doing it rather than thinking, "Oh, I can't, I'm helpless." If you thought you could do, you wouldn't cry. If you have the determination that you can do, you won't cry. It's good not to give in to grief. Cancel grief when it comes by affirming that you can do.

* * *

There's no such thing as a mistake — we do it! There is no such thing as an accident — we do it!

* * *

To be interested in things outside of yourself you must get your interest off your little self.

* * *

You shouldn't support people in their weaknesses — it boomerangs.

* * *

Any advice comes back to you karmically.

* * *

If you explain something, do it through the other one's point of view.

* * *

That which you embrace becomes a part of you.

* * *

It's so much faster for your growth to know that only you can do it for you.

There's nothing bad; there's just making errors on the way back Home.

* * *

Advice is ego playing God.

* * *

Outlook differs according to the sight of the person. In gross eyes, mass is gross. In mental eyes, all is mental. If the eye (I) becomes the Self, the eye is infinite and all is seen as your infinite Self.

* * *

Attitude toward a child and an adult should be the same.

* * *

Behavior is general. We don't behave one way with one person and another way with another.

* * *

Everything one does is motivated from their basic motivation; therefore, one behaves similarly in all situations. Only a freed person doesn't. That is why a freed person is an enigma to others.

* * *

Your behavior with the world will be the same as it is with your parents.

* * *

One is a fool who doesn't use the experience of others. It is a wise man who learns from others' experiences.

Your attitude toward anything will be your blessing or your curse.

We look for confirmation of our feelings, positive or negative. Better look for the reality of things.

* * *

Fully trust a crooked person and he will be honest with you.

* * *

He who excuses, accuses himself.

* * *

Don't defend yourself — reform!

* * *

Sympathy is something we should never feel, as sympathy is supporting the other one in his misery. Compassion is understanding him and wanting the best for him.

* * *

If they think that sympathy is love, you have to grant them their right to think that. When they want sympathy there is nothing you should do. You can't join them, so you just let them be.

* * *

Complexity is the lack of understanding.

* * *

Tension is caused by wanting to go in two opposite ways at the same time.

Being a skeptic is good if it causes you to prove things.

* * *

Non-attachment is the way to happiness. Disown all things from your heart while taking care of them. Consider them borrowed for use only. Use them with gratitude.

* * *

Perform material duties with service. Otherwise you are limiting yourself, your consciousness, your growth.

* * *

When you act in the world, you shouldn't care for the fruits thereof. If they are good, O.K. If they are bad, O.K. It shouldn't matter how it comes out. Whatever you do, don't have attachments or aversions to it and you will transcend this world.

* * *

Action does not cause bondage, but the sense of doership does. It is the wrong identifying of yourself as the doer of the action that causes bondage.

* * *

It doesn't matter what we do in the world so long as we remember what we are.

* * *

If your interest is in God you should talk only about God. If one is on the path one should never talk about anything but God or the things necessary in living. Other than that the lips should be sealed. Talking not about God sends you in a downward direction. Anytime you are not talking about God, you are actually talking about the opposite.

* * *

Nothing said should ever bother you.

* * *

Anything that bothers you is not outside you. The bother is within you.

* * *

Rebellion is better than the inability to rebel. Best is acceptance with no wish to rebel.

* * *

Gratefulness is a very joyous state. Want to be always happy? Maintain a state of gratitude.

* * *

Have no doubt and you can do anything.

* * *

There is no doubt when you have radical reliance on God.

* * *

See no obstacles and there will be no obstacles.

* * *

He who gets elated necessarily gets deflated.

* * *

Everyone should be your friend. We've got to attain equal-mindedness toward all beings to reach the top.

Our attitude should be the same toward all life.

* * *

Almost everything that we do lessens God.

* * *

When all are included, one is not deluded.

* * *

There's one thing we cannot do and that is to give up our mastership. We only blindly believe we can. We blindly give our power to others to hurt us.

* * *

Discussing good actions and bad actions is discussing whether you should be good in the illusion or bad in the illusion. Realize that there is no illusion!

* * *

When your understanding is high enough, you see only confirmations of truth in everything you hear, see or read.

* * *

Isolation does not give quietude. Elimination of thought does.

* * *

Escape, by moving away from problems, is not quietude. It's momentarily escaping the disturbance only to meet it again.

* * *

The only quietude is within. Get to the place where no one and no thing can bother you.

* * *

The highest compassion is to know that no compassion is necessary.

* * *

Rightist action is completely selfless.

* * *

The two greatest things you can do are to keep up the quest of, "What am I?" and to be not the doer but be the witness.

* * *

The greatest act is to only be.

* * *

Beingness is higher than doingness, and doingness is higher than havingness.

* * *

The more you just be, the more you realize that you are the world, every one and every thing. The more active you are, the more you are being limited by the particular act you are involved in. You are that personality involved in that act doing that particular thing which is quite infinitesimal in the realm of infinity! The greatest action is in the realm of inaction — being the All. A master is aiding every being on this planet. By his seeing every person as a master he is supporting them as being a master. So seeing and supporting nearly four billion people as masters is quite an activity, isn't it?

* * *

A contented person needs no action. One who is not content must do.

* * *

In Reality, there's nothing to be done, nothing to be achieved. If you can realize that, you've got it made!

* * *

The best behavior is that which is in accordance with the way a master would act — dispassion, seeing all as equals, being the witness, being not the doer. Maintain the state which is natural in the realized state!

* * *

Be what you really are! Be your Self!

* * *

You can be — when there is no striving!

* * *

All behavior should be that which is characteristic of the egoless state or the state of the Self: changelessness, equalmindedness; seeing only the Self, seeing only perfection; having the same attitude toward good and bad fortune, identifying with all, indifference to praise or censure; having joy only in your Self, having complete passivity, complete humbleness; being not the doer, having desirelessness, dispassion, non-attachment, forbearance.

* * *

"The world as world is one long sad-ness. The world as self is one constant joy."

Lester Levenson

Session 22

THE WORLD

THE INCENTIVE

We perceive the world through our physical body, more specifically, through our five physical senses. If we perceive the world and our physical body through our physical senses, then we cannot be the body vehicle that we are perceiving through, it being an instrument that we are using. Our prime objective then is to discover the perceiver.

Say to yourself, "I am not that body, I am not that mind — what am I?" In the background of all seeking and thinking, always keep this quest going.

As we do this and the more difficult the world gets, the more incentive there is to seek the true Happiness — the Self. When life is easy, the incentive is not as strong. This human, physical life that we are now in, is the most difficult of all living that we will ever experience and therefore presents the greatest opportunity for growth and realization. However, if one does not seek the Self and goes along with the world, then one's delusion and ignorance increases, and that is the extra hazard of being in this difficult world.

Now when things get worse, an important thing to remember is that if you lose your head, the Masters cannot help you. If you do not lose your head, you can see it as a motion picture and grow through it.

Here are some additional thoughts on the world and the illusions we create. Let them build inside you.

* * *

The world has a slave consciousness. Man is convinced that it is necessary to work for a living and therefore it is. Were this not so, nature would freely supply all needs.

* * *

If you want to know how much hatred there is in the hearts of total Americans, look at the present conditions. However, we are not going backwards spiritually; we are advancing, in spite of what you see. We have been in a docile state of deep apathy holding subconscious thoughts of hostility, and now we are moving up and out of it. This is

204

shown by our ability to express our hostility. Expressing is higher than suppressing. And this is what is happening in the world. You see it throughout everything today. The people are growing.

However, the important thing for you to know is that there is nothing out there in the world but your consciousness. Let go of hostility and war and see the peace and harmony just behind it. A Master, a Christ, sees no hostility and destruction; He sees the Truth. He sees God as all. Now, if God is all and God is perfect, where is there imperfection? In Truth, in Reality, there is none. You must get to see this. You have to start with the correct assumption that God is all and God is perfect, and if you look through that consciousness, that is all you will see.

* * *

We should not get too interested in this world if we want to know the Truth.

* * *

The more you want and have of the world the more you let go of your limitless joy.

* * *

The things of man are not the things of God. And man wants to foolishly hold onto the things of man.

* * *

The world is nothing but a grinder-up of bodies.

* * *

Desires bring us here and keep us coming here until we tire of it and have no more desire for it.

* * *

To play with this world, to try to make it a good world, as is generally done in metaphysical teachings, is fruitless as far as Realization is concerned. However, it is useful in giving us a life that is more conducive to seeking the Truth.

* * *

Accepting people's limited ideas of the world is injuring the World (and yourself).

* * *

Accepting worldly limitations adds your force to them by your validating them.

* * *

Education today is mis-education. We are taught limitation and illusion. The most important things are not taught. Colleges have no courses on the most important subjects: happiness and love, and the life-principle itself.

* * *

What we call knowledge in the world is ignorance. Everything that man is trying to learn is constantly changing, so therefore, all of it is incorrect. That which is true never changes. The knowledge of your Self requires dropping all knowledge of the world.

* * *

The world authorities are generally those who don't know.

* * *

The more multiplex one is, the more multiplex the world.

When we want to change the world, it is the ego playing God.

* * *

People set the vibration of a place.

* * *

The whole world is thrashing, dashing, gnashing, gashing and slashing, which in the end, results in ashing.

* * *

Exclusiveness is a blight on the world. Oneness is its salvation.

* * *

You cannot exclude even one percent of the people in this World and attain Realization.

* * *

A frustrated person is one who attempts to do and carry out things by himself instead of letting the forces of the Infinite do it.

* * *

The real history of the World is not a series of dates, battles and events. It is the continuous story of its spiritual growth. Someday the history of this World will be rewritten correctly by a Master. But not until the world wants it.

* * *

Clairvoyance and TV are similar except that clairvoyance is on a much higher frequency.

* * *

People are like dogs with a mean master. No matter how much the world beats us we keep coming back for more.

* * *

The World has moments of pleasure with far more pain in between.

* * *

Chasing after joy in the world is an extremely frustrating thing. Has anyone attained full satisfaction in this world?

* * *

Never let anyone know or tell anyone your weaknesses. People accept us at our own values and their mind goes to work to support the concepts.

* * *

Our vision of the world is our own. No one sees this world as any other one sees it.

* * *

If the world pulls you down it is because you have its negativity in you.

* * *

Weather is caused by the total of all people's consciousness.

* * *

The World beats you until you know your Self.

There is no such thing as a good world. It's the extremist limitation man can impose on himself. It is the helliest hell that he can live in.

* * *

The World is a grand graveyard. Everything in it dies or disintegrates.

* * *

If the world is real to you, you are all the time validating ego.

* * *

All knowledge of the World is knowledge of delusion and must be let go of for Realization.

* * *

The highest enjoyment in the World is a mere pittance compared to your natural inherent state of joy.

* * *

The realer the World, the greater the misery.
The realer the Self, the greater the joy.

* * *

There is much more to this world than meets the physical eye. That which the eye sees is the least.

* * *

The world is only God chopped up into little nothingnesses.

* * *

The world is one long misery when seen as world but eternal joy when seen as your Self.

* * *

The world is powerful only because we have been in the habit of it for a long, long time.

* * *

Progress in the world lifts us from the physical agonies to the mental agonies. The world is a trap, attempting to trap infinity into finiteness — an impossibility!

* * *

The true view of this world is intense joy. The deluded view is misery. See the world aright and have nothing but joy!

* * *

The Absolute Perfection is above the perfection of the world.

* * *

The only good world is a transcended world.

* * *

When you take your attention off the world, you can see what you are.

* * *

If you do not know the World is in you, how can you let go of it? If the world is out there, what can you do about it?

Any pleasure in the world is a momentary ego satisfaction.

* * *

The world is a limitation no matter how high you go, until you see the truth of it.

* * *

People who have enough spiritual understanding don't need laws, don't need parliaments.

* * *

The only way to get a good society is to get the individuals composing it good.

* * *

All legislation is to control acts resulting from selfishness. When all are selfless, no laws are necessary.

* * *

In the not-too-distant future, the president will be the highest spiritual person in the country, the vice-president the second highest, and so forth down.

* * *

The world as world is one long sadness. The world as Self is one constant joy.

* * *

World equals misery. Self equals joy. The cause of misery is that you thing the world is real. The cause of joy is the knowing that the Self is real.

* * *

In the world we are seeking to know the truth about the world as we see it. This is tantamount to wanting to see the truth about a lie. There is no truth, no changelessness, that can be found in the world. Only within our Self can we find the truth of the world.

It should be obvious that with all the tremendous increase in knowledge of the world acquired in the past 25 years, man has become less happy rather than more happy. Any knowledge other than knowledge of one's Self is not right knowledge. It is because of the aforesaid that our authorities of today are of muddling minds, are constantly changing their knowledge and theories. Someday they will discover that they are about 90% wrong. Only the knower of his Self can be correct in the knowledge of the world. He can change the 90% to 0%.

* * *

The world is a play act. You have written, in your imaginative mind, the script, the acts, and the actors, and yourself as one of the actors. Recognize this and dwell in your authorship.

* * *

The limiting of infinity gives the appearance of matter and energy.

* * *

You have to master the world; otherwise, it is master over you.

* * *

If there is anything in the world we like or dislike, it is master over us.

* * *

Use the world to transcend the world. Look at your attachments and aversions to it and drop them.

Not seeing the world as it is, is an aversion to it.

* * *

You have to start mastering the world because you are convinced the world is master over you. You must see that you are the one who determines it. That makes you master over it. The next step is to become master over your mind, and then you are a Master. (It's a nice feeling when you start mastering the world, isn't it?)

* * *

The world is a tremendous magnet.

* * *

Primarily, you have to unwant the World and want your Self.

* * *

You don't have to be subject to anything because you are master of everything.

* * *

The truth is, we created the stars and the planets. The important thing is to run them. Don't let them run you.

* * *

Look at the earth's influence on you and undo it.

* * *

Rather than be automatically locked into the world, keep up your vigilance of remembering your true Self.

* * *

The world is a very good place for rapid growth because your ego is being presented to you every time you talk to someone or someone talks to you. Daily, look at your ego motivations and let them go!

* * *

Every act in the world is motivated by your ego, until, of course, there is no more ego. Then action goes on egolessly.

* * *

After you scorch enough of the mind, then the world doesn't trap you.

* * *

There is immediate realization of the Self the moment one sees the unreality of the world.

* * *

When the eye sees the world as "I" — that is Realization.

* * *

Now you see the World as a very variegated variety. When you see the singular substance just behind it, you see the reality of it. Seeing the reality, you will see the singularness as the Self — your Self.

* * *

When you see the Self, the world does not disappear; your view of it changes. It will not look like it does now. You will see it as your Self.

* * *

The only reason people do not get Realization is that they have more desire for the world than for Realization.

It is the belief that the world is real that is the cause of one's difficulty in keeping out habitual thoughts. Were it not for this belief, realization of your Self would be easy. And this is your prime difficulty — this belief that the body, mind and world are real.

* * *

Our pleasures must be taken directly, not attributed to things outside of ourselves.

* * *

Looking for joy in the world makes Realization impossible. The source of that joy is you, and it is not outside of you.

* * *

Only desire for this world keeps us in the world.

* * *

You are causing everything around you — even when someone else seems to be doing it. When you realize this, you'll take responsibility for everything.

* * *

If you don't like the world, change your consciousness. That is all there is out there (your consciousness) and it's the only thing that you can change, the only thing that you should try to change. Make the World perfect by perfecting your consciousness and all will be perfect.

* * *

The Truth of the world is just behind what you now see.

* * *

Declare your mastership rather than be a victim.

* * *

The whole world is just a mere thought — think on that!

* * *

I and world, seer and seen, rise simultaneously, concurrently, co-dependently, and necessarily exist co-existently. The creation is instantaneous with the creator. Realize this. There is no world without the one who sees it. Realize the seer, within whom the apparency, the world, was imaged. The reality then is only the Seer.

* * *

"If you could let go of thinking, and in just one easy thought with no other thoughts around think, 'I am perfect,' you'd instantly have a perfect body."

Lester Levenson

A PERFECT BODY

PERFECT UNDERSTANDING

Should we try to achieve a perfect body? I would say yes, definitely yes. We should be able to perfect the body. But once we are able to do that, then it is better to let the body be the way it is, healthy or sick, and not be affected by it. When one has enough understanding, no matter what happens to the body, it is all the same to them.

Having given you an over-all approach, let me now go into it in more detail. If we want a perfect body and we don't have a perfect body, it means that we don't have the conviction that we can make the body perfect. It means we are subconsciously holding in our mind a consciousness of an imperfect body. The body is an exact copy of the mind, the body being only our consciousness projected outwardly. We must change our subconscious thinking until we subconsciously have the conviction that our body is perfect. That will do it.

Now, is it necessary to have a perfect body? No, it is not. However, it is necessary to have a perfect understanding. To get this understanding is if you cannot have a perfect body, then learn to make your body perfect. When you can, then go beyond the necessity of a perfect body by getting the spiritual understanding of, "I am not the body" and, "The body does not affect me." This is a much higher state. In fact, this is one of the highest of states: to be able to maintain your equanimity regardless of what is happening to the body!

FINITE FORM

This body is not infinite. It is an extremely limited vehicle and very, very delicate. Change the internal temperature 12 degrees and it dies. Put tiny amounts of chemicals (poisons) in it and it dies. Cut out oxygen and it dies. So this body is an extremely limited vehicle. It is much better to not be the physical body, to be what you really are, and get out from under the fear of death, the basic fear behind all other fears.

The discipline of having an imperfect body and not allowing it to bother you, is a very high spiritual discipline. Many fully realized masters go through life with a sick body, setting an example of non-emphasis on the body, because the body is a cage of limitation. We are not in the body, but the body is in us. Our greatest limitation is, "I am this body." Not only is the body a limitation, but also associated with it are hundreds of other limitations. So, although at first I corrected body imperfections instantly, I now prefer not to correct the body, but to have it touch me not, not even in the slightest, regardless of what is happening to it. This is something I started three or four years ago.

I can tell you what happens when you do not identify with the body. I was just thinking of the time I was loading trees for firewood onto a truck and the tree wouldn't go. I said, "I'll make this go," and I gave a tremendous push while I had my shoulder against a tree trunk. The tree went on and I slipped a disc at the bottom of my spine. The reason I mention this incident is that this was an excruciatingly painful one. Immediately, I almost collapsed from the pain. Then I said, "Lester, be not the body."

Now, the body doesn't bother me if I am not the body. I was aware that there was a pain, but it was like a weak distant pain and it did not bother me. I could immediately load other trees. The body acted just as though it were not imperfect.

I have done that at other times. I once sprained an ankle and it swelled. That's painful too, and when I did not identify with the body, I walked off as though the foot was perfect, and yet there was a sprained ankle there. When I had that slipped disc, I would awaken in the morning and, forgetting, I would not immediately not be the body and the pain would be severe. To get out of bed, I would actually have to fall out on hands and knees. I remember doing this the first day or two. Then I would shake my head and say, "Wow, what is this!" Recognizing the situation, I would say, "Oh, I am not the body"; then I would stand up, move through the day as though the body were OK and the body could do any thing and every thing; and yet, there was a weak distant pain that I knew was there, but it did not bother me. Now, this type of disciplining is excellent if one can do it. Be not the body!

Do you have any questions?

QUESTIONS AND ANSWERS

Q: Wouldn't it be so much simpler to simply say, "The body's perfect," and then have a perfect body? After all, you control your body — why even have the pain or feel uncomfortable when you get out of bed?

Lester: Well, when I got out of bed, I was identifying with the body; that's why it pained so. But the moment I didn't, everything was all right. I'd stand up and the body would do anything. Now, this is a test of your spiritual knowingness. This is much higher. This is being not the body.

Q: How can the body be imperfect when you said before your body is a reflection of your mentality, and if you know that there's only perfection, how can you have an imperfect body?

Lester: At first, I identified with the body and then, after minutes, I did not. A perfect body is not the highest state. A body is a limitation even when it's perfect. It's a perfect body. It's still a body, but perfect. A higher state is not being the body, but being the All. Ah, you're shaking your head now. Have I answered it?

Q: I'm beginning to follow what you're getting at.

Lester: So again, it's a matter of level, but because we're not into a level that is high, I want to stay there. Be not the body! Be what you really are! Be infinite! Be the All!

Perfection is not a perfect body. Perfection is absolute perfection. Although you have a tendency to bring it down into perfect things, perfection does not relate to things. No thing is perfect. Every thing is a thing of limitation, confined to form and space. So the top state, the absolute, is a state of no things. It's just beingness, or pure consciousness, pure awareness. That's not being a body, a thing. It's just being.

So to sum it up, we should have perfect bodies! If we have bodies that pull on our attention all the time, it's difficult to seek the Truth. So rid yourself of body demands. Make the body as perfect as you can; however, it is a higher state when the body does not affect us because of our not identifying with the body.

Is it clear now, these two different aspects of body? It's great to make a perfect body. It is far better to be not the body.

Q: You see, it's very difficult for me to be beingness or awareness without being something or aware of something.

Lester: That's true for most of us. But the top state is just beingness,

only beingness, or consciousness, only consciousness. It's consciousness conscious of all consciousness. It's beingness being all beingness.
And consciousness and beingness mean the same thing at the top.

Q: Well, can't we enjoy the limitation at the time?

Lester: You can. You can if you choose, but that's not the ultimate
joy. If you want more joy, don't enjoy the thing — enjoy the joy. Be
joy! Happiness is our natural inherent state. We are the All.

We artificially create a lack and then a desire to relieve that lack,
which, when that lack is undone, seems to make us feel better. It's
like sticking a pin into your skin until it hurts and then when you take
the pin out, you say, "Gee, that feels good." This is exactly what
enjoying things and people is. We hurt ourselves by creating a lack
and then remove the lack and the pain, and say, "Gee, that feels good.
That makes me happy."

Every time you feel happiness, you feel only your real Self, more
or less. The happier you are, the more you feel your real Self. But you
wrongly attribute it to things and people outside of yourself.

This is very important so let me restate the mechanism. When
you create the lack, you start up thoughts: I need this person or this
thing to make me happy. This causes a bit of pain, which you experience as a need, a lack. When you are relieved of that thought of lack,
you return back to being your Self, and this is what you call happiness. So that what you have been calling happiness is really only a
doing away with a correlation of happiness which is your inherent
natural state, restoring it and then wrongly attributing it to external
people and things so that we become attached to these external people
and things.

So, if you want to enjoy a body, that's your privilege. But, if you
want more joy, don't enjoy the body, just be joy, which you naturally
are. That's your natural state. When you see that you are the All,
there's nothing lacking. It is not necessary to need things. So, take
your joy directly — be your Self. That joy is infinite.

Q: Would you discuss your experiences of changing your body
because really, many of us are in a stage of development where we
don't quite understand this. Or maybe I should talk about myself —
not about "us."

Lester: OK. What happened to me was that I saw that there's as much life in this body as there is in a piece of wood. It's composed of carbohydrates and minerals, the same chemicals as in a piece of wood. I saw that the only life in this body is I. I put the life into the body. I saw that the body is my consciousness, and my consciousness puts the life into it. When I saw that I make the body, then I saw that I can change it. I can mentally change it.

The body I have now is the accumulated education, body-wise, that I have gathered up to date. This is my concept of a body. That's your concept of your body. It's deeply subconscious right now. This is why it can be difficult to change the body. To perfect it requires the seemingly impossible task of letting go of all these past concepts of imperfection of body. But this can be done when you release.

Another way, is to put in your mind what should be there, a picture of a perfect body. Now, this picture of the perfect body must be put in with will power. And it much be more powerful than the sum total of all the pictures in the past of an imperfect body. You must image the picture of a perfect body with a thought that's stronger than all the past thoughts. Does that make sense? This is the mechanics of it.

All right, now what is a powerful thought? A powerful thought is a concentrated thought. The more concentrated, the more powerful the thought. A concentrated thought is a thought without other extraneous thoughts present at the time. The very best way to get a most powerful thought is to let go of yourself, your little self; let go of your feeling that I have this or I have that. Then say, "Yes, there is only perfection, and that includes this body." Let go of the world; let go of your thinking as your mind is your biggest obstacle. Your mind is going all the time, whether you're aware of it or not. When you're not conscious of it, it's going on subconsciously. You've trained yourself to think, think, think. You've got the mind spinning with all these thoughts. You've given a lot of importance to this thinking. The importance of it is also subconscious, so it's not easy to let go of the importance of thinking. And this is an obstacle to your concentrating.

If you could let go of thinking, and in just one easy thought with no other thoughts around, think "I am perfect," you'd instantly have a perfect body. It'll take a continuous trying until you achieve it. An almost effortless thought is the way it is affected because your mind is quiet at the time. And you might not even be aware of it when it happens. You might become aware of it later on.

I was just reminded of a case of a man who was in a wheelchair for many years, I believe ten. His house caught on fire and he packed two bags, ran out of the house and sat down on them. It was after he had sat down on the bags that he had realized what he had done. He had forgotten that he couldn't walk. See, when it does happen, you're accepting the positive so much that the negative is forgotten for the time being.

To sum it up, the thing that will effect a perfect body is a very strong conviction, "My body is perfect." Saying it in another way, it is a concentrated thought, which is a thought undisturbed by other thoughts at the time. And the feeling is a feeling of let-go. You just let go and let the perfection be.

Q: So, what you're really saying is when I see all-perfection, my thoughts are so based upon perfection that my body automatically takes that perfection.

Lester: Yes, if you see the all-perfection, then everything is absolutely perfect... everything.

Q: Then, I cannot have an imperfect body.

Lester: Right.

Q: And this being very, very peaceful — if I go into psychosomatic medicine, they claim that the body difficulties are caused by turmoils in the mind. And if these are quieted, then the body may be corrected without any thought about it.

Lester: Yes, if you quiet the subconscious mind. You see, the body is working on an automatic pilot. Everything happening in the body, we are doing subconsciously, automatically. So, you have to straighten out the subconscious thinking.

Q: When you were in New York and you accomplished a lot, did you do it systematically? Did you just see perfection so completely, or did you realize the power of your mind? Just exactly what method did you use?

Lester: Well, when I did it, it was almost like a by-product. I sat down with a determination to get the answers to "Who am I?" "What am I?" "What is this World?" "What is my relationship to it?" In the process which, I saw Perfection and this universe, including this body,

223

was a product of consciousness, my thinking. I therefore imaged the body as perfect and instantly it was. Gone were the ulcers, the jaundice, the coronary trouble and other imperfections. It was very easy. It was like an almost effortless thought.

There are different levels of healing the body. Spiritually, it's instantaneous. There's only perfection and that's all there is and it is instantaneous. Mentally, it is done from instantaneously to very fast, in days or in weeks, depending upon your mental concept of how fast you can do it.

Q: When you're using the word "body," it also would include all our environment, wouldn't it? There's really no difference between our body and our environment.

Lester: That's true in the sense that it is all our consciousness, but I'm speaking specifically of the body because we're talking about that. Actually, the whole material world and the body are very similar in creation. They are the physical out-projecting of our mind.

Have I answered all your questions on it? See, it does not help you much when I tell you what I did. You've got to do it your way. And as I see it, your way is overcoming the accumulated wrong body-thinking of the past. This is a carry-over from a prior life. This is how deeply ingrained it is in you. If you can perfect it, good. If you can't, don't make a big issue of it because it's better to live with it and not be it. Get your spiritual understanding. That's far more important.

What's so great about the best of bodies? They decay sooner or later. The very best of bodies becomes awfully stenchy sooner or later when it starts decaying. So, what's this big thing about bodies? Approach it from a higher point.

Q: As I understand it, if I have a sense of perfection, which would include my body, the body could not be imperfect.

Lester: That's correct. Get it! And when you get it, not only the body but everything becomes perfect, which is far better than having just a perfect body. Then you have the whole universe perfect and that's a very, very high state. To see the perfection where the imperfection seems to be is the highest state.

* * *

"Discover who the sufferer is and on discovering this you will find all joy."

Lester Levenson

GROWTH CAN BE EVERY DAY

THE WORLD AS A MIRROR

Most of us do not realize that every day we are presented with wonderful opportunities to make major steps in our growth. Were we to look at and see this, the Goal that seems so difficult and elusive would soon be in our possession. Awaken to this fact and be done with worldly miseries!

To do this, we must accept the worldly happenings as they relate to us as our means of growth, as our teacher. We must look at all the unpleasantries; we must face them squarely with an objective eye and seek and find both their cause and their gift.

The method should be either or both of two approaches. Whenever someone or something bothers us and we are unhappy, or whenever we react to someone or something, ask, "How and wherein did I cause this?" Look within the mind to find the past thought, now subconscious, that caused the event. Discover the originating thought and discover mastership over the event.

The second approach is more readily available. Every time we react or experience something unpleasant, it is always because of some ego motivation. Ask, "What is my ego (selfish) motivation behind this? What, in this situation, do I want to be different from what it is?" When you discover it, let go of the ego desire or of wanting it to be different. Use your daily unpleasantries for growing freer every day. The more you do this, the faster and easier it is to do.

Either or both of the above methods will free you and return to you your mastership in a relatively short time. Make it a habit of using both, or one or the other, every day.

Here are some additional thoughts for your consideration:

* * *

Whenever you're unhappy do not look for escape from it via the distraction of doing something else, or seeking entertainment. This is the worst thing you can do. You will never be able to let go of o eliminate unhappiness in this way. Either discover your mastership of the event or see the ego motivation behind the misery and thereby undo that particular unhappiness.

Almost everyone, when unhappy, looks for escape and calls the escape or relief from the misery, happiness. This allows the unhappiness pattern to continue in the future. It postpones the time indefinitely as to when one will have to eliminate the unhappiness. Escape is the worst palliative in the world, worse than drugs. Every escape is a complete waste of time and furthers the continuance of the misery. The more you feel misery, the deeper it becomes ingrained. Therefore, one should not escape from nor remain in misery, but should use one of the above two methods to get out of it permanently.

* * *

All unhappiness is caused by our trying to be limited — an ego. The more we are our Self, the happier we are. We will never be completely happy until we are completely being our Self.

* * *

Why waste time in entertainment, escape? Looking to entertainment each time delays and pushes the Goal a bit further away. Only a realized non-attached being can enjoy things in the world without creating bondages and miseries.

* * *

What everyone is looking for in entertainment is escape from misery and the happiness of the Self.

* * *

Escaping misery keeps you forever miserable.

* * *

Problems are a constant reminder that we are moving in the wrong direction.

Every pain arises basically from limiting your Self.

* * *

A person cannot be happy if he has inner anxieties. Anxieties are expecting to happen that which you do not want to happen. Expect only that which you do want.

* * *

It's the ego sense of being a separate individual that is the source of all trouble.

* * *

All unhappiness is separation.
Limitation and misery are the same.

* * *

Misery is caused when an infinite being tries to be a limited being.

* * *

If, when you are miserable, you would think and feel the opposite, that is what you would effect.

* * *

Misery is complexity. Happiness is simplicity.

* * *

If you see misery, it's your misery. When you see the perfection where the seeming imperfection seems to be, the misery is only an apparency.

The more miserable you get, the less you should look for an escape (socializing, entertainment). Rather isolate until you see and let go of the reason for it — or, move into your real Self. Never let go of, through escape from misery, a good opportunity to grow.

* * *

Misery is just the whip we set up to whip ourselves into happiness.

* * *

The more we move away from our Self, the more miserable we become until finally we get so miserable that we cannot take it any more and then we begin to move back into our Self.

* * *

You create a lie when you say, "I don't have," and that starts the unhappiness of not having.

* * *

Anytime you're miserable you're dwelling in your ego. Just being miserable should be a re-aligner for you. Say, "Here I am in the wrong direction." Then change it and you'll be happy again.

* * *

Anyone can feel happy; anyone can feel miserable. You don't have to see why — just change it!

* * *

Every worldly attachment is a dedication to misery.

* * *

Misery is the setting up of limitation.

Misery is to the degree that we think we are limited.

* * *

Every pleasure in the world has an accompanying pain because there is associated with it the feeling that this pleasure may not be sustained in the future.

* * *

You turn your feelings on and, if you take credit for them, you can turn them off, that is, control them. However, be careful not to suppress them.

* * *

If you really see the reality of a problem, it is licked.

* * *

You can resolve any problem here and now.

* * *

Every problem is an ego problem. In order to have a problem there has to be an ego frustration.

* * *

Martyrdom can be ego.

* * *

Suffering is the opposite of godliness.

* * *

Suffering is not spiritual.

God is joy. Suffering is Satan.

* * *

The more you suffer, the more you will suffer.

* * *

Suffering karmically develops and leads to more suffering.

* * *

Suffering is good when it drives you to God, or to seek your Self.

* * *

Every time you feel miserable, there is presented an excellent opportunity to make a big step forward.

* * *

The less we allow our Self to be, the more miserable we find ourselves.

* * *

Feeling sad about anything is holding onto it. Say, "This is something I have to let go of," and immediately you will feel better.

* * *

When you are miserable you shouldn't try to escape it. Get quiet and go within until you see the reason for it, or better, be your Self.

* * *

If you will take full responsibility for feeling bad, you will feel like a master.

* * *

Every time you feel restless or unhappy, there is ego desire behind it. If you can get it up into view, you'll let go of it with a chuckle. It's an opportunity to let go of something that's running you. Look for the ego-motivated desire and when you see it, let go of it and immediately feel lighter and happier.

* * *

Every time you drop ego, you experience joy.

* * *

Discover who the sufferer is and on discovering this you find all joy.

* * *

"Marry to help the other one get realization. Marry only to help the other one fully know God — that should be the basis for marriage."

Lester Levenson

Session 25

FAMILY RELATIONSHIPS

THE SEARCH

Why do we marry? Why do we have children? What are we seeking in marriage? In children?

The answer to all of these questions is: We want the greatest happiness. We believe that in marrying and in having children we will be happy. Were that true, all married people would be happy. But a mere look at our institution of marriage belies this.

Wherein lies the fault? Is it in marriage? No, the fault lies within us. We wrongly look in the wrong direction. We externally seek happiness outside of ourselves in others. We will never find a continuous happiness with no sorrow so long as we look to others or to things outside of ourselves. A happy person is one who takes his happiness from within and he is happy whether married or single.

Should we marry or should we not marry? That is a moot question. You will do exactly what you will do. You have predetermined precisely what you will do on this point. Therefore, the important question should be: How can I attain the ultimate happiness?

Marriage affords an excellent opportunity for growth and should be so used. One is constantly confronted with situations where one may increase one's love for one's family. Every day we should make it a practice of increasing our love, using all the situations we find ourselves in wherein we are not loving to the best of our ability, but consciously increasing our love for the other one until it is completely selfless. When we reach the state of selfless love, we have reached the Godhead.

QUESTIONS AND ANSWERS

Q: Why is it a difficult thing to be married, Lester?

Lester: Some people find it very easy. The difficulty is in us and not in marriage.

Q: It has a positive aspect, hasn't it? Isn't there a release from selfishness?

Lester: Yes. Marriage should teach us selflessness.

Q: So in that way there is a positive step if it's handled correctly. It teaches love of one person, therefore you can enlarge it in the family and then to a larger unit. Isn't that true?

Lester: Yes. It's a positive step wherein you're involved in a situation in which you can learn non-possessiveness. It's a very positive step in that direction. The thing we're looking for in a mate is the thing called love. Love is the Beingness that we are. Love is God. Looking for it in a mate — we never find it. However, if one is married, one should very definitely love his or her mate as much as possible. When we learn how to love a mate properly, we can love others properly.

When we realize what love is and what we are really seeking, we stop seeking it externally in a mate or in the world, and we seek it within. The very best marriage is to marry God. Could you get a better mate?

Q: Should we be married?

Lester: I don't talk against marriage; I don't talk for it. I want you to have what you want for yourself. A married person can find God, but has more obstacles than a single person. A single person can more easily concentrate on the path. A married person is forced to be concerned about his mate and children, if there be children. Now, most people who say, "I'll get married and continue on the path," almost invariably get so involved in their marriage they don't have time nor inclination for the path. So, in that sense it's an obstacle.

Q: Unless you married someone who was searching for it also, wouldn't it be a very difficult thing?

Lester: Yes. The very best situation in marriage would be to help the other get realization. Marry only to help the other one fully know God — that should be the basis for marriage. And the other should do the same for you. It should be mutual.

Q: It should really be a spiritual state, not a possessive state?

Lester: Love is a freeing of one, not a possessing. That would be spiritual.

Q: How best could you guide children into the path?

Lester: The best thing you can do is to set an example. That's the very best way to teach children — by example. They want to be like their parents. So it always comes back to: If you want to help your children you must help yourself. Then you'll find out you don't have to consciously do anything. Just help yourself and you'll see them grow with you.

Q: We have two children and they're really different. They desired to be our children and we desired them, right?

Lester: Yes. We often choose parents who have characteristics similar to ours so that we can have a constant lesson in front of our eyes. This is why we find parents so difficult sometimes. If there's anything that I see in you that annoys me, it's because I have it in me. If I didn't have it in me, I couldn't even see it in you.

Because we choose parents who have characteristics similar to ours is one reason why people believe in heredity. (We only inherit our physical appearances). Every child is so different from every other child. Parents know this, that each one is a completely different individual. And if the present environment and heredity had any appreciable effect they would be very similar.

Q: A thought struck me that a child is born an absolute stranger to the parents. They don't know anything at all about that child. They are a stranger and it is up to you to make them love you. It is the amount of love that you pour out that induces the amount that they can pour out, isn't it?

Lester: Yes, assuming that our memories are cut off and we begin at the beginning of this lifetime. But I have to say "No," if you take the history before this lifetime. We keep regrouping together. Attachments and aversions to each other keep us coming together lifetime after lifetime. An attachment between two individuals will bring them together again. Or, an aversion will do the same thing because an aversion is a holding on by holding off. Attachment is holding them to you; an aversion is holding them away from you. But either way you're holding them.

Q: Lester, as a parent, am I loving the flesh or loving the spirit of the children?

Lester: You're basically loving your own ego.

Q: Because they're part of me.

Lester: Yes. You did it. You created them. You did that tremendous thing. And you want them to be a good example of you. See? Now, if we love our children we free them; we allow them to grow, to bloom and come out like a flower does. We don't try to fence them in. We free them and guide them and love them, unattached to them, knowing that they are God's beings. They are just as much God as I am is the way you should feel. Also, they are going to go through life just the way they have set it out anyway. But you should strive to free them, to feel non-attached. This is a higher love than a love with attachment.

Q: Of course, as you say, you do have to lead them.

Lester: Guide them. And they'll ask you for the guidance if you just free them. But they resent being dominated and dictated to. They resent having to walk the same path you are on, or the same way you did it when you were a child. They don't like to be ordered around. But they want to learn. They have a natural curiosity. They'll ask you. And if you can start from the beginning by freeing them from the first day, what to do and what not to do, they behave like an adult does when he or she is told what to do and what not to do. They resent it. They oppose it. Oppositional patterns are set by the time they're able to walk around; they've got this oppositional pattern well developed. That's what makes bringing up children so difficult.

Because of all our attachment we're trying to steer them, and they resist. We were trained that way; we train our children that way and they will train their children that way and it goes on and on.

Training could be accomplished without opposition if it starts right. Show them the possibilities, the alternatives, and let them make the decisions. Then they're working with you from the beginning and they don't develop oppositional habits.

Here are some additional thoughts on marriage and relationships. Reflect on them. Allow them to assist you.

Families are regrouping of people who have been together before. Strong loves and strong hates bring us together again and again.

237

Our attitude toward relatives should be the same as that toward all beings.

* * *

The first place to practice love is at home with the family. We should try to love our family more and more by granting them their right to be the way they are.

* * *

It's a great thing for spiritual growth to resolve relationships with parents (even if they have passed on). Parents present excellent opportunities for growth if and when we try to resolve our differences until there's only love with no attachment.

* * *

Family is excellent for bringing up to us all our reactive automatic behavior because there is where we developed most of it.

* * *

Giving unselfish love to a child will develop unselfish love in that child this lifetime and will condition the child for a most happy life.

* * *

The main thing that a child wants from us is love, and we cannot fool a child. Children know our feelings and that is what they read. We fool ourselves with words, but we don't fool them.

* * *

When children are contrary, it is because they are seeking to get attention from their parents. In early years, this meant survival: If I am approved of by my parents, they will take care of me, and I, the helpless child, will not die. A child tries to be good and to get approval and, if impossible, becomes bad and in that way gets attention. This attention subconsciously implies approval. It becomes an aberrated pattern of behavior.

If you can get to see your parents the way they really are and then love them the way they are, you would be accomplishing tremendous growth.

* * *

You behave most automatically with parents. You'll find your parental behavior patterns applied to the world. You carry on the automatic behavior patterns set up before the age of six for the rest of your life (unless, of course, you change them).

Normalize your behavior with your parents and family. You've got to see your parents the way they are and accept them that way. Nothing should be blamed on your parents. No matter what they do, you should accept responsibility for what you are.

* * *

Total non-reaction to parents is close to realization.

* * *

It doesn't matter how we act as long as the feeling within is love. The attitude is more important than the act. Use this with family.

* * *

If we were capable of selflessly loving, instead of conflict with children, there would be complete harmony. But it is only because we have lost sight of what selfless love is that we are in this difficulty of opposition between parent and child.

* * *

Parents want to do wrong and yet want their children to do right. This makes the parent look dishonest in the eyes of the children and disconcerts them, causing rebellious feelings.

A child will learn no better than the parent's example.

* * *

Our responsibility toward children, because they cannot take care of themselves, is to feed, clothe and guide them until they are old enough to take care of themselves. But after a person is an adult, we should let go and let God take care of them, even though they seemingly can't take care of themselves. They need to learn that they, too, are taken care of if they take responsibility for themselves, or better, if they surrender to God.

* * *

The only real difference between children and adults is size and experience.

* * *

When parents say "don't," they are instilling inhibitions. When parents say, "do," they are instilling compulsions. Both cause feelings of inability in the child.

Children we see as an extension of our ego. We should see them as individuals and extend to them the rights we do to individuals.

* * *

You want to help your child — help yourself.

* * *

Every child is a whole, complete, infinite individual.

* * *

Seeing Truth doesn't belong to married people or single people. It belongs to those who seek and discover Truth.

* * *

Married people can get Realization — if they are determined to get it.

* * *

The only happy couples are those with an understanding of Truth. They know that their joy is within and not in the other one.

* * *

What people are really looking for is love of God. Not knowing this, they look for it in a mate.

* * *

Once you get the taste of God, it's easy not to marry. You feel no need for a mate. Being married to God, you reach satiety.

* * *

It's an obstacle to have a mate. It's an added obstacle to have a child. It doesn't have to be; it can be an aid to growth, if we so use it

* * *

There is no one married whose unhappiness does not come from looking to the other one for happiness.

* * *

The only ideal marriage is when each marries to help the other grow spiritually.

* * *

The top attainment is to have nothing but love for each parent, each sister, each brother, each child. Resolve this and you will resolve your relationship with the world.

* * *

*"The unrealized person sees the world
as running him, the realized person sees it
as his own projection and therefore he can
run it, it cannot run him."*

Lester Levenson

WORLDLINESS VS. SPIRITUALITY

THE DILEMMA

What is the difference between the divine and the Worldly, the spiritual and the material? Is there a difference? Is there a difference between being spiritual and being in the World? There is a tendency for us to separate the two. That is a gross error. There is no difference between the spiritual and the material when we look at it from the viewpoint of Truth.

The difference is in our outlook, in the way we see the world. It is the way we look at it, that's all. We can look at it from the ego point of view, or we can look at it from the Self. A realized person sees the World only as an out-projection of himself; therefore, it really is his creation. And as an out-projection, it's like a cinema screen out there with this whole universe projected on it and which, at will, could be changed or withdrawn. To the one who does not see the Truth, this cinema, this moving picture, seems not self-created and as such, one makes himself subject to it and becomes a slave to it.

A Master is very much in the World. A Master has His feet firmly planted on the Earth, but He sees the basic substance just behind the apparent World as His very own Self. And when He does that, everything is in harmony, everything is perfect.

SEEING THE TRUTH

It is not a matter of separating one from the other, or having one or the other, it is merely seeing the truth of the world. When one does, one is realized. When one does not, one is forever shadow boxing with his self-created world of opposition. Both see the world. The Master sees the Truth just behind it and there is nothing but harmony! The unrealized one sees separation and opposition and there is much disharmony! The unrealized person sees the world as a thing running him; the realized person sees it as his own projection and therefore he can run it and it cannot run him. Being a Master over it, He resides ever the same, in peace and tranquility, and lives in complete ease all the time.

We must, in our everyday lives, be in that state of tranquility, and until we can be in that state while in the details of daily living — we have not reached the top.

So there are no two categories, the world and spirit; it's all one and the same. It is just a matter of the way we look at it. We should strive to get to the place where no one and no thing can perturb us. When we get to that state, we are at the top. We are in the world and no thing and no one can disturb us in the slightest. Develop this. Make this a practice. Make this your way of life. Do not react to people; do not become angry, jealous, hateful and so forth. Remain ever the same, ever the same; no matter what happens, no matter what goes on, you really are ever the same, serene and poised.

QUESTIONS AND ANSWERS

Q: But Lester, when I look at the world, I see differentiation?

Lester: Any time we see any difference, or a difference between the spiritual and the worldly, it's because we don't have enough understanding of the spiritual as yet. We are separating. The highest state is when we are in the world and in the spirit at one and the same time and there is no difference. When we're there, we don't see it as world and spirit. We see it as one and the same thing; we see a oneness; we see it all as our very own Self; or, if we want, we see the whole world as being within us, as a dream is within us in sleep. No matter what happens in the dream, we remain the same. We see absolutely no difference in anything; there's a singular oneness throughout everything. Nothing changes. Ever-the-same is our feeling.

This can be used as a yardstick to know how far we are on the path. Is everything ever the same? Do things really not change? It is a little shocking when we start examining it from this point of view. How far am I on the path toward seeing the sameness, the Oneness, the no-otherness, the nothing but God, God in all, the God in everyone?

When you accomplish that non-duality, you lose the feeling of separation of "I." If you want to recognize the "apparent" others, you use the word "We." But more than that, you would rather talk about yourself in third person. That is the feeling a Master has, and He talks that way. Certain Masters will not speak of Themselves by name; they'll speak of Themselves in the third person as Their disciples do. For instance, if everyone called me what Ken jokingly calls me, I would talk about Father Divine. Instead of saying "I," "Me," or "Lester," I would talk about him, (pointing to himself) Father Divine. That's just the way you feel when you're in the state when all is one and all is the same. You don't identify yourself with just your body.

I've been emphasizing this point because quite a few were asking questions and talking about the two, the world and spirit, not knowing that in Truth they are one.

Q: There is no difference?

Lester: Right. It's one and the same, when you see it right. If you see it through illusion, if you see it wrongly, you'll see separation; you'll see the differentiation that this is spiritual and that is worldly; that this is divine and that is mundane.

Q: The "Me's" are our ego?

Lester: Yes. The "Me's" are a condescension on the part of a Master in order to communicate with the apparent egos. A Master sees nothing but Masters; specks of infinite light, all looking alike — blazing effervescent radiant Beings, points of Beingness all being One. This is the way a Master really sees everyone; He doesn't see people the way we see them.

Q: Does He see them as different shades or all one shade?

Lester: Identical points of light, of one ocean of light, brilliant, effervescent, emanating, with center everywhere and circumference nowhere. Are you trying to imagine what it's like?

Q: Well, I had an experience of seeing something like that and it's a light like a burning sun.

Lester: Yes. A bright blazing sun. Masters can see nothing but a Master in us, and at the same time, they can go through the pretense of seeing it otherwise by saying, "Harry, yes, you do have problems." or "Harry, you do have a body and you do live in a house." But as they say it, it's like a dream voice talking, or apparently talking. For it's all an apparency. It's a pretense — they're actually pretending as their view of the omnipresent, infinite One never changes.

Q: They are pretending a duality, then, actually, where we're more or less living it?

Lester: Yes. However, we're pretending it too, but we don't know that we're pretending it. A Master pretends it and he knows that he's pretending it. But we are ignorant of our pretense.

Q: In that way, He's coming down to our level?
Lester: Yes. And He does it only to help us.

Q: Well, why can't I as a human being say, "I will play a game of baseball?" When I say I'm a baseball player, I can make myself subject to all the rules. But I don't' have to play baseball. So, why can't God say, "I will play the game of being Bob?" And then He puts Himself subject to the limitations of Bob as He defines it, as when I play baseball, I make myself subject to the rules. Now, why can't God, to entertain Himself, be a Bob? Or be a Lester? And be limited in a sense — the thing is, if I play baseball, I limit myself to all the rules of being a baseball player. Well then, I will play baseball and have a good time and be Bob.
Lester: God can — and does — but never forgets He is God! Do you ever forget?

Q: Therefore, I am God who is playing Bob and for the moment I forgot?
Lester: You only are if you know that, not if you state it. Giving it lip-service doesn't equate with knowing that.

Q: I see.
Lester: So theoretically, you are right. Now, the important thing is to carry it out practically — to know your Beingness in God while you are playing the game, to know that you are God and that you are pretending to be limited as a body and so forth.

Q: And any time I don't want to, I don't have to play, and I don't have to take that particular step of being limited because I am the creator of the game; I make the rules and I don't have to play anymore than I have to play a baseball game. I can quit just like that! (finger snap)
Lester: That's the way it is. All right now, when you don't really know that you are God, you can discover it by tracing the source of

"Me." If we trace the source of the ego "Me," we'll discover it's the infinite Being. If you'll trace the source of the mind, you'll discover the same thing. The infinite Being is putting this pretense of limitation, ego and mind, over Itself, so that we don't see this statement of Truth: that this world is only God — playing a game of apparent limitation. The way to discover it is to seek the source of the ego "Me," and if we stay with it, we'll discover that it is really the Infinite I, that I am.

Q: Well, according to your book, and let me use Bob's words, if I play the game of ball looking up to God, then I don't have it made. If I do anything at all looking out from God, then I know who I am. But if I play the game looking up to God, from the outside, then I don't know.

Lester: You are right. Translating that into Christ, if I look up to Christ, or believe in Christ, that isn't it; I have to look out through the eyes of a Christ; I have to believe as Christ believed; I have to be as a Christ.

Q: It's in your book. I read it in the Gita this morning, and also in your book, so you get your stuff from a good source.

Lester: In the beginning of the book, there is a disclaimer stating that the knowledge is not mine. It is Truth, but I can't make it and I can't unmake it. I can only recognize it or not recognize it. That's the choice that we have — to recognize the Truth or not to. We can't make it; we can't do anything to it; but we can recognize it.

Q: All the books that I read say the same thing; Patanjali says it, Yogananda says it, the Gita says it and the Vedas say it; they all say it.

Lester: Yes, they said it a thousand years ago, a million years ago, a billion years ago, a billion, billion years ago, and in the future, they'll say the same thing. Because Truth is that which never changes; It is changeless. The basic Truth will never ever change in all eternity and you can know this for the entire universe. If somebody comes from a planet billions and billions of light-years away and tells you otherwise, no matter how high he looks, acts and talks, if it doesn't fit in with what you know of the changeless Truth, you can be sure he's wrong, even though he's acting and looking like a god.

Do you know what I'm saying? Even if an angel tells you something, if it's not in accordance with Truth, reject it, because there are so many high appearing beings that look like gods that you can be very easily fooled — until you know the Truth. Truth is the same throughout from infinity to infinity.

Q: We're trying to get ahead as quickly as we can, and we listen and read and we think the right thing to do is to be on the path, but I go to church and I see a priest, a monk, up there and he's been struggling on the path for twenty years. How can I make it quickly when I see in front of me someone who has been on the path much longer and he's struggling?

Lester: Look at it this way. If you want to go from Los Angeles to New York City and the direct route is not known to you, you start probing; you might go up to Washington State first, then cut eastward, then come down to Nevada, then go up to Montana. However, if you know the direct route, you take the direct way and get there much sooner. Probing may take you a whole lifetime. Going directly, you could do it in three or four days' time.

Q: Don't say another word to me, because I got the answer.

Lester: All right. Now the priest or monk doesn't see the direct route and he's probing and he's learning bit by bit. He'll get to New York eventually if he keeps trying and wandering all over the United States.

Q: But doesn't each of us have different abilities? One person gets over something very easily, very quickly, and someone else has a problem that's deep-seeded and it's been with him a long while, which takes a very active struggle to get over it?

Lester: Yes. However, quickness of realization is determined by the intensity of the desire for it. How far have we gone in our desire for it? If we've gone very far, the realizations come fast and easily.

Q: And we stick by them then?

Lester: Yes. They really stick with you. I say to you: I'm not teaching you. You're getting something you've known; you are doing it; you're just re-remembering things you've always known. I can't give you this knowledge; no one can. I just suggest and you open yourself up to that which you already know, have always known and always will know, subconsciously.

Q: In other words, you just read a page of your true Self.

Q: Well, it's Self-realization, actually.

Lester: Yes, and this is also true: If you haven't grown much, or as much as someone else, you can go way beyond that one if you have a very strong desire for it. Only a very strong desire for full realization will give it to you this lifetime. Anyone who has only a desire for Truth will get full realization quickly. You can override your past conditioning when you want to.

How long should it take an infinite omniscient Being to know that he is omniscient, omnipotent and omnipresent? How long should it take him to do that?

Q: One realization.

Lester: When man so wills, he's immediately set free — totally!

So, really what this growing turns out to be is that we play with the path as we're doing now, getting more and more realizations and then one day we say, "Oh, my gosh, look at this tremendous thing I've always been! What silly playing around I've been doing! The heck with it!" And boom! It's finished!

Q: And at that moment you're looking out from God!

Lester: Yes. You are looking out from God and seeing the whole thing, seeing the silly dream you have been going through of playing the game of limitation, and you just drop it, lock, stock and barrel!

* * *

"The more we develop love, the more we come in touch with the harmony of the universe and then our life becomes more beautiful, more bountiful and more delightful."

Lester Levenson

ABOUT LOVE

THE MISUNDERSTANDING

Love is one word I do not often use, primarily because it is so misunderstood. Defining it, we normally add more words to the usual words, and these words do not really convey the meaning for only through growth do we understand what love is. But love is an absolutely necessary ingredient on the path. If we ever expect to get full realization, we must increase our love until it is complete.

Now the love I talk about has little or nothing to do with sex. Sex is a body gratification. However, most of us confuse it and tie it in with love. When you see what sex is and what love is, you will see that they are two different things. They can be tied together and also they do not have to be.

The love that I talk about is the love of Jesus Christ. It is complete love which expressed in the extreme is: "Love thy enemy." I think the best definition of the word is: "Love is a feelingness of givingness with no expectation of receiving for the giving." It is a very free giving. And it is an attitude that is constant. Love does not vary, not the type of love we are talking about. The amount we have, we apply to everyone. We love our family as much as we love strangers. This might sound odd, but this is the truth. To the degree we are capable of loving strangers, to that degree we are capable of loving our family.

The concept of possession is just the opposite of the meaning of love. In love, there is never a holding onto, a fencing in, or anything like that. Love has a sense of freeing the ones we love. When we are giving in our attitude, we want the other one to have what the other one wants. I guess the best example of this type of love is the love of a mother for a child. A mother will sacrifice and give everything to the child without considering herself.

OTHER DEFINITIONS

There are other definitions for love. I think acceptance is a good one. When we love people, we accept them as they are. If we love this world, we accept the world the way it is. We do not try to change it. We let it be. We grant the world its beingness the same way we should grant every other person his or her beingness. Let them be the way they want to be; never try to change them. Trying to change them is injecting our own ego. We want them to be the way we would like them to be.

Identity is another definition. Love is a feeling of oneness with, of identity with, the other one or all other ones. When there is a full love, you feel yourself as the other person, and you treat the other person just like you treat your own self. There is complete identity.

A constant state of gratitude accompanies a state of complete love. We are thankful for everything. We even thank God for the bad as well as for the good. To understand this requires reaching the state of high love. Only then does thanking God for the bad have any meaning to us. The practical aspect of this is that the more we practice being in a state of gratitude, the more loving we become. Try this and learn the truth of it.

Love is not only a feeling, love is a tremendous power. This is so little understood in the world. We had an example of this type of love by Martin Luther King. No matter how much he was attacked, he gave out nothing but love to his attacker. He taught non-violence. Perhaps the greatest demonstration of this type of love was Mahatma Gandhi's winning a war against Britain. He did this without any arms and through his teaching: "The British are our brothers. We love the British. Non-resistance to the British and to the British soldiers, only love for them." Yes Gandhi well understood this and was able to win over enough followers in India to make this effective.

THE MOST POWERFUL FORCE

The power behind love, without question, is far more powerful that the hydrogen bomb. That is, once you know what love is, Love is the most powerful force in the universe. When expressed as love really is, not as we have been taught to think of it, it is extraordinary.

It is said that God is love, and I add, "One with God makes a majority." One individual, with nothing but love, can stand up against the entire world because this love is that powerful. Love is nothing but the Self that we speak of. Love is God. When we are only love we are God. To quote the Bible, "God is love. God is all powerful." So there's some authority for what I am saying besides my saying it. Love will give not only all the power in the universe, but also all the joy and all the knowledge.

Now, how do we make this practical? The best way of increasing our capacity to love is through wisdom and understanding. Also, we can do things in our every day life that will increase our love. The first place to practice love is at home, with the family. We should try to love our family more and more and more. I think everyone knows the wonderful experience of love, of loving one person. Can you imagine what it would be like if you loved three billion people? It would be three billion times more enjoyable! Home is the first place to keep trying to increase our love for the ones around us, by granting them their beingness. That's the most difficult thing, I believe, to do in a family, especially if the other one is a child. But every child is a whole, complete, infinite individual, and a child of God.

Next, after loving the ones in our home, we should try to love our neighbors, then our larger group, our state, our country. Then we should try to love all people all over the world.

QUESTIONS AND ANSWERS

Q: The Russians?

Lester: Even Russians.

Q: The Chinese, too?

Lester: I heard Oral Roberts say something on that some time ago. He said, "People ask, 'What would the attitude of Jesus be toward the communists if He came back today?'" And he answered, "He wouldn't be the way people expect. He wouldn't have anything against anyone. He would not hate the communists. He would talk against doing wrong, doing evil, but He would never say anything against any human being."

I believe that if we understood the power of love, and that if the majority of Americans loved the Russians, and the Chinese etc., the world would be won over by the Americans without any arms.

After we learn to love all the people in this world, there are many more people outside of this world. I think loving all the people in this world would allow us to meet with our brothers and sisters of other worlds, because in this universe there are many, many mansions; many, many places of abode. And because of our inability to love on this planet, we have cut them off.

So, to come back to the point of being practical: The more we develop love, the more we come in touch with the harmony of the universe, and then our life becomes more beautiful, more bountiful and more delightful. It starts a cycle going where you spin upwards. Love begets love! Love falls in love with love!

There is another thing. If we want to be loved, the way to get it is to love. It is not only the very best method, but it is, I think, the only method. To receive love we must love because what we give out must come back. Looking for love without loving does not bring love to us, does not satisfy us. This is a basic error in many, many people's thinking. They go through life wanting to be loved, never feeling that they are even when they are really getting the love. The feeling has to be in us. If I love you, I feel wonderful. If you love me, you feel wonderful. It's the one who loves who feels great. So wanting to be loved is getting into a direction that can never be satisfied. The happy one is the one loving, the one giving. Blessed is the giver because he's so much happier.

Love should be felt equally for all. When we say we love one person more than another, if we would trace it through by going inwardly, we would find that the one we love more is a person whom we think we need, who has something that we would like to have, and therefore, we say we love that person more. This is propitiation in the guise of love.

Actually, love cannot be chopped up. If you want to test your own state of love, look at your enemies. This is the real test. Or, if you don't want to go that far, look at strangers. Examine your attitude toward strangers. It should be one of: they are me; they are my family; every mother is my mother; every father is my father; every child is my child. This is the attitude we achieve through understanding. This is the real sense of the word love.

Q: Lester, it seems to me you're talking about love as giving, giving of yourself and so forth, and yet the conflict that I have occasionally is that it seems that as you give of yourself, people tend to take more and more. And eventually, if you don't put a stop to it, they bleed you dry, emotionally, mentally, financially, and they use you as a crutch.

Lester: That's impossible. We feel real love. If we have the correct attitude of love, that doesn't happen. What you're saying I often hear. What is needed is for us to know what real love is. The givingness is an attitude. We can always maintain an attitude of love. Most people who give are not giving lovingly. They're giving because of the recognition they think they will get for giving: "Look at me; I'm doing good," or "I may get my name in the paper," or something like that. You see, that kind of love will get us into trouble. People will drain others on that, because they're looking for something in return. We're looking to advance but they pull us down.

Q: Don't you think it's easier to love somebody five thousand miles away than somebody next door to you?

Lester: The easiest thing in the universe to do is to love everyone. This is what I think. This is what I've discovered. Once we learn what love is, it is the easiest thing to do. It takes tremendous effort not to love everyone, and you see the effort being expended every day. But when we love, we're at one with them; we're at peace, and everything falls into line beautifully.

The main thing is to know love in the sense that I'm defining it, then those things don't happen. But when we love in the sense that humanity understands the word, then you're right. But I don't call that love.

Q: What do you call it? Or do you have a name for it?

Lester: Selfishness, actually. We are doing things really to help ourselves.

And yet in the real love, in the spiritual love, there's no self-abnegation. We don't have to hurt ourselves when we love everyone, and we don't. When we love, there's a feeling of mutuality. That which is mutual is correct. If you love, you'll hold to that law, and therefore people won't take advantage of you. If you are loving, you're applying the most powerful force in the universe. But it's the love of a Jesus Christ I'm talking about, not the everyday selfish love.

Practically speaking, if people are trying to hurt you, and you just feel love for them, if they continue, you will see them hurt themselves. If they continue further, they'll hurt themselves more. They won't be able to oppose you any more. But we have to practice this love that I'm speaking of, not the love as we have known it.

Q: It's a basic attitude. It's nothing you physically or even mentally do?

Lester: It's a constant attitude that evolves in us when we develop it. However, we should try practicing love, as said before. First, on our family. Grant everyone in the family their own beingness, if you can. If you can't, keep trying; keep trying until you can. Then apply it to friends, then strangers, then everyone. By doing this, you will develop it, although it isn't something you can turn on just like that.

Q: In a way, all of us have it, but it's just layered over by many attitudes?

Lester: Yes, it's smothered by wrong attitudes. Now this love I talk about is our basic nature. It's a natural thing. That is why it's so easy. The opposite takes effort. We move away from our natural Self and smother it with wrong attitudes.

Q: Isn't love almost like a selfishness, because when you love somebody, it's such a wonderful feeling for you?

Lester: Well, this is a matter of semantics. The way you put it, yes, but not in the general sense.

Q: I know when I love somebody, I feel so good. It's such a wonderful feeling.

Lester: It's true after you discover what love is. It's the greatest thing in the universe. It's the thing that everyone wants, only because it's his basic nature in the first place. Every human being is basically an extremely loving individual.

Q: To understand this thing of joy, is it the same type of thing as when your mind becomes stilled in one avenue of thought, of acceptance of the other person, and therefore the mind is stilled?

Lester: Yes. The more we love, the less we have to think. If I'm not loving you, I have to be on guard. I have to protect myself. If I'm not loving the world, I'm always protecting myself from the world which causes more and more thoughts. It puts me extremely on the defensive, and subconsciously it builds up year in and year out, and then I'm a mass of thoughts protecting myself from the world. Now if I love the world, the world can't hurt me. My thoughts get quiet; the mind gets peaceful, and the infinite Self is right there. And that's the experience of this tremendous joy.

Q: In other words, it's not the object, that brings this out. It's the quieting of the mind that actually lets the beingness come through a little more, and that really is the love experience, isn't it?

Lester: Yes.

Q: The light shines through!

Lester: Yes. What you mean is that we take our infinite Beingness, our infinite joy, and we cover it over with thoughts. We take the natural state which is unlimited, and we cover it up with thoughts of limitation. The thoughts smother this infinite Self that we are. It smothers the capacity to enjoy just being. And so all we need to do is to quiet the thoughts, or rid ourselves of all thoughts, and what's left over is the infinite, glorious Being that we are, which is our natural state. That's the way we were, that's the way we're going to be. We are actually that now, but we don't see it. This infinite, glorious Being that we are, being absolutely perfect, can never change. It's always there. We just don't look at it. We look away from it. We look far away from it. What we should do is turn our mind inward, and begin looking at It, and the more we look at It the more we see It.

Everything seems to point to the same direction, does it not? That happens as we get more understanding of what life and the universe are. Everything fits together more and more, and gets simpler and simpler, until there's just one absolute Simple called God. God is simple; everything else is complex. The greater the complexity, the further we are from God. God is One and only One; One without a second.

Q: If someone else has a desire and there's a feeling that if I went along with him that I might lose something, then that isn't love. But if my love is complete in the sense of whatever they wish I wish, then I wouldn't be afraid?

Lester: Yes. There's a word for it today — togetherness. It's a very good word. Doesn't that fit what you're saying? Togetherness?

Q: The thought occurred to me that when I know my beingness, I can't get hurt, so how can anybody else hurt me?

Lester: That's true. It's impossible to be hurt when we love fully. We only feel wonderful when we love, in fact, we feel the greatest!

Q: If you feel a sense of togetherness with one more than another then you begin to separate?

Lester: Yes, it is not full love. It's partial love, and the more partial it is, the less good it feels. When we love fully, we love every being. We have nothing but a tremendously wonderful, warm attitude of: everything is fine; every person is just right. We see only perfection, and that's the way we see the world. When we hate, we see the same world in just the opposite way.

Q: When you speak of giving, are you speaking of giving things or spiritual understanding?

Lester: Love is an attitude of givingness. When things are given with this attitude, it is love. If I give you something because I want you to like me, that is not love; that is trying to bolster my ego.

The greatest givingness is giving understanding, giving wisdom. If I give a meal to a man in poverty, four hours later he needs another meal again. However, if I give him the principle of how to produce a meal, he will never go hungry again.

Let me end with a quote:

"Love is patient and kind. Love is not jealous or boastful. It is not arrogant or rude. Love does not insist on its own way. It is not irritable or resentful. It does not rejoice at wrong, but rejoices in the right. Love bears all things, believes all things, hopes all things, endures all things."

* * *

"Karma comes to an end when one realizes it as all in the mind and one is not one's mind."

Lester Levenson

Session 28

KARMA

A TRIED METHOD

Our method is one of question and answer. The reason why I use questions and answers is that I find it to be one of the very best methods of discovering Truth. The most effective teaching is individual teaching, rather than group or mass teaching. For the knowledge or Truth we are after cannot be picked up intellectually. It cannot be gotten from books. Were it possible to get it from books, we would all have it — for we certainly have books.

Instead, I find that the only really effective teaching is accomplished when the teacher gets the pupil to experience the answer. Only when one experiences the answer can one really understand. This experiencing is also called realizing.

So, do you have a question?

QUESTIONS AND ANSWERS

Q: I'd like to know a little more about how karma works and why it works. I'd like to know what puts it into effect; what starts the wheel. In your book, you mention that it's the thought.

Lester: The word "karma" is a Sanskrit word meaning action. Its general use means action and the reaction to the action. Other explanations are cause and effect; what you sow you reap; what you give out comes back to you.

Karma is initiated in thought. Thought is the cause. Action is the effect. When we create a desire, the desire initiates the thought of wanting something. Wanting something then causes us to act to get that something. When we get that something, it often does not satisfy us and therefore we increase the desire. This process goes on and on and on, until we become bound by desire. Since we can never satisfy it, it's unconscious. If our desires were capable of being satisfied, we would have no desires, right?

Q: Would you say that again?

Lester: If our desires were capable of being satiated or satisfied, we would soon fulfill all of our desires. They would soon be satisfied and we would have no more of them!

Q: Which is the state we should attain?

Lester: Yes. We should attain the state of no desire, of no longing. Then we are happy always.

Q: I understood you to say that karma is a law of action and reaction and could be used, not in the sense of punishment for a wrong deed, but as a reward for a good one.

Lester: Creating things we don't like we call punishment. Creating things we do like we call reward. Creation is initiated in the mind. The mind doesn't know good or bad; it just creates. When we create things that are distasteful to us, (and we don't take responsibility for the creation,) we say we're being punished.

Let me get back to the question of what karma is. To every action there's an opposite and equal reaction. It's called the law of compensation. It is initiated in the mind. Every thought we have creates a vacuum. The pace at which nature fulfills it is also determined by our thought. And every thought is initiated by a previous desire.

Since a desire is not real but is an assumed lack, an assumed agony of need, it can never be satisfied and it actually becomes stronger the more we try to satisfy it.

The only way we can be happy is to let go of all desires. Then we become perfectly content.

Q: So it takes the two; the thought alone without desire won't do it?

Lester: Without a desire, would you have a thought?

Q: I guess not.

Lester: Correct. You wouldn't have any thoughts without desire.

Q: Well, there are intellectual desires, aren't there?

Lester: Yes, but they are desires. Otherwise, there would be no thought. You desire to be heard; you desire to communicate with people. It might not be a desire for ice cream, food, for things that the body needs, but it might be a desire for approval.

So, desire initiates a whole cycle. Way back in the beginning, it started with a thought of lack. Then there was a desire to fulfill the lack. The desire caused more thought. The thought caused action. Since the action does not fulfill the desire, we increase the desire and action, keeping it going until we are apathetically spinning in an endless cycle — with satisfaction impossible.

All our present thinking is initiated by something from the past. Our total feelings now are all from the thoughts and actions of the past. So, all thinking is now motivated by something that has already happened. Action and reaction go on and on that way and we are caught. It's almost impossible to have an original thought any more since every thought is based on past thoughts.

Q: So then, it started way back when?

Lester: It's beginningless and it's endless. I'll take you a step higher. Let us look at the example of the rope being mistaken for a snake. You're walking along the road; there's a rope on the ground and you think it's a snake. Karma is in the realm of the illusory snake.   When did that snake begin and when will that snake end — so long as you think it's a snake? It's beginningless and it's endless, because in reality it never was; it was always a rope. If you are in karma, it is a forever thing. If you are not in it, it never was. Does that make sense? Karma is beginningless and endless.

Hence, it's impossible to work out karma. Some schools of metaphysics teach that you must work out your karma. While you're trying to work it out, you are creating new karma for the future. So, it's impossible to work it out.

Well, what can we do? Only one thing — awake from the illusion and see the Truth! See the snake as the rope! Once the rope is seen as the real, the snake isn't. When we see the Truth of our Being, all this action and reaction turns out to be a dream-illusion and therefore, as such, cannot touch us any more.

Q: Didn't you say we become the observer? I understood that the cycle still must be performed, regardless of enlightenment, is that correct?

Lester: No. That is, once your understanding is full, from that moment on, there's no more karma. When I say, "Be the witness,"

262

that is still in the realm of duality, witnessing the duality, but it's a giant step forward. It's a method of letting go of the ego-sense of being the doer. It's a mode of behavior that's very conducive to growth.

However, when you are fully realized, you'll look at the world and you'll see only a singular oneness in everything and everyone. And you'll see that it is nothing but your very own Self. And the Self is only the Self. So, what happens to the world is that you see it as it really is; you look at it as the rope instead of seeing it as the snake. Then you are out of karma and there is no more karma.

So, from the highest point of view, when you see who and what you are, there is no karma. When you see your real Self, there's only Beingness; action and reaction are only apparently going on.

Q: Let's say I'm driving out onto the freeway and I see a guy coming and I step on the gas and get in front of him. What does this do to me? Is there a reaction coming back from this?

Lester: In this dream-world, to the last ounce there's action and reaction.

Q: One of the big things with any human, and I know I am no different, are thoughts of sex. This is quite a strong interplay and quite a strong force. How does this all get worked out?

Lester: It's one of the most difficult things to transcend. However, it is possible and it is relatively easy to do it once you recognize that all that joy that you're seeking through sex you can have all the time, but much more so, once you're out of the trap of desire. That's why I say, "Get to the higher place where, in order to have sex, you give up joy." Then it's an easy thing to let go of. Meantime, moderation is the best guide.

Happiness is only your very own Self; happiness is your basic nature. You don't need anything external to have it. But you think you do because you've covered over this happiness with layers and layers of limitation: I must have this to be happy; I must have that to be happy. And this has been going on for a long time. But the more you see who and what you are, the less desires have a hold on you.

Q: You have shown the way or method for me, by which I have realized that there is something greater than sex. I have now realized that sex is actually a giving up of something, giving up of a higher feeling for a lesser feeling. It's much easier to understand in that light.

Lester: Sex will keep you earth-bound. It's necessary to get above it. Having sex will not prevent you from moving toward realization, but while you are engaged in it, you are a slave to it and can never get full realization. You are making the physical thing the joy and it isn't. The real thing is that you are that joy, only a million times more so! As high as the feeling is that you get from sex, you can go way, way beyond that feeling in joy, and have it twenty-four hours a day. And it is this unlimited joy that you are really seeking, but you sacrifice it for sex.

Q: When we do things and realize that they should not be done, can we dispose of them by doing the opposite?

Lester: Well, if you're doing the opposite, you're involved in action again, creating the opposite for the future.

Q: You just have to be desireless?

Lester: Yes, that's it! Being desireless, you will see who and what you are; you'll see that you're above all this illusion of karma and then it can touch you no more.

Q: When you see that, the release is so tremendous, it's like a sex release.

Lester: Much greater, much greater. I'll have to get some testimonials for you.

Q: If you drop the desire for some thing, will it still come your way?

Lester: No. The desire is the cause for it. You can mentally undo karma by mentally undoing desire. Karma is caused by desires that remain in the subconscious mind. Dropping desire drops all thoughts of it. If you take desire out of the subconscious mind, the seeds of karma are no more there. This is the fastest, the very best way of undoing karma. If you want to undo karma, do it mentally. Why experience it again and again and suffer it? If you let go of things mentally, you let go of them forever; then you don't have to experience them.

As Jesus said, "Whosoever looketh on a woman to lust after her hath committed adultery with her already." The act originates in the mind. Every negative thought we have creates karma that we don't like, and we call it bad karma. If people only knew this! It doesn't matter whether we carry out the act or not. The seed is sown in the thought.

Here are some additional thoughts for you to reflect on about karma.

* * *

Karma sows the seeds of its own destruction.

What we go through is determined by what we have gone through. This is the law of compensation or karma. In between physical bodies, we choose a certain part of what we have been though to go through the next time around; we set up similar situations, hoping that this next time we will transcend them. You always get another opportunity — ad infinitum.

* * *

Bad karma keeps us so miserable with negativity that we change our bad karma to good karma, and that turns out to be a golden chain instead of an iron chain. Freedom is above karma.

* * *

Whenever we move up, something happens to test us. What actually happens is that we subconsciously feed ourselves more karma because we have become stronger and can face it.

* * *

Karma is nothing but the accumulated past habits of thought that are going on subconsciously.

* * *

Karma is the conglomeration of all the subconscious thoughts running you. Get rid of these thoughts; quiet the mind totally and there is no karma.

Where is karma? It's in the world of illusion.

* * *

Anything karmic is really comic.

* * *

Karma is a harmer. It is a bondage maker.

* * *

We hurt ourselves when we judge others because it is karmic and returns to us.

* * *

The fastest way out of karma is to grow.

* * *

Karma and reincarnation are part of the illusion and have no part in Reality. Past lives should not be gone into. It is playing with the unreality, making it seem real.

* * *

Get to accept karma. The idea that you can fight it is contrary to the accepting of it. If you accept it, your fears, frustrations, tensions, miseries etc., are alleviated and you are no more holding onto it by attempting to avert it. Since there is nothing you can do about it, you just let it be. Everything this body is going to go through, it will go through. Understand this and remain as you really are — free.

* * *

You can't change what the body will go through. That was determined by you by prior action. However, you can choose not to be that body, but to be your Self.

* * *

The ego doesn't like to hear that it doesn't have free will. But the ego itself is a product of karma.

* * *

If karma is, what does advice mean?

* * *

Examine karma and you will discover that karma and destiny are one and the same.

* * *

Acts performed with no interest in the fruits, thereof, produce no karma.

* * *

If action is being done without attachments and aversion, there is no karma being created.

* * *

Once you reach the state of non-attachment, you can enjoy the world and do it without creating any karma.

* * *

It is when we rise above karma, good and bad, that we move into being our real Self.

* * *

How can an infinite Being be subject to karma, karma being an extreme limitation?

*　*　*

Get above karma; don't work out karma.

*　*　*

Karma comes to an end when one recognizes that it is all in one's mind and one is not one's mind.

*　*　*

There's one act that will do away with all karma — be your Self!

*　*　*

All actions that the body will perform have already been concluded by you, before it came into existence. The only freedom you have is whether or not to identify yourself with the body and its action.

If an actor plays the part of a king or a beggar, he is unaffected by it because he knows he is not that character. In exactly like manner should we carry out our part in the world, and whether we are king or beggar, we should be unaffected by it, knowing that we are not that character but are a grand and glorious being, our very own infinite Self.

*　*　*

"The stability of one's peace is the best measuring stick for one's growth."

Lester Levenson

Session 29

GROWTH AND RECEPTIVITY

HAPPINESS VS. GROWTH

Happiness is not necessarily an indication of one's state of realization. Aborigines and natives are as happy as we are, and sometimes more so. We who are supposed to be at the upper end of civilization, as a whole, might not be as happy as they are. They enjoy mostly through the physical senses. We enjoy more through the mind and hence in some ways we are capable of more joy. However, because we are capable of more joy we are also capable of more misery.

Many of us think that the things we do that give us a state of happiness are giving us spiritual growth and therefore are the right things to do. This could be true and it could also be false. The happiness we get from a new realization is definitely growth. We are delighted in the new revelation because we have become a little freer and therefore permanently a little happier. However, the happiness we get from avoiding or escaping unpleasantries is not growth. In fact rather than furthering our growth, it keeps us bound to the unpleasantries we are avoiding. For until they are faced, looked at, and dropped, they will remain in our subconscious and emerge from time to time until we finally deal with them. Therefore, in order to be undone, unpleasantries must be faced and not avoided. Then no escape is necessary.

However, is it also true that the greater our growth the happier we are. We gain an accumulative total happiness that doesn't vary from day to day. It is freedom from the constant nagging of our compulsive subconscious thoughts; it's a sense of well beingness; it's a sense of security; it's a sense of peace. Even when things are outwardly being expressed against us, when the world seems to turn against us, we still feel a greater peace within than we did before.

It is that inner state that should be used as a measure of growth. A miserable person can, for the time being, for the moment, be laughing happily. But you cannot use that as an indication of that person's constant state of freedom.

How can we tell a person's state of freedom or happiness? By checking when everything is against one. Use this as a method for checking yourself. When things go wrong in the world, then check your state of happiness.

QUESTIONS AND ANSWERS

Q: It seems we are inclined to be almost irritated when we see someone else who is happier than we are.

Lester: Yes, it is called jealousy and when we see some one who is happier than we are, we don't like it. Sometimes we attack that one indirectly, even if it is our mate.

This goes on between couples as they grow. When one moves ahead, the other unconsciously resents it, does things to try to undermine the first one. The motivation is often subconscious. But even if it does it becomes conscious, we sometimes don't understand why we're doing it. The reason is that whenever two people get together, the higher one automatically tries to lift the lower one up a bit and the lower one tries to bring the higher one down a bit; they move toward each other. This is an unconscious behavior that goes on whenever two beings meet.

To come back to what I was saying before, the stability of one's peace is the best measuring stick for one's growth. Peace under circumstances not ideal, peace under circumstances in which the individual is being tried is a good measure. If you maintain your peace while everything out there is going against you, then you really have it. This peace that I'm talking about is the real happiness and can be measured by its imperturbability. If a person cannot be disturbed in his peace, he's got it! He has let go of much ego, because only the ego can be disturbed. The Self can never be disturbed. And when we abide as our Self, we allow the whole world to be as it is.

So if you want to know your state, check yourself under adverse conditions. Measure your growth by the bottoms, not by the tops. You'll find that your growth goes in cycles, up and down. You should get to the place where the bottom is happiness, and that makes the top even higher — a state of serenity, tranquillity, bliss — all with a deep imperturbable peace.

Q: Where is this bliss, joy, and peace felt?

Lester: People feel it in different places. Actually it's at the very center of your beingness. Normally we go from a low point at the start, to a very high point at the end.

Q: Do you know why?

Lester: Yes. This is something I'd like to explain to you. Why go down? We're supposed to be intelligent people; we know the ways. Why go down? Somewhat stupid when you know how to be high and happy the way you feel now; in fact, it's stupid not to be the way you are now all the time.

The reason why you go down is that you have not undone enough of your unconscious thoughts. I direct you toward the infinite being that you are. As you see it, you undo the contrary thoughts and feel freer and higher. But later when you are alone, the remaining unconscious thoughts of limitation re-emerge, take over, run you, and you feel lower.

What is necessary is that you continue to eliminate the unconscious thoughts until there are no more, until you are totally free. Only then you will be satisfied.

I'm pointing up now what you need to do to further your growth. The intellect is excellent for growing and is necessary at the beginning; it sets you in the right direction; it takes you forward. Then you reach a place where it can take you no further. So, what do you do? Do you stop at the top of the intellect, or do you go on? I'm saying let's go on! This doesn't mean let go of your intellect, forget it, or suppress it. No, I'm saying go beyond it. I'm suggesting another giant step forward.

I'm trying to get you to see what this next step is, by first telling you what it is not. It is not intellectual. Intellectually there's nothing more I can give you.

What is it then? It is becoming aware of your Self by actually experiencing your Self. I could lead you much higher than we've ever gone before if you would draw it out of me. This would help you to experience a higher state than you have ever known before. Then the experience would be your knowledge, and after you experience it, it would leave you with a stronger desire for freedom, a stronger incentive to move faster toward the Goal.

Now, I don't want to talk in riddles or intangibles. What is it that will draw out more than the intellect has drawn our so far? It is your state of receptivity. Receptivity determines the amount of the Power that flows into you. Stated another way, it is letting go of your reservations. As you become more receptive, more of the power flows through me into you and lifts you to the place where you experience your Self.

I, Lester, do not do it; it flows through me to the degree that you receive it. It can help lift you to a higher state, by experiencing that state, you definitely know it. You better know that, "Thou are That."

Q: How do we do that?

Lester: Greater acceptance of the direction coming through me, and of the fact that happiness really lies within you and not without. The direction up to now has been to quiet the mind by looking at, and letting go of, subconscious thoughts. As you let go of these thoughts, you become freer, your mind is quieter, your real Self is less obscure and you're more able to be the real Self that you are. Also, the more you have this experience, the more you are capable of being drawn into your Self by the Power flowing through me into you. This could go on to the Ultimate.

You have quieted the mind to quite some degree, but there is much more to be done. That's why I ask, "Who can sit down and immediately quiet his mind and have no thoughts come in?" If you can do that, you're a Master. To the degree you can quiet your mind, to that degree you are a Master. But everyone is quieter now then they were. Our next step is to get even quieter. And I say we're not going to get it through intellectualism any more, through bandying words up and back. We're going to get it through a method that directly helps you experience the quietude of your Self.

Q: When you quiet your mind and no thought comes in, then what happens? Is it a blank?

Lester: No, it's not a blank; you have no mind to go blank! You're in the realm of All-Knowingness; you don't have to think any more; you just know everything and everything falls into line perfectly — every moment. You operate on a feelingness, called intuition. Everyone in this room has experienced it at times.

Mind is nothing but the total bundle of your thoughts; a small part conscious; the major part subconscious and held out of view. Mind is not complicated when you see what it is; it's simply the totality of thoughts.

Q: Isn't it true that subconscious thoughts are thoughts that are not being thought of at the moment?

Lester: No, they're being thought of at the moment, but they're not consciously being thought of; they're subconsciously being thought of at the moment.

Q: So that's the difference between conscious and subconscious thoughts?

Lester: Yes, subconscious thoughts are active right now, but we're not looking at them. Are you consciously pumping your heart? Breathing? Running that chemical digestive factory you have? Are you doing these things consciously? Well, then you're doing them subconsciously.

Q: I didn't have that in mind exactly.

Lester: I know, but I want to show you how all the thoughts on the body, even though you're not conscious of them, are active right now, and there are many, many thoughts connected with running a body; there's a lot of action going on there. They're active right now, even though we're not conscious of them.

Q: That's automated; that's what I call automation.

Lester: Right, But who is now running the automated action? We are. It was originally useful in that we didn't have to consciously operate the body. Then we lost sight of the fact that we threw this onto automatic; and therefore it is now running us. It's difficult to change it because we have made it unconscious. As we become aware, we see this and then we change it. We become free of it; we reestablish our control over the body.

Out object is to let go of unconscious thoughts, these habitual things of the past that keep us automatically bound. Every habitual thought is a bondage that takes away a certain amount of freedom, happiness. We must let go of all these old habit-thoughts until we are totally free of them. Then we are liberated, fully-realized Masters.

Q: That's why some words will trigger us. If we hear a certain word, we fly into a madness, or if we hear something else, we feel good.

Lester: Right! So, our objective is to let go of all these subconscious thoughts. We have done a beautiful job so far, through using the thoughts, the mind. Now I'm suggesting that we move on; that we get the mind yet quieter by doing that which does it directly, that is, by experiencing your Self.

It can also be done in meditation. I ought to re-define the word "meditation." When I say meditation, I mean holding one thought to the exclusion of other thoughts, and that one thought should be a question. As other thoughts drop away the mind gets quiet and concentrated. When the mind is concentrated, you will experience your Self and It will answer any and every question. It will answer the questions that we need to have answered to show us the way out of the bondages.

Now, in meditation, the moment you sit down to quiet the mind, it seems to get noisier, which is natural. The thoughts come up for us to drop, to let go of. And each time we let go of one, that's one less that we have to let go of. And each time we let go of one, that's one that we have to let go of. As time goes on and we keep dropping these thoughts, we have less and less to drop. Someday the mind becomes quiet enough so that we fully see this infinite Being that we are; and then in one lump sum, we drop all that is left. And when there are no more thoughts, we are free and there is left only our infinite Self.

Q: My mind keeps getting noisier and noisier.

Lester: No, it is just that you are looking more at your subconscious thoughts. You don't get more thoughts, you just become more aware of them. The unconscious thoughts that control you will come up. Every time you meditate this happens, and through practice, some day you will be able to hold one question, one thought, without other thoughts coming in. When you get that far, you are moving rapidly. When you have dropped all subconscious thoughts, then you know what God is, that your beingness is He.

Q: I'd like to identify the feeling in meditation. Is it similar to a feeling you get while listening to a fine piece of music?

Lester: Yes, it is one of the nicest and quietest feelings you can have.

Q: Then the process of meditation, as I'm seeing it now, has not to do at all with thoughts, but with identifying with this feeling and allowing it to expand.

Lester: Yes! However, this nice feeling is accomplished by quieting the thoughts. Someday the meditative feeling will be far more enjoyable than the music was.

Q: I feel that it would be such a tremendous welling up that you would almost explode!

Lester: Well, you won't explode because you take it on as much as you can accept it. There is such a tremendousness in us, that if it came all at one time, we just couldn't take it.

Q: Is meditation related to receptivity?

Lester: Definitely yes! The better we are able to meditate, the more receptive we are, and the more receptive we are, the better we can meditate.

I'm stressing meditation with the hope of helping us to become more receptive. We should let go of the queer ideas we have about meditation. You don't have to be a Hindu or a Yogi; you can be one hundred per cent American and be a very good mediator.

Meditation is simply holding one question or thought to the exclusion of all other thoughts, and when that question or thought is on your beingness, that's right meditation. Before we attain good meditation, we have to work to let go of extraneous thoughts while we're trying to hold one question. Then that one question will be answered, whatever that question is. "What am I?" is the final question. When we get the full answer to that, we are in the ultimate state.

Q: Don't you automatically try to answer that when you ask yourself the question?

Lester: Yes you do, but your mind cannot. The mind can never give you the answer to the question "What am I? Why? Because Realization is elimination of the mind and the mind posing the question is not going to eliminate itself. It's almost like saying "eliminate yourself." The mind does not want to eliminate itself, therefore, when the mind poses the question, "What am I?" the mind will never in all eternity, give the answer.

This is another reason why the intellect can take us only so far. The mind cannot give us the answer because it, itself, is in limitation, in finiteness. The answer is in infinity. The mind can pose the question, "What am I?" and when the answer comes, it's from beyond the mind. It's only by quieting the mind that you will be able to see who and what you are. The mind is the blinding cover over this infinite Self that you are.

Q: But underneath it all — I'm trying to find something to hang onto here — is it this glow, this feeling?

Lester: Yes. If you will examine the glow you'll discover it to be a feeling of "I - ness", of beingness.

Q: Assuming this feeling that we all get occasionally is our true being shining through, even though it's a very small part we're experiencing, this is the constant experience we should attain to, right?

Lester: Yes! Make it nothing but that and that is It. Then there's nothing but the experience of "I..." all the time, and you are There.

Q: Up until now, I've only had an intellectual understanding of these things and this is the first concrete experience I've had.

Lester: Well, that's not really so. There was always a feeling of experiencing when you got a realization.

Q: Well, that's what I'm finding out; I've now identified with this glow, this feeling.

Lester: Yes, the glow is the experiencing and is higher than the intellect. It's simply experiencing.

Q: That's the way I want it because books make it sound awfully complicated. How does that fit in with the Self Realization Fellowship teachings?

Lester: SRF teachings will say the same thing from a different approach. Their approach is for the majority of seekers. Christianity is in the realm of love, devotion and surrender to God. So are the SRF teachings. Instead of working so hard to eliminate the ego, they say, "Just surrender to God." If you really surrender, it's only surrender of the ego. "Thy will, not my will" is simply surrender of the ego.

SRF directs you to quiet the mind, mainly through meditation, so that your infinite Self becomes obvious. Its main teaching is its methodology, called Kriya Yoga, an integral method that can be used by everyone.

If you understand the overall picture, you'll see that there's no disagreement. I'm trying to get you to quiet the mind, to let go of the mind. Their teaching will end up doing the very same thing. And it's a good balance to have our intellectual, wisdom way and their devotional, love and surrender aspect. However, you can't really have one without the other. So approaching it from both sides is beneficial. And we should use every aid possible. We need it; we're in an earth period that is extremely low. We're having opposition going on all day as long as we associate with the world, and therefore any aid that is helpful should be used.

There is no greater aid than the actual, wonderfully exhilarating experience of being your Self. Be more receptive — surrender your little self and allow the Power of your real Self to flow, until It, the Power, is the only power flowing through you. Glory in that Power! Remain in the Power! Remain and abide as your infinite, glorious Self!

* * *

"The all-quiet state is such a tremendous state, that it can never be put into words. The words ecstacy, euphoria, bliss, nirvana don't describe it really — they only allude to it."

Lester Levenson

Session 30

THE QUIET MEDITATIVE STATE OF BEINGNESS

CATEGORIES

Humanity is divided into three general categories of havingness, doingness, and beingness. The lowest of the three is the havingness state. Most human beings think that if only they could have, they would be happy: "If only I could have a million dollars, I would be the happiest person in the world." "If only I could have a strong, healthy body." "If only I could have."

The next higher state is a doingness state; instead of saying, "If only I could have," we rise to the place where we want to go out and do, and we are capable of doing things in the world. There, we are more interested in doingness than we are in havingness.

The highest state is the beingness realm. This is the state that I am trying to get you into. Beingness will have no meaning until you experience it. Only then will you know what it is and you will want beingness more than anything else in the world. This reminds me of something someone said to me.

We visited a friend we had not seen for over a year. She is very interested in metaphysics. While we were visiting her, she said, "Let's cut out this talking; let's meditate. Why waste time talking?!" She had already experienced this realm of beingness. When you are up there, it looks silly to talk. Why talk? Why not just be?

THE HIGHEST STATE

Havingness is the category that roughly 90% of us live in most of the time. "Oh, if we only could have those almighty dollars, more and more of them, or a million of them — then we would be free and happy." But, what is the experience of those who do accumulate a million or more? Are they happy? Well, a lot of them have many problems, and are loaded down with non-freedom. They are more unhappy than happy. The proof of their not attaining happiness is their compulsive drive to get more and more, even though they cannot use the amount already accumulated. Were it true that material things brought happiness, the wealthy would be so happy that they would be incapacitated by it, and the poor would be so miserable that life would not be worth living.

As I said, the next higher state is the doingness state. Here we are the real doers in the world, and are the leaders. Here we are found as big business men, small business men; big politicians and small politicians; people in the arts; and professional people. Here we are out on our own, more independent than the job holder. Are we happy? No! Happier than the job holder because more independent — but not free. Still we are compulsively driven. I think the proof of this is the number of actors and actresses who, on attaining the height of fame and fortune, find themselves so unhappy that they commit suicide or go through life frustrated.

We come now to the only state that can give us happiness with no sorrow — the state of beingness. Beingness is the highest of the three states and it is the very highest state possible. In the ultimate state we are Beingness, being all beingness. States another way, it's Awareness, aware of all awareness. When we are just that, when we are only that, that's the highest state. It is in this top state of Beingness that we reach our ultimates of perfection contentment, perfect satiation, perfect joy, perfect peace. It is the state of highest felicity.

THE WAY

There is no giving up of anything on this path. You always take on more. Those who tell me, "Well, I don't want to give up," are refusing to hear what I have been saying. But why don't you hear it? It is very subtle ego-sabotage saying, "I don't want to grow anymore." When this happens, I should present it to you so that you may see the ego-sabotage. Then you may let go of it and go further.

We are moving toward an infinity, and until we are absolute and infinite, we should keep moving — if we want the ultimate happiness — and who doesn't? We will never be fully happy until we reach that state. The ultimate happiness and your Self turn out to be one and the same thing. There will always be a subconscious, below the surface, nagging that pushes us on until we achieve it, until we are There.

What the world today calls happiness is escape from misery — alleviation of misery. The relatively small amount of happiness the world has is only relief from misery. All entertainment, all socializing, is relief and escape from our thoughts! Look at, examine, and discover this. Stop chasing rainbows!

In the havingness state, one has the least happiness; in the doingness state, one has more happiness; in the beingness state, one has the greatest happiness. I cannot tell you what it is; it is an experience and you just must experience it.

The best way I can help you to experience it is to get you to do what will put you into that state. It is a very deep, quiet, meditative state; it is a state wherein we let go of thoughts. Through my helping, guide you in such a way that you may fall into it, you can experience and know what this state of beingness is. That guidance is to lead you into right meditation and to support you while in it.

My objective is to try to show you how to get a deeper and deeper feeling of this state of beingness. Now, some of us have gone very deep into the state of beingness and know what it is. Yet, if I asked you to describe it, you would have difficulty; you could not tell what it is. You could talk around it, describe it by saying it is nice; it is peaceful; it is serene; it is delightful. But what is it? You cannot put it into words. It is like trying to explain to someone what an orange tastes like: You just cannot do it. Once one tastes the orange, then one knows. It is the same with this deep meditative state of beingness. Once you taste it, you know it. And after you have tasted the deep state of meditative beingness, you will want it more than anything else in the world.

THE KEYS

For best results, meditate at least one hour in the morning and one hour before retiring. The morning meditation sets you in a mood and prepares you for a better day. The evening meditation helps undo the turbulence of the day and carries through the night. You will find yourself sleeping better. For maximum results, increase the length of your set time of meditation until the meditative state stays with you all the time and remains with no effort.

When you want "Beingness" more than anything else in the world, it is a sign that you have gone deeply into your beingness — your Self. This experience is so much greater than anything else you've ever experienced, you will find yourself preferring it to anything and everything else. Then you will see and know that this is what you have been blindly seeking for through indirect external means in the world. And then you will discover that it is right where you are. You do not have to have anything. You do not have to do anything. You only have to be what you are. It is your natural state!

As you may have noticed, I have not spoken about ways and means of meditation, nor have I been asked questions on it.

QUESTIONS AND ANSWERS

Q: Do you want questions on it?

Lester: That is up to you. I know that some of you joined various organizations and are beginning to get some of the methods. There are organizations whose root teaching is meditation; how to meditate and how to do those things that will prepare you for meditation. These have many methods and means of helping one meditate better.

This is important for when thoughts come into our mind unwanted, when we cannot keep them out, we are not free. Whereas, when we can cause thoughts to enter or not enter, we are free and a master over mind. Until then, the mind is the master and we are the slave and the victim of our thoughts.

In such a state, we are actually being pushed around like automatons by our habit-thoughts. People talk to us and it's just as though they are pressing our automatic buttons. They praise us and we go up; they berate us and we go down. And we think we're free willed! Anyone who goes up on praise and down on condemnation is behaving like a robot, because, whether I praise you or condemn you, I don't do a thing to you but send out tiny bits of sound energy, and you give it enough power to make you happy or miserable, making you nothing but an automatic robot.

So, an easy way to become master over your mind and over this automatic state is through meditation. It's the practice of quieting the mind by seeking that which we really are. This we should do until we reach the Goal. Our direction from here on should be learning how to better meditate.

I can give far more potent guidance while you're in the meditative state than I could through my voice. But you will never know it until you experience it. The help you've gotten so far is small by comparison to the help you can receive when you get quiet; then I can communicate to you directly — Self to Self. Then I can help you be your real Self. Not only I, but also the Masters. Whether They're here in body or not, this is exactly what They do. When we are quiet, They come in and They help establish us in our Self. And by our experiencing it, we go deeper and deeper until it's complete — until we're in the quiet meditative state 24 hours a day, regardless of what we are doing.

In this quiet state you never lose consciousness. When you go to sleep, you're fully aware that you're sleeping. When you are dreaming, you're fully aware that you're dreaming. Should you decide to cut the dream, you can cut the dream. The same with the sleep. Or, while you're fully awake, if you decide to go to sleep this moment, you go to sleep this moment.

This is not giving up anything; this is becoming a master over the three usual states that we all go through every day: the waking state, the dream state, and the deep, dreamless sleep state.

Let me sum up what we have been talking about. First, we talked about our havingness, then our doingness, and now, we're talking about the top state of beingness. The beingness state should be developed from here on. Any questions about what I've been saying to you? Is it understood?

Q: The main purpose of meditation is to learn to quiet the mind?

Lester: Right. Purely, simply and wholly to quiet the mind until it's totally quiet. When it's totally quiet, that's the Goal.

Every thought is a thing of limitation, is a cover, a veil, over our infinite Beingness. When we remove all the veils, there's nothing left but our infinite Beingness. The veils are only our thoughts. Mind is not mysterious — except when you don't understand it. When you understand, it's nothing but thoughts; it's as simple as that. It's the sum total collection of thoughts that is called mind. Stop the thoughts and there's no more mind action.

Meditation is simply a method of quieting the thoughts and meditation should be continued until all thoughts are quieted. The all-quiet state is such a tremendous state that it can never be put into words. The words ecstasy, euphoria, bliss, nirvana do not describe it really. They only allude to it. But as I said, when you once experience a certain depth of meditation, you have experienced the greatest thing you ever have experienced in your life. And you will want to repeat that experience, want to establish and maintain it so that it is all the time. This experiencing turns out to be only your very own real Self, now called happiness and creeps up very quietly.

When you gain this beautiful depth of quietude, don't spill it out in conversation. Most people do not see how much they let go of this beautiful quietude when they pour it out, lose it, in conversation. The same is true of thinking. When one gets involved in thoughts, the thoughts take one away from the quietude. Then one has only the memory of it being a nice feeling. Instead, one should maintain, sustain and retain this feeling and the best way to do this is, after meditation, remain by yourself.

Just keep quiet; stay in it as long as you possibly can, until you become fully established in it all the time. Then it's all right to talk; you won't lose it. But as it is now, you let go of the depth of quietude you get in meditation when you talk to people. You just waste it and it's so valuable to get that feeling. Hold it and develop it further and further, until it is there all the time.

You'll know when the state of beingness is complete. You will see yourself as all beingness. It comes in stages. First, we get a little of this beautiful state of quietness, peace, serenity, tranquility; then, as it develops, we begin to see more and more that we are all beingness. In the beginning, it might be for the briefest instant. Then for a minute, or maybe five minutes. Each time the experience will last longer and longer until it's the only thing. Then you will see yourself only as beingness being all beingness. Then you'll know what God is; you will know your real Self.

Q: This whole thing is like trying to tell somebody what the orange tastes like?

Lester: Yes, but most of us have experienced this quietude of beingness to a degree, so it has a certain amount of meaning. To the degree that one has experienced it, it has that much meaning to him. Then I add to it by saying: someday you're going to have such a tremendous experience of just Beingness, that after it, you will want only to reestablish it permanently. Everything else in the world becomes secondary to it. You also recognize that what you have been seeking in the world is right where you are — it's not out there; it's within, right where you are; it's your natural, inherent state. It's your Self and it's all the glory of gloriousness.

Q: Can this state be reached without direct conscious effort toward finding out who you are?

Lester: Yes, in a slower way, by seeking God through devotion and self surrender. Surrender yourself wholly and completely unto your God and you will reach it.

Q: I am trying to understand where I am now.

Lester: I'll tell you where you are now. You are at that place that's equal to how well you can remain quiet. To the degree that you can remain quiet, imperturbable, to that degree is your growth. In meditation, how well you can keep your mind on one thought without other thoughts coming in, shows you how far you've gone.

Q: Well, I'm experiencing thought, so I can't see it.

Lester: There are indirect ways of telling. How easily you're disturbed by others. How much you react to what people say, and so forth. When your mind is really quiet, it doesn't matter what people say about you; you don't mind.

Q: But you already are that which you are seeking. It's just a matter of knowing it, isn't it?

Lester: Yes, it's a matter of re-remembering it, recognizing it. We have to experience it to recognize it. Meditation is the way to experience it.

Right now, we are convinced that we are limited to being our body. That is the biggest lie of all lies. We are infinite! It is just wrong perception, wrong seeing. It is an illusion. The lie is not real. The reality is that we are the Beingness behind the body.

Q: What we really should do when we get into meditation is to see what we are and not see the limited being? What should we do to get away from the sense of limitation?

Lester: Let go of the concepts of limitation. By doing this, you experience beingness more and more until you experience only the Being, You, just behind the body and mind.

Q: Our thoughts of limitation are what's restricting us from seeing what we are?

Lester: Yes, our thoughts, which themselves are limitations. And not just our thoughts of limitation, but our thoughts — every one of them — is a limitation.

Q: How do you differentiate between consciousness and thought?

Lester: Consciousness is general awareness. Thought is awareness of a particular thing.

Q: To me it means more if, instead of using the word "meditation," you say, "I want you to begin getting rid of your sense of limitation and get a feeling of being all; of being all knowledge, all consciousness."

Lester: That is what meditation does and achieves.

Q: I have to put it into words, and I suppose you know it instinctively.

Lester: No, I put it into words. I define meditation most simply as keeping one's mind on one thought. Now this makes sense to you: Hold one thought such as, "What is God?" Just stay with that thought, and only that thought, and keep other thoughts out; that's meditation. Take another thought: "What is this world?" Just hold the thought: "What is this world? What is it?" You keep questioning: "What is this world?" When there is only one thought, the mind is quiet. When the mind is quiet, the answer comes from beyond the mind.

Q: You are not saying what we have been taught elsewhere, to think about a rose and not let any other thought come in. You're really saying think about God, or about "I."

Lester: Yes. "What am I?" is the very top question. When the answer to that comes fully, that's It. By holding that question in your mind and awaiting the answer to it, you are doing the very best of meditation. No matter what method one uses, no matter what path one takes, in the end, one gets the answer to "What am I?" But know this: the mind will never give you the answer. Any answer the mind gives has to be wrong because the mind is an instrument of thought, and every thought is limited. Therefore, you mentally pose the question and you await the answer, and it is from beyond your mind, from your Self, that the answer comes.

Q: Because you already know, so you just stop the nonsense?
Lester: Yes, you stop the nonsense of not knowing.

Q: And in recognizing, "I know, I know," I'm getting rid of being limited.

Lester: That's it! That's the whole thing in a nutshell. As you said, you already know it and you just let go of the thoughts that are contrary to it until this knowingness is self-obvious. This is called realization or revelation.

Q: Is beingness no thought of consciousness?

Lester: Beingness, when complete, is without thought. However, beingness and consciousness are the same, which one cannot intellectualize on, but which one can experience. Beingness and consciousness are the exact same thing. That's why I said: If you want to know a cow, be a cow. If you want to know what a tree is, be a tree. And you can, because you are. How better can you know something than to be it?

The real answer will come when you get there; then you'll see that beingness and consciousness are the same. Don't intellectualize on it. Do it! Do it!

Q: It's awfully boring when, in meditation, nothing comes.

Lester: It shouldn't be boring because, as you're doing it, you're quieting thoughts. The more you quiet thoughts, the happier you are.

I think by now we can all examine and know what our joys really consist of. If we're listening to music, our mind concentrates only on the music; all other thoughts and problems of the day are let go so the music seems beautiful. It is really dropping our discomforting thoughts that makes the focus of our attention on something external seem so wonderful.

Q: I must express a thought I just had when you were talking. In other words, it's like all electricity going one way, with no side issues, no interference. When you listen to music, you think about nothing but the music.

Lester: Yes, all other thoughts, bothersome limitations, are let go of for the time being and you feel your real Self much more. You'll never know the real beauty until you see the Beauty behind the beauty, the Source of the beauty.

Q: Which is "I?"

Lester: Yes, your real Self. When you develop the ability to meditate, it leads you into the most beatific, blessed state; into nirvana, tranquility and serenity; into your quiet meditative state of knowing what you are — you, the real Being of the universe, being your infinite, glorious and magnificent Self.

* * *

"A person can control a whole nation, but if they cannot control their own mind, what kind of control do they have? They are victims of their own mind."

Lester Levenson

MEDITATION

DROPPING THE MIND

The greatest thing, and the most difficult thing we have to do is to drop the mind. It is a junkyard full of refuse from ages past; refuse of thoughts of limitations — I am a limited body, I have troubles. All thoughts contain limitation. We pile them up in the thing we call mind. Mind is nothing but the total accumulation of all these thoughts. So mind is kind of a junkyard of limitation.

All right, so how do we get rid of the mind? By quieting it. When we quiet the mind we discover our infinity. The more we see our limitlessness, the more we recognize that junkyard called mind, and the more we let go of it. We let go of it until we go so far that we drop the whole remaining mind at one time.

However, before that, we keep battling the thoughts as they come up. As the thoughts come up, we let go, let go, let go, until we let go of enough of them so that the Self that we are, is obvious. Then it takes over and takes us all the way. The greatest thing is quieting the mind, which is eliminating thought, which is eliminating the mind.

Meditation is a necessary step in quieting the mind. This is the major point I am stressing: Meditate. Learn how to meditate and in that state learn how to release. The deeper one goes, the more one discovers the innate joys to which there are no limits. No matter how joyful you get, you can always go further. If you were a thousand times more joyful than you are now, you could still go on and on and on in joy. Joy is unlimited because you are infinite.

But the major thing to accomplish is the ability to control the mind, to meditate, to release, to drop into peace at will. A person can control a whole nation and if they cannot control their own mind, what kind of control have they got? They are a victim of their own mind. Rather than being in free control over their thoughts, they are an effect of them. They are actually pushed around by past habits. They are no Master. Only the one who can control their mind is a Master, a Master not only of themselves, but of anything and everything they do. Meditation is the way.

Here are some additional thoughts. Let your time with them be a meditation.

* * *

Meditation is directed thinking.

* * *

Meditation is putting your mind on the way to find God.

* * *

Meditation is looking for the answers in the right direction.

* * *

Meditation is basically thinking in the right direction and holding to it so that other thoughts keep dropping away until the mind is concentrated. When the mind is concentrated the answers become obvious to you.

* * *

Concentration is holding one thought to the exclusion of other thoughts and will lift one and help one grow.

* * *

The ability to hold one thought concentrates the mind so that it can crack the secrets of itself.

* * *

Meditating to get the mind quiet is good. Meditating to let go of ego-wants is better. Meditating on "What am I?" is best

292

Meditate, actively seeking.

* * *

Meditation should be on: "What am I?" "What is God?" "What is the World?" "What's my relationship to the world?" "What is the substance of this World?" "What is infinity?" "What is intelligence?" "Where is this World?" or on some of the statements you've heard like: "I'm not in the World but the World is in me." Question and ask, "How come?" Try to see it. Try to see the meaning behind these statements of Truth.

* * *

We get to see the perfection by looking in the direction where the perfection is. Now, the perfection isn't out there; we know that. The perfection is in here where we are, where the "I" of us is. So first, we have to direct our attention inwardly; we should pose a question and hold it until the answer comes. When the answer does come, you know, and you know you know. And to get the answer to "What am I?" it is necessary to still the noise of the mind, to still the thoughts. The thoughts are the noise. The thoughts are concepts of limitation and there are so many of them that they're constantly bombarding us, one after another all the time. Keep dropping them until perfection is obvious.

* * *

All these extraneous thoughts wouldn't come in if we weren't interested in them.

* * *

We must learn how to quiet the mind. We can never learn how by constant conversation. The less conversation, the better.

* * *

Meditation does not have to be formal to be meditation. It can by any time one gets quiet and seeks. Some of us find it is easier to meditate when it isn't formal because sometimes we unconsciously have objections and resistances to formal meditation. However, we should work to drop the objections and resistances, and be free of them.

* * *

Reverse your negative thoughts as they come into mind. Let go of negative thoughts by reversing them and then eventually, let go of all thoughts.

* * *

What you gain remains. Even though you've undone one thought, one idea, there still remains multitudes of thoughts and so another one comes up. Undoing one limiting thought doesn't undo all the subconscious thoughts. What remains must be let go of. By dropping a tendency of predisposition, you drop all the thoughts motivating it.

* * *

Meditation should always be with a seeking.

* * *

Everything that everyone is looking for through work is far better gotten through meditation. Meditation will sooner and better get you what you want than working in the world for it will.

* * *

It is the doorway to the Infinite when you go inward. When you go outward, it is the doorway to limitation.

* * *

Internalize your attention. All externalized attention is wasted.

* * *

What you do to yourself, being your own doing, can only be undone by you.

* * *

God is known only through your effort and direction. Look concentratedly within for the kingdom of God.

* * *

With meditation, you will discover that you've covered up your unlimited Self with your limited ego.

* * *

Meditation is the road to omnipresence.

* * *

Meditate to get into the practice and habit of meditation. We should meditate as much as we possibly can. Meditation is getting the mind one-pointed in the direction of who and what we are. It's taking the mind away from the worldly things and focusing it on the direction that we're in. The more we do it the more we like it. And the more we like it, the more we do it, until it becomes a thing that goes on effortlessly all the time. No matter what you're doing, that meditation continues in the background. Then you are really moving. Until then you're not moving very rapidly, because most of the time you're in the world and in the direction of limitation.

* * *

There's only one way to get to the high state, and that is by quieting the mind. The method of quieting the mind is meditation. It's very difficult; the moment you sit down and want to quiet the mind, up pop the thoughts. Well, as the thoughts pop up, keep knocking them out, putting them out, dropping them, until you reach a state where you can sit relatively quiet. Then you begin to like meditation because it's a deeper experience of your real Self. Once you like it, the main obstacle to the practice of meditation is eliminated. But you should never stop until you reach the place where meditation is delightful. Then you will go on with ease.

* * *

The most effective meditation is when you are by yourself. Group meditation is for beginners, for the purpose of accustoming one to meditation.

* * *

Meditation really should be communing with your Self.

* * *

You'll see your Self to the proportion that your mind is quiet.

* * *

The way to get rid of the ego is to get the mind so quiet that you can see what you are. Then you know that you are not the ego and you drop it.

* * *

Intense meditation will get you to your realized Teacher, to your Master.

To expand from being just a body is so difficult because of the state of the world today. We do need the help of the Masters to lift us, actually to help pull us right out of it. They cannot do that unless we are receptive. We cannot be receptive unless our mind is quiet. And our mind becomes quiet through meditation.

* * *

Just go into meditation, get quiet and expect that higher help and it will come. God and Gurus are constantly helping us. If we just get quiet, with their help we are lifted into experiencing our Self.

* * *

Meditation has to get to the point where it is the most important thing. However, even a little meditation will go a long way, especially if it is concentrated.

* * *

Spiritual things are spiritually discerned. Spiritual knowledge does not come down to a lower level. We have to raise ourselves up to it. We raise ourselves in meditation. Meditation should be used to get higher understanding by raising ourselves up to where higher understanding is.

* * *

Meditation is wonderful. Things happen in meditation that never could happen while you are talking or active.

* * *

You can make the mind quiet by the desire to discover what you are. When the interest in knowing what you are becomes stronger than the interest in this world and body, then you discover you. Desire, intense desire for it, is the key.

The concept of meditating by making your mind a blank is in error. You cannot make your mind a blank.

* * *

Meditation is a stepping stone to the knowledge of the answer to, "What am I?"

* * *

Someday the most delightful thing you will know of will be meditation.

* * *

Meditate until it becomes constant, i.e., until it continues in back of the mind regardless of what you are doing.

* * *

There is a meditation of just getting quiet. Just get quiet, not in a passive way, but in an active way of just being. It's awfully nice to just be and be and be. It's a tremendous experience. It's a wonderful feeling of just being. However, don't stop there. Keep dropping ego until there is no more.

* * *

You'll reach a point where you'll like meditation better than anything else, because you'll reach a point where you're being very much your real Self. That is the greatest of all joy which you formerly thought was external in the world, in your wife, in your children. You'll see your wife and your children as nothing but your very own Self; you'll see that. And the joy will be direct and constant all the time.

* * *

The answer won't come from reasoning. It will come from quiet meditation. Someday, sometime, it will come. It will just present itself to you, so simple, and you'll say, "Oh!"

* * *

Meditation is thinking, but thinking on one thing so that other thoughts drop away. When you are intensely interested in one thing, other thoughts drop away.

* * *

The quieter we are, the more we are the Self. When meditation becomes constant, all the time, even though we are outwardly active, we go through life and work automatically, all the time remaining in our Self.

* * *

The mature seeker of the Self starts with: The reality is that I was never bound; I was always free and perfect — and takes off from there.

* * *

Just look at what you are instead of what you are not. When you discover what you are, you simultaneously discover what you are not and drop it.

* * *

Say, "I am not this body; I am not this mind," and stay with it.

* * *

Seeing that you're not the ego, you're letting go of the big chunks of ego.

The depth to which you go in meditation determines how much you wipe out the ego.

* * *

Depth of meditation is the degree of quieting the mind.

* * *

The longer you can meditate, the deeper you can go.

* * *

Once you reach peace, then find out what you are.

* * *

Getting the good feeling is good. The higher you go the better the feeling is. But when you look for the good feeling as the end, then that is the end. Growing is more than dropping into the good feeling of the Self; it is dropping the nonself — the ego.

* * *

Enjoying meditation is a step, but don't stop there; go beyond it. You have got to get the answer.

One could possibly meditate forever and forever.

* * *

Meditation in itself can get to be a trip, can be used as a crutch. You've got to get realizations.

* * *

When you get full realization, you're in the meditative state all the time. Actually, meditation is the natural state.

Constant meditation is a constant remembering of God, Self.

* * *

Meditation is extremely difficult at first, but it gets easier as time goes on — then, one day you'll say, "This is great! This is what I want!" Then you do it all the time. Then you're really on the spiritual path.

* * *

Very concentratedly dwell upon your Self. Turn the mind back upon the mind to discover what the mind is, and then go beyond the mind and dwell in your Self. Each one must experience it. It's a perception, but it's not really a mental perception. You get recognitions, revelations, realizations by keeping the mind pointed in one direction until it gets very quiet, until other thoughts drop away. Hold one thought until that takes you to the realm just behind thinkingness; the answer is there. We call it an experience, a revelation.

* * *

We must learn to quiet the mind so that when we sit down, we let go of the world. Only then do we really begin to move at high levels on this spiritual path. We've made this world a better world; we've made this dream a happier dream — but we're almost as bound as we were before. We have replaced bondages to bad things with bondages to good things. Now we must learn to let go of thoughts, all thoughts. The way is through meditation, right meditation: quieting the mind, stilling thoughts, and finally, eliminating all thoughts.

In group meditation support is lent one unto the other. The power is multiplied and you can get more deeply quiet as time goes by. But the very best meditation is when you are by yourself and you need no group support. Then you are not confined to any time period. You get with it and you might stay with it five, ten, even twenty-four hours. And this should happen. When you get to like it so much that you stay up all night continuing it, it has become more interesting than sleep. Then you've got the momentum going. Then you'll get to see and be your real Self.

* * *

A way to dominate the mind is to drop into the Self. You reach a place where it's so delightful you just don't want to do anything but remain in it. It gets to be very easy. Once you get to the point where it's easy, then just continue it. Stay with it until you go all the way. By the constancy of it, each day, you get quieter and quieter, and then the Self, as you see it, keeps scorching the ego, which further quiets the mind.

* * *

You know, it's said that your spiritual growth really begins when you are able to drop into samadhi. I don't like to say this because it's discouraging to some people. Samadhi is complete absorption in your thought. It's total concentration.

* * *

Meditation at first is holding the thoughts on God, Self, to the exclusion of other thoughts. When one is realized, meditation is the awareness, not of anything by anyone, but only the current of awareness of awareness where there is no otherness and no action, yet compatible with full use of the mental and physical faculties.

* * *

At the end of the road of meditation you discover your grand and glorious Self!

* * *

"All of a sudden it's there and you real-ize it's always been there, that you have been looking away from it by deluding yourself into thinking you are a body and mind."

Lester Levenson

Session 32

THE GAME

LIMITATION

We are all infinite, perfect Beings. I assume that most of us accept this, at least theoretically. We are told this by the scriptures, especially the Hindu scriptures. The Masters tell us this. I come along and say the same thing. But why do we not express this infinite, perfect Being that we are? The reason we do not express it is that through habit of lifetimes, we have played a game of limitation. We have played it so long that we have completely forgotten that we have been playing a game of limitation and that our real basic nature is infinite. We do not, however, look at this infinite Being that we are. We continue, every day, every moment, looking at this little puppet that we set up, called the body, and assume that we are that body. So long as we keep looking at this body as being us, we are stuck right there; we cannot see our infinity, we don't know that it is; and we go on and on, lifetime in and lifetime out, assuming that we are a body.

We have done this for so long, in fact, that it takes a super will to move in the opposite direction, to look at and see the infinite Being that we really are. This super will can take us away from assuming every moment that we are a limited body. If we would do it for just one second and see this infinite Being that we really are, we would use that second to undo much limitation. But first we must assume that we are infinite. Then we must start undoing the limitations. We must actually accept that we are not this body, that we are not this mind, and until we do that we have absolutely no chance of getting out of this trap called "The Game of Being Limited Bodies."

So, as the scriptures say: Thou Art That. Be still and know it. Every thought we have is necessarily a thought of limitation. Let go of thought — get still.

MORE METHODS

The methods are, as we know, to quiet the mind. The way to do this is to hold one thought — the highest one we can find — and then let go of all other thoughts. The moment the mind is quiet enough, this infinite Being that we are becomes self-obvious. So the method is very simple: quiet that mind enough so that you see this infinite Being that you are. The moment you see it, the moment you see this infinite Being that you are, you'll immediately go to work to undo the remaining thoughts that suggest that you are not infinite. And when there are no more thoughts of limitation, there will only be the infinite Being left.

Strangely enough, what you are seeking is the very closest thing to you. Every time you say "I," that's It. When you say "I," you are talking about the infinite Being. When you say "I am a body," you are saying "I, the infinite Being, am a limited body with a limited mind." It is really as simple as that. But simplicity does not mean it is easy to let go of the habits that you have been hanging onto for aeons.

This thing that everyone is seeking, this thing that everyone calls happiness, is nothing but the infinite Self that we are. Everyone, in his every act, is seeking this infinite Self that he is, calling it by other names: money, happiness, success, love, etc. Having been told this — and again, we've been told this many times before — why don't we just be what we are and stop trying to be what we are not — a limited body? Can anyone answer that? Why don't we stop being limited?

QUESTIONS AND ANSWERS

Q: Because we can't.

Lester: You mean an infinite Being can't stop being limited?

Q: Because we don't want to.

Lester: Right. We don't want to!

Q: The infinite Being doesn't want to?

Lester: Yes. I, the infinite Being, think I am a limited body, and I've been doing this so long that I, the infinite Being, do not want to let go of constantly assuming I am this limited body. Does this make sense?

Q: Yes.

Lester: Every time you say "I" without going any further, you're talking about the infinite Being that you are, but you immediately add to it "am this body." If you would only just say "I-I-I" from here on, you'd get full realization, because as you're saying "I-I-I," you're concentrating on "I" and not saying "am a little body with needs."

So there's no one who is not every moment experiencing the infinite Being that he is. As long as he experiences an "I," he is experiencing this infinite Being that he is.

However, you don't want to see that. You want to be the body. So, what is required? First, saying to yourself "I am not this body, I am not this mind; then what am I?" If we reject this body and mind enough, what we are becomes self-obvious.

We can never become an infinite Being because we are that. We can only let go of the concepts that we are not it. We can just let go of the concepts that we are a body, a mind. The first thing needed is the desire to let go of this limited beingness that we think we are. A very strong desire to be the infinite Being that we really are is the only thing that we need to get there quickly.

But, we don't want it. If we really wanted It, we would have It. There is difficulty, of course. And what is the difficulty? It's the habit; it's the unconscious habitual thinking; it's the mind. So we attack it by attacking this very unconsciously thinking mind. The mind is the only cover over the infinite Being that we are. We must stop thinking long enough to see what we are, and that "long enough" can be just one second. If you would stop thinking for one second (thinking includes the unconscious thinking too) — if you would stop thinking for one second, the tremendous liberating shock of seeing what you are would cause you to use this infinite power that is yours, to scorch the mind. The mind can be scorched in large amounts, each and every time we will, just for a moment, drop into that unlimited state of no thinking.

I guess the next question is: How do we create the desire for it? If the desire is strong enough, anyone can see and fully be the infinite Being in a matter of weeks, months, a few years. If any one of you had a strong desire to see this infinite Being that you are and just kept that desire only, in a few months you would see and remain as the infinite Being that you are. You would stop imagining yourself to be a limited body. So the key is desire.

When you desire to be a body-beautiful, a body-healthy, you can become these things, but all these thoughts generally prevent you from seeing the infinite Being that you are. So to go further, you simply exchange all your desires for the one desire to discover your infinite real Self.

Are there any questions on what I've said so far?

Q: While doing, "What am I?", I looked at the stars and I got an idea that I could be the stars.

Lester: You are talking about a method called Self Inquiry, which is really the very top method. The final question we all have to answer is: What am I? And when that answer comes, that's It. So, why not pose that question at the beginning? However, it is important to remember that when you pose the question "What am I?" the answer the mind gives cannot be right because the mind is the cover over your real Self. The mind is the thing that limits you. So the method is to hold the question "What am I?" and only this question. If another thought comes in, quickly drop it by saying to yourself, "To whom is this thought?... Well, to me... Well, what am I?" And you're right back on the track. Keep following this track until you move beyond thought to knowing.

Q: I see. Thank you.

Lester: Now, there are just a rare few on our planet who successfully use this method. Therefore, I suggest we use it this way. Always seek the answer to "What am I?" No matter what you do during the day, whether in meditation, reading, or so forth, in back of your mind always keep that question poised and be ready and waiting for an answer: "What am I?... What am I?" I use "what" rather than "who" because "who" is a personal pronoun and tends to lead us into being the body. "What" is more impersonal. But this question should always be held. No matter what path we follow, no matter what method we use, we should always hold in the back ground "What am I?" And if we do this, eventually we will see the full answer.

Q: Lester, pertaining to this method, how many times does one ask the question?

Lester: Every time a thought, a stray thought, comes into the mind, we say, "To whom is this thought?... Well, it's to me... Then, what am I?" This will have to be repeated after each stray thought.

Q: And if no thoughts come, then it's not to be said?

Lester: Right.

Q: Then you wait for an answer.

Lester: Wait to see; you don't wait for an answer; answers come from the mind.

Q: You wait to see?

Lester: Yes, you wait to see. The Self becomes self-obvious. All of a sudden It's there and you realize It has always been there, that you have been looking away from it by deluding yourself into thinking you're a body, a mind. And then you see yourself as all beingness. You become every person, every animal, every insect, every atom in the universe. You discover that the beingness of the universe is only your beingness. It's here; It's here right now! So stop looking away from It. Quiet the mind. The "I" that I am is there. There's nothing closer to you than this. Stop seeking It out there, through a body. It isn't out there. The "I" in here, this is the infinite Being.

And when you hold only this question, it is not easy and therefore I suggest holding it all the time. Get in the habit of always seeking what you are, no matter what method you're using. And when quietness of mind comes, to the degree that there's no other thought on your mind but "What am I?" this stilling of all the other thoughts makes your Self obvious to you. It's right there where you are, wherever you are — right where the "I" is.

So again, hold this question — no matter what method you use — until the answer shows itself, until it becomes obvious.

Q: It seems very hard.

Lester: It is hard. It is hard to let go of the habit of thinking every moment that you are a limited body. We bombard ourselves with the thought: I am a body; I am a body; I am a body. This goes on all the time so that we don't see the infinite Being that we are. It's a constant bombardment of: I am a body with involvement.

Meditation is an attempt to quiet the mind by holding one thought so that other thoughts die away. By holding that one thought — if we can get to the place where just that one thought is there — that's enough quieting to see the infinite Being that we are. There isn't a method that doesn't try to effect the quieting of the mind so that the infinite Being that we are can become self-obvious.

Q: When you say "self-obvious," what does your real Self feel like?

Lester: When you get toward the end, as Vivekananda said, you see that there never was anything but "I" all along. Now, if there's nothing but "I" all alone, then "I am everything, everyone." You look upon every other body as equally as your body. You see everyone as you; just as you see your body as you, you see everyone as you.

The feeling is indescribable. It's such an intense experience, far beyond anything that limitation today will allow, that you'll never know it without experiencing it. But, from the level where we are, it's the thing we call happiness. It's joy unlimited — infinite joy. At first it comes on as an elation; it's over-whelming; it's hard to contain; it gets to be uncomfortable. You get slap-happy, punch drunk, ecstatic; it gets to be annoying. And then you work at it until it falls away and what's left is a very deep, profound, delectable peace. It's a peace that is so much better than the extreme joy that you had before, that you don't look for that joy any more. The joy state is not the ultimate; the ultimate is the peace state. Everyone of us can get a taste of it at times.

Q: Then it's possible to come across this and then lose it?

Lester: Oh yes. Many people do. The first time we really drop into it, we are not able to maintain it because the habit of thinking takes over again. And the moment we're thinking, we are limited. Every thought must be a think of limitation.

Let go of the game of being limited; let go of the world. Don't try to control it. Don't try to enjoy it. Take all your joy from within. Then, what was formerly the game assumes a sameness picture. Everything becomes the same. If everything is the same, and it is in the Absolute Truth, where can there be a game? If you get caught up in a game, you're caught up in an eternal illusion. The game will never end. And if you're in the game, you're away from your infinite Beingness. There is always a certain limitation in the game that will always keep you from being fully satisfied.

So there is a step above the game of playing we are bodies and that step is where everything becomes exactly the same. And that exact sameness is only you, your beingness. There's an infinite One-ness left and that infinite Oneness is you and is your beingness. It's beingness being all beingness. And there's no separation; there's only beingness, being all beingness.

Now, of course, it take experiencing it to really know what this beingness is. I am convinced that the best description of the top state is Beingness being all Beingness.

Q: How can I increase my desire for It?

Lester: Only you can do it. No one can do it for you. This is the unique thing about it. You have to do it.

The grace we hear of is always existing. It's the inner beingness that we are making us uncomfortable until we reestablish the original state. Desire for happiness is the grace. It's always there. All we need to do is to recognize it and take it.

Q: How does God get made into man? Isn't it somehow sacrilegious to try to change back?

Lester: No. Anyone who tells you that doesn't want you to attain the top state. But it happens this way: It's like going to sleep at night. You dream you're borne into a little infant body; then you are a week old, a year old; then twenty, then forty; and you dream you have problems and problems and problems. Remember, this is only a night dream. This goes on and on, and you get so tired that you dream the body dies. Then you wake up. Where did you ever change yourself while in that dream? You didn't! You say it never was; it was all concocted in the mind.

That's exactly how we do it in this state we call "Waking." In Truth, this waking state is a sleep state. We are totally asleep to the reality of this infinite Beingness that we are. We are no more awake to the Truth right now than when we are asleep at night. We are just dreaming that we are awake. Actually this is a sleep state that we need to awaken from, and when we do, then we say, "Oh, my gosh, it never was! I never was a limited body! I was always that infinite Being that I am!"

So we mentally create a dream called the Waking state of the world. However, it's just a dream-illusion. But to recognize that it's a dream, you must wake up out of this state. Does that make sense? So the answer to "How did we do this?" is that we are dreaming it!

Q: Deliberately?

Lester: Yes. Deliberately. You see, we start off as infinite Beings in a passive way. We go to the bottom — that's where we are right now — then go back to the top and again see our infinity. But after going through that, there's a positive knowingness of our infinity, whereas before it was a passive knowingness.

It's something like this: "Perfect health" is a meaningless term to someone who was born perfectly healthy and stays that way all his life; he doesn't positively know what it is. And yet, it's a nice state when he's in it. But he's passively healthy; he cannot fully appreciate it. However, if he got very sick and was on the verge of dying for many years and then reestablished the perfect-health state, then that perfect-health state would be far more meaningful to him than it was before he got sick.

And this is the silly thing we do to ourselves: We go from infinity down to where we are and back up to infinity with a positiveness of knowing the infinity that we are. But we pushed, on the way down, in a way that we lost sight of what we were doing. And if we look within, we'll discover this.

Q: That's the first time I've heard a sensible explanation of the whole mess. First time it's ever been explained why we've been pulled down.

Lester: OK, now go back up.

Q: Is there one person doing this?

Lester: There is one Beingness doing this. I think the best example of this is the ocean and the drops. We, the ocean of beingness, imagined little tiny circles around parts of us that we called drops; and this drop says, "I am separate from that drop and separate from all the other drops." It's an imagined circle around part of the ocean calling itself a drop. But actually every drop is the ocean. It has all the qualities of the ocean: it's wet, it's salty, it's H_2O, and so forth. I think that example might make sense. Or, it's like a comb and each tooth says to the other, "I am separate from you." It's all one comb, and we are the teeth saying that we are separate, when in actuality it's just one comb. Remember, you are the one infinite ocean of Beingness. It is the "I" that you are. Seek It, see It, and forever hold It!

* * *

"The reason why so few of us make it is that most of us have a stronger subconscious desire to be a physical body than we have a conscious desire to be a free unlimited being."

Lester Levenson

REALIZATION THROUGH DROPPING
THE UNCONSCIOUS

YOUR BASIC NATURE

Our subject is called many things by many schools. I like to call it happiness and that which gives you the ultimate in happiness is the discovery of the Truth. When you come to completely know you, you reach this ultimate joy and with it the peace of satiation. You discover that you are All and that your former worldly search was you trying to find your real self; and that you never could discover the real you then the consequence of which was that you were never satisfied.

I have said it repeatedly — you are this thing called happiness. Your basic nature is infinite joy, far beyond anything your mind could comprehend. That is why we are all seeking happiness. We are all trying to return to that wonderful inherent state. However, we do not find it because we are looking away from, rather than toward it. To find it we must look within. There we find that we are infinite Beings. We have no limitation. We have all knowledge. We have all power. And we are omnipresent, here and now. There is no one who does not possess these three things.

The difficulty in discovering our purpose and goal in life lies in the fact that because we are infinite, we can make ourselves infinitely small. And this is exactly what we have tried to do. We could not be much more limited than we are right now. In this universe, which is infinite in size, we are at the most extreme end of limitation. We have imagined ourselves, and frozen ourselves, into physical bodies, and because of so many millennia of looking at ourselves as bodies, we have become convinced that we are these physical bodies.

Beings are capable of seeing all realms that are denser than their's. In the subtlest realm, the causal world, beings can perceive the denser astral and physical realms. In the astral world, beings can perceive the denser physical world. And because we in the physical realm cannot see a denser realm, we are in the densest, most limited realm possible.

THE PHYSICAL BODY

The physical body being at the extreme end of limitation possible to us, we feel cramped. We hurt. We reach out. We try to express our freedom in the physical world. We try to eliminate time and space, to go faster and further.

I am pointing out how far we have gone in accepting limitation since we came into a physical body, and that this is the reason why it is so difficult for most of us to discover the Truth of ourselves, which is: we have no limits.

However, there is an advantage to being in this very limited state. Because we are so cramped we have more of a desire to get out of it than we would if we were living in a harmonious heaven where everything was easy and immediately available; where life does not prod us into trying to get liberation. We have a very distinct advantage in being here. We are forced to seek a way out. We are trying in many ways and with many methods to get free.

No matter what the methods are, they all must end up doing the very same thing: freeing us from our concepts of limitation. The methodology must quiet our mind, must do away with thoughts. Every thought is a concept of limitation. When thoughts are undone, what's left over is the infinite Being that we are. Unfortunately, we set into motion an automatic way of thinking called the subconscious mind. There, we relegate thoughts to the background and let them operate without needing to pay any attention to them, and we have lost sight of them.

In the beginning it was an advantage in operating a physical body, because originally we had to operate every part of the body consciously, — every cell, every organ — and to eliminate all that attention, we put it on automatic control via the subconscious mind. And the subconscious mind is the real difficulty when we try to let go of thoughts. It is difficult because we are in the habit of not looking at them. Looking at them we don't see them. Since we don't see them they go on and on, lifetime in and lifetime out. In fact, one could say that we are so married to our thoughts that we never even think of divorcing them. And until we do, we will continue — blindly attached to physical bodies — and as a result, having a miserable life. For every ounce of pleasure we take, we get pounds of pain; and it must be that way because the pleasure we are trying to get is by seeking our very own Self externally in the world and through the body, and it just isn't there.

314

BEYOND THE BODY

The methods, to be effective, must be in a direction of first quieting our thoughts; then actually getting rid of our thoughts. Make a conscious effort to bring up subconscious thoughts and when they are brought to the conscious plane, drop them. When they do come up, because they are very limiting and very negative as a whole, you want to drop them and you do. After you have dropped an appreciable number of them, then you can drop thoughts in large amounts.

To drop thoughts in large amounts requires dropping the tendency or predisposition that has evolved from the accumulated thoughts on that one particular thing. Dropping the tendency or predisposition, one drops all the thoughts that caused that tendency or predisposition. In this way you may, at one time, drop a large accumulation of thoughts.

For instance, if one has a tendency to like sweets, one could bring up from the subconscious one thought about one kind of sweet one at a time and continue letting each go until there are no more. As you can tell this takes as much time! However, if one drops the tendency itself, if one eliminates one's attachment to all sweets, then all the subconscious thoughts that made up that tendency are dropped, and one is totally free from desiring sweets.

Later, you reach a point where you can drop all the remaining thoughts at once, because having infinite power, you will have reached the point where you can see that you have this infinite power and you then can use it to wipe out the rest of the mind. That is why it is sometimes said that Realization is instantaneous. When you get that far that you can see that the power is yours, you wipe out all the remaining thoughts at once. Then you are totally free; you've gone all the way.

When this happens, you do not become a zombie and you do not disappear or go up in a flash of light. What you do is let the body go through that which you preset for it; and when you reach the end of the line of the action for the body, you will leave it with joy. You will leave it just the way you leave and let go of an old, worn-out overcoat.

You will never die. People around you might say so, but to yourself, you do not die. You consciously drop the body the way you would drop an old, worn-out overcoat. But, again, you will not do this until you run the course that you preset for it. Now, I tell you this so you will not be fearful of dying if you get Realization.

So, attaining the ultimate state is not disappearing into a nothing-ness. It is moving out into your omnipresence and letting go of con-finement to only a physical body.

THE VALUE OF DESIRE

Now, to do this you must have a strong desire to do it. The only thing that keeps you from being the infinite Being that you are is your desire to be a limited physical body. When you desire shifts into wanting to get free of the extreme limitation, it's a start; but to go all the way you must have a desire to be totally free, that is more intense than your desire to be a physical body.

The reason why so few of us do make it, is that most of us have a stronger subconscious desire to be a physical body than we have a conscious desire to be a free unlimited Being. Until you confront this and see what your desire really is, it is impossible to achieve total Freedom, total Realization. You should dig into the subconscious to bring up your desires, because unless you see them, you cannot let go of them. The only reason why you are limited to the physical body is that subconsciously, you have a strong desire to be this limited physi-cal body. When your conscious desire to be free becomes stronger than your subconscious desire to be a physical body, then you will quickly achieve your Freedom. And therein lies your ultimate happi-ness.

I think that is an overall presentation of the subject. Now, if you have any questions I'd be very happy to do what I can to answer them.

QUESTIONS AND ANSWERS

Q: How do you dig into your subconscious?

Lester: Good question. You do it by first, wanting to do it. It's very difficult when you begin, but as you do it, the more you do it the easier it becomes. You can actually reach a place where it becomes easy. Practice will do it. By practicing bringing up subconscious thoughts, the more you do it, the more you're able to do it.

There are many aids to doing it. In the book The Eternal Verities, there are ways and aids like: "Get to the place where no one and no thing can disturb you." When someone disturbs you and you don't know why, the thought is subconscious. Bring up the thought. By constant trying you will develop the habit of actually getting it up; you'll see that there's a limiting thought, an ego or selfish motivation behind it and you'll drop it.

Q: Is just seeing the subconscious thought or motivation enough?

Lester: Just looking at it is not enough. You must consciously drop the thought or consciously will out the tendency or motivation. I'm assuming you'll want to let go of these thoughts because they're all limiting and negative.

One reason why we don't like to dig them up is that we don't like to see how awful we are. But there's nothing good or bad; there's just moving in the right direction or the wrong direction. When we move in the wrong direction, we move toward more limitation and that's really so-called bad. But everything is experiencing. And when we don't judge ourselves, we move much faster.

Q: When we don't judge ourselves?

Lester: Right, when we don't judge ourselves. Whatever comes up — so what? To get this far in your limitations, you have run the gamut of everything bad. It'll come up, but it's from past experiencing. Also, when you wake up you'll discover that you never ever were apart from your real Self, which is whole, perfect, complete, unlimited; that all these experiences were images in your mind just like in a night dream you imagine everything that's going on. But while you're in a night dream, it's real to you. If someone is trying to kill you in a night dream, it's real; you're struggling for your life. But when you wake up from that dream, what do you say? "It was just a dream; it was my imagination." This waking state is exactly as real as a night dream. We're all dreaming we are physical bodies; we're dreaming the whole thing. However, in order to reach this awakened state, it is first necessary to drop a major part of your subconscious thinking.

Q: How do you see it when you come back after realizing it is a dream?

Lester: You see it like you now see a dream you had last night. You see it as a dream, and that's how important it remains to you. The before and after picture is simply point of view: before you thought you were limited to a body and all these bodies and action were so real; after, you see it as a dream, like a moving picture. When you see characters on the screen you can lose your awareness of yourself by identifying with one of the characters on the screen and you'll emote with him and feel unhappy.

Q: But don't have all the desires that you had before?

Lester: You have no desires because you wake up to the fact that you are infinite, you are the All — there's nothing to desire. Desire limits you: "I don't have the All, therefore I must get it and I create desires to get it." So desire is only a limitation. When you see the full picture you naturally lose all desire; there's nothing to desire if you are the All.

Now, practically speaking if you choose to go along with the dream you can act out a desire for the time being, and then act as though it's being satisfied. However, it's just an act and you play act.

Q: How does the mind distinguish between bad and good?

Lester: By saying, "This is good and that is bad."

Q: Is that an individual thing?

Lester: Of course. What's right in one country is wrong in another; what's right to you is wrong to someone else. It's a very individualistic approach. Of course, there's some general agreement on right and wrong; we generally agree we shouldn't kill each other. So right and wrong is a very individualistic standard. If you need a right and wrong, doing that which helps your growth is right; doing that which hinders your growth is wrong. That should be the right and wrong.

Q: Do we learn the right from experiencing?

Lester: Yes, you learn the right by doing the wrong. And also by experiencing the right. Unfortunately, most of us do it by actually doing the wrong thing. We learn to keep our hand out of a fire by burning it. This is what seems to prod us more than anything else — the hardships of life. We all want to get away from the misery of it, don't we? It should be the other way, that the wonderfulness of the right way should be the attractiveness of it. When you do get that far, then your growth is very fast and you're approaching the end of the line.

Q: What did you mean by "After you're Realized, you live your life as you preset it?" What does that mean?

Lester: We preset the behavior of this physical body before we enter it to put us through experiences that we hope to learn from.

Q: Knowing that you would attain Realization this time?

Lester: No. Knowing that in past lives you subjected yourself to the law of action and reaction, cause and effect, karma (they're all the same thing), and that you want to continue that game. You did certain things when you were in a physical body before, so next time you want to set up similar things in a hope of undoing some of the things you don't like, instigating the things you do like. But you cannot change anything that the body was preset to do by you. You're going to do exactly what you preset for that body before you came into it. There is no free will in worldly living. However, there is a free will. The free will we have is to identify with the real Being that we are, or to identify with the body. If you identify with the body, you're in trouble. So the free will is one of identity. Knowing this, it makes life much easier; you don't fight it. You aim for proper identity.

Q: The desire for bliss, would that be enough to start your search for happiness?

Lester: Sure.

Q: If one is sincere and isn't succeeding, will a Guru help them?

Lester: A realized Teacher is the greatest of all help; but He can't help you any more than you will help yourself. This is most important: He cannot help you any more than you will help yourself. When you try to help yourself, He joins you and helps you to a realization that you're ready for.

Q: He helps?

Lester: He or she helps you get a realization that you're ready for. If you're tapped on the chest and you get cosmic consciousness, it's because you're ready for it. Of all help, a Guru's is the greatest because He has gone the direction and He can help you go the same direction.

Q: How is it that when you see the dream structure of maya and you see the real Self, then all of a sudden you're caught in the dream again and you believe it? What happened?

Lester: It is possible to see your real Self and fall back into the world. Why? Because you have not let go of the subconscious thoughts "I am this physical body; this world is real." You must go into your subconscious and make conscious all these thoughts and keep them. Or, see your Self to the degree that you see that your mind is external to you, something that you created, and then you just wipe it out. If you can't wipe it out, and very few of us can, keep picking away at it; keep bringing up the subconscious thoughts and dropping them. Or, you can make it ineffective in large chunks by willing out tendencies. Take a particular tendency like smoking. If you've been smoking for years and years, you have thousands of little desires to smoke. The tendency is strong. However, you can say to yourself with will power, "This is ridiculous! I am through with this!" and never again have a desire for a cigarette. That's getting rid of all the thoughts of desire to smoke by willing out the tendency. That's one chunk: smoking.

Q: That's one chunk; the whole thing clear back?

Lester: Complete. I've seen many people do this on smoking with no problem. They just made that decision and that was it!

Q: And that's how you get rid of each thing that's bothering you?

Lester: Yes. If you're jealous, look at it. If you're disgusted enough with being jealous you say, "Finished! Done! It is gone!" and you can undo the whole thing. That's letting go of a huge piece of mind. That's letting go of many, many thoughts of jealousy that you've had in the subconscious mind. It takes some maturity to undo that tendency.

Q: And it won't come back if you really do?

Lester: Right. If you, with resolve and determination, really drop it, it's gone.

You can try it on smaller things first, and when you succeed then go to something larger. Do it on one thing. Then you can do it on two, then on all. Do that which you can do. Keep doing this every day and it won't take you long. Make this a way of life. Grow every day.

Every incident is an opportunity for growth. Everything you're experiencing is an experience of limitation. Every annoyance you have is an excellent opportunity to transcend that. Develop the habit of digging into your subconscious for the causative thought of the annoyance and then dropping it. Daily striving assures quick arriving.

* * *

"Those who did go all the way, they did not abandon their bodies, homes and families. They only abandoned their former feelings of bondage and attachment to their bodies, homes and families, and in place of it felt free."

Lester Levenson

Session 34

WHY NOT GO ALL THE WAY?

You have been given the direction and some tips on how to go all the way. The question is, is it enticing enough? Is it promising enough? Can you go all the way? Let's get right to it!

QUESTIONS AND ANSWERS

Q: Well, I'd like to go all the way, but it's always over the next hill. I get to this point and it's not there; and I get to the next one and it's not there.

Lester: Not really, because it's right where you are. Over the next hill is where it isn't. Right where you are, where the "I" of you is, is where it is.

Q: How come we don't know it?

Lester: Yes, how come? That's what I want to know.

Q: That was my question.

Lester: Yes, but what is the answer? I say it's silly not to, because once you do, you'll never, ever have a moment of unpleasantness, ever again. It becomes impossible to be unhappy. What's wrong with that? Why don't we do it?

I would say you don't believe it enough. You don't believe that you have no limits; you don't believe that life can be, every second, ecstatically happy; you don't believe that it can be totally effortless; you don't believe that you can do things mentally.

Or, is it that we keep procrastinating? I say that if we really do want to go all the way, we do it. So, again, why don't we go all the way?

Q: Well, I think, in my case, I've probably hypnotized myself into believing the opposite. I've associated with the finite me all my life, in all my conscious awareness, to the degree that it is real to me.

Lester: Oh, then to you the Infinite would do away with finite?

323

Q: Yes. Because the finite is what I believe in; it's real to me. What you say about the Infinite has infinite possibilities but until I can totally accept that, it's like when you touch a light bulb and it burns you and somebody says, "Now touch it and it won't burn you"; it's difficult to overcome your subconscious reaction not to touch it.

Lester: Well, let me tell you then, that the Infinite includes the finite, and is the basis for it. You see, you can hold onto all the finite you want when you're infinite; you don't have to lose a thing.

Q: Then, I'd be glad to give it up for the Infinite.

Lester: Give it up? Maybe this is what's bothering us; that we're afraid that we're going to give up our bodies; that we're going to give up our families and homes. It doesn't happen that way. When those who did go all the way achieved it, they did not abandon their bodies, homes and families. They only abandoned their former feelings of bondage and attachment to their bodies, homes and families, and in place of it felt free.

Q: If there's happiness greater than what I've experienced in a body, to heck with this!

Lester: Well, again, you do not give up your body. Your happiness gets more intense the more you move toward total freedom, until it reaches a point where you just can't contain it any more. Then you resolve it into a very beautiful peace that is never, ever again disturbed. And that peace is really far more delicious than the intense joy was. And then, when you choose to be active in the world, you'll never, ever lose that background peace; you will feel it all the time. And you are free to do anything in the world; you can act angry, scared; be poor or rich; you can do anything you want; but you do not disappear.

Q: It doesn't affect you?

Lester: The world can never, never touch you again, because you have imperturbable peace.

Q: I understand.

Lester: So then, why don't you come along?

Q: Whenever I identify my source of income with the effort I exert in my business, I say to myself, "You're a stupid idiot. This isn't the source of my infinite supply." However, I'm not strong enough to just say, "Well, this isn't it; I'll do it the other way," because I think, "What if it doesn't work?"

Lester: You would have exactly what you had before you tried it. However, you expect it not to work if you say that.

Q: Yes, but that's where the hang-up is. Maybe it's a lack of faith, not that it hasn't worked for you, but whether it'll work for me, I am not convinced. If you could only help me, just one little infinite bit of strength that you could give me...

Lester: Oh, now wait a minute; you have the support and I've given you many directions, any one of which would take you all the way. I could give them to you again.

Q: That's like the sign "San Francisco." I'll bet there are probably a hundred signs that point the way to San Francisco; but if I get to the sign and sit down underneath it, it would take more than just knowing where San Francisco is, and that's where I bog down.

Lester: Right, you don't take the direction; you look at it and sit down. Now, the direction: "Get to the place where no one and no thing can disturb you" would have taken you all the way.

Q: Yes, but that's like going to the moon.

Lester: It is easy — if you would do it. It is your decision to be disturbed or not to be disturbed.

Q: That's quite a challenge!

Lester: Do you want more? I'll give you new ones.

Q: Yes.

Lester: Be totally selfless. Be interested only in others; have no interest in yourself. That would take you all the way. If we would be totally selfless in our behavior, act not for ourselves but for the other ones — this would do it rapidly.

Q: I don't mean to be argumentative, but this is really nitty-gritty.

Lester: I'll give you another one: Get to the place where you have no more desire; keep letting go of desires until there are no more and that's it! You don't like that one either, do you?

Q: Well, part of it. I've got a lot of things I'd like to let go of.

Lester: If anyone would carry that through until there are no more desires — and it's just letting go of them as they come up — you'd go all the way.

Q: Lester, what about the one that you and I discussed, about the mind? You see everything out there in your mind, right? So that's where everything is. So, that thing out there is just your mind. When you discover this, you change your mind and it changes out there.

Lester: Yes, that would take you there.

Q: What about no attachments and no aversions?

Lester: That will do it too. That will take you all the way. But why haven't we used these things? They are not new to us.

.

Q: That's what I'm earnestly trying to decide for myself. This is ridiculous; all this intellectual knowledge that I've acquired and what little I've actually done with it. It's alarming. I've asked, "How many people have their own private Master in their family." You've given us all this stuff and I say "It's my responsibility what I do with it; why haven't I used it?"

Lester: Yes, and your private Master is you! This is important: Your private Master is you!

Q: Isn't there only One any way?

Lester: When you see what you really are, you'll see the Oneness and no more otherness.

Q: I try to squint, and no matter how I do it, I still see separation.

Lester: That's the way you are approaching it, with squinty eyes; you won't look at it full view, wide open, because you are afraid you're going to disappear. So what you have to do is dig down within, pull it out and see it. Once you see it, you'll naturally let go of that fear. You're also afraid you're going to lose your individuality. Your individuality is something you'll never, ever lose. It's with you through eternity. The "I" that I am, is never, ever lost. What happens is that we just expand it to include more and more until it includes the entire infinity.

I say you're more afraid of losing yourself, your body, your mind, your family, your business, and all your little things; you're subconsciously afraid you're going to lose them. If it were conscious, you'd look at it, drop it, and be free.

Q: Well, you reached me when you added those other things. The physical body attachment I don't see, but when you included my family and my business and these other things...

Lester: Do you want me to show you how attached you are to that physical body? Just imagine, don't do it, but just image throwing your body over a cliff. Can you now see your attachment to the body?

Q: Yes. But do you have to have that desire to get rid of it?

Lester: You don't get rid of it; you see what you are and then you'll see that you are not the body, that the body is one infinitesimal part of you.

Q: Why can't I go all the way?

Lester: Because you're afraid that if you do, you're going to disappear. Does anyone feel that? That you'll disappear if you go all the way?

Q: I'm afraid I'd lose my mind.

Lester: You actually do lose your mind, and then you reestablish it so that you can communicate. It's far more difficult to reestablish the mind than it was originally to let go of it because the mind itself was such a clamping down of you, you don't want to come back to it. But you will; you'll start thinking again. The only difference in the before and after picture is that now your thinking is unfree, determined by subconscious, compulsive thoughts; in the after picture there are no more subconscious, compulsive thoughts. Every thought is totally free and without any conditioning by your tendencies and predispositions.

That leads me to another great one: Rid yourself of all your tendencies and predispositions, and you will go all the way.

I have never talked much about miracles, have I? I don't feel as though I'm imposing on you now, as I used to feel, were I to talk about miracles because having moved up, you are more able to accept them. When I first moved to Sedona and lived by myself, most things were done by thought and I was unaware of it. However, others began to come in, and it was because of them that I became aware of these unusual things. To me they were natural, but not to the others.

I might have told one or two of you about the teleportation incident. This one is interesting because it involved two others, one who is following this path, and another one who is not. The one who is not I'll call Harry. Harry came to Sedona from Phoenix and asked me if I would take a walk and naturally, he chose a direction uphill. The three of us walked a mile and a half uphill, and when we got to the end of our trip, we sat down to have our sandwiches. We had only a pint size canteen of water for the three of us and we drank most of it on the way up. We had left only about an eighth of an inch of water in the bottom of this pint canteen, hardly enough for half a cup. But the three of use were thirsty, and so I let go with the feeling, "Everything is perfect!" I received the inner knowledge that the water was abundantly there. Then I asked, "Do you want a drink, Frances?" "Sure." I gave Frances a cupful. Then Harry drank a cup, then I. We kept drinking until each one was satiated. We each had seven drinks! I curiously looked into the canteen and the same amount of water was there as originally — just about an eighth of an inch on the bottom of the canteen.

We then started the downward trek for home. I was so tired that I felt as though the body would not walk any more. I just let go and I said, "Oh, Lord, there must be a better way!" And the thought again came to me, "Everything is perfect." As I thought "perfect," we, the three of us, had one step up there and the next step was down near my home, where the surroundings were similar to the place we had left so as not the make it obvious to Harry. Frances caught it and said, "Lester, we teleported!" I said, "Oh, you're crazy, Frances, you're imagining it," because Harry's mind was in turbulence; his face showed a frown and a consternation. For his sake I had to again say, "It's your imagination, Frances." Frances knew. Later, when we were alone without Harry, I said, "What made you think we teleported?" And she laughed. She said, "Don't you remember, on the way up Harry and I were collecting rocks and in several places we put them on the left side of the road on the way up (the road was cut into the side of the hill). I wanted to pick up those rocks on the way back, but we by-passed all of those places."

Now, to do these things, it takes a mere effortless thought; you surrender, let go, and have a thought with no effort, no drive. It's the easiest thought you could have. And then it happens.

During the early days in Sedona I was living this way, unaware of it. To me it was natural. Whatever I thought, I expected. It seemed natural, just the way everyone thinks he lives naturally. It is really the natural way and it is meant for us to live that way. Although, if we did, we wouldn't fit very well into our present society, would we? So, if you want to stay in communication, you go the way of people.

Miracles are just this dream world effected immediately. And miracles don't necessarily mean spiritual development because the majority of people in the universe use these things; they use them on other planets where they're not necessarily more spiritually advanced than we. It is their natural way of life.

But the easier way to live is purely mental; mentally do everything. You should be able to do all this. Why not go all the way and have nature serve you? Why do you do things the harder way? I think it's because you're afraid you're going to disappear. I'm saying to you, "Look, I have been through these things. And I still have a body here. I didn't disappear."

Q: Can you demonstrate your infinity for me, too?

Lester: You must demonstrate your own. You have had ample witnessing of these unusual things. If I do it for you that would mean you can't do it. I just finished saying that you can do it! It's surrendering, then mere effortless thinking! You have the feeling that it is not I but the Father who worketh through me.

I can go on and on. I'm trying to entice you. When I moved into the mobile home on my grounds, a girl, now living here in Laguna Beach, asked me, "How often do you fill that butane bottle?" (It was a five-gallon bottle.) I said, "Every month." Then I remembered it had been eight months since I had last filled it. Becoming aware of it, I let go of it.

When I was trying to show Frances how to conserve water, I let her take charge of and keep filled my 55 gallon water drum alongside my mobile home. It took care of all my needs, including a shower every morning. The reason why I wanted her to take care of it was that I wanted to show her that you can live on very little water. But I lost track of time and when I brought it to her attention, she laughed. It had been four months since she had filled it last. I kept using the water and the tank wouldn't empty out! When we opened it and looked, it was still full after using it for four months! It never would have emptied out if I had not let go of it.

Q: "Had not let go of it," what do you mean?

Lester: Let go of it by letting it be "normal."

Q: You thought again of it as being a limited thing?

Lester: No, I let it be as usual, or as is normal to people. I want to remain in communication with people and I choose to live like people live, because if I live in an unusual way, I'm out of communication. It even scares people.

Q: This wouldn't scare anybody.

Lester: I know by experience that it scares people. When it first came to me while I was living in New York City, some people wouldn't come near me because of these things happening.

What's wrong with this way of life? Why won't you take it? It is yours for the taking. I hope to allure you by making it so tempting that you will go all the way. Look at the difficulties you go through to make a living.

Ask yourself, "Why don't I go all the way?" "Why don't I take things directly, just for the thought of them?" "Why don't I express my total freedom?" And maybe the answer will come up and you'll see what you're doing to hold yourself down.

Q: One reason is that we are so used to being hamstrung that we don't realize that we can get out of it. I was just thinking of the motel, of getting it sold, and then I thought, "Do I really want to leave it?" and I know I upset it every time.

Lester: That's true and that is why I'm telling you of the easy way. Your habit of thought runs you the hard way. One way to undo all habits of thought, which are in the subconscious mind, is to see that you are not the mind, and you will scorch it.

Q: Tell us a little more about scorching this mind, which I have found out is most important.

Lester: I see you've gotten a realization just recently.

Q: That's right.

Lester: And yet, you didn't carry through on it. With that realization, you should have continued and said, "I can do it; I am infinite!" With that infinite power, you just pass your figurative hand over the mind and it's finished. It's just a mental wipe-out that you do. And that's it. You know how long it takes? Less than that! (finger snap) Less than a second.

When you get your full Realization, it's instantaneous. Before that, you play around, dropping a little bit at a time. This goes on and on, year in and year out, until you decide to let go of the whole thing; then you've got Full Realization. It really comes instantaneously — when it comes. You will it. Will is your power. You turn on your will so strongly that you just undo the whole mind, and you are totally Free.

Q: It just doesn't make any sense at all. It's just as though you're handing me all the money in the world and saying, "Here!" and I'm sitting and saying, "Why don't I take it?"

Lester: Yes, why don't you?

Q: What's wrong with me?

Lester: What is? That's the big question. What is wrong? I know you think that this is possible, otherwise you would not have listened all this time.

Q: It's the intellect that's in the way.

Lester: That is it. Why not wipe it out? The intellect is the mind. We have to see we're not the mind and that it is external to us, and then just make it ineffective. Just like that; that's the way you'll do it.

Q: You said something the other night, Lester, which was a help

331

to me and that was "I am going to put Lester to bed."

Lester: I always think that way. I'll send Lester and this body around and make it appear to be doing things.

After I got the realization that I am not the body, it was years before I could use the word "I." People would laugh at me because I would talk about Lester; I would talk about "him" and sometimes I would say, "it, Lester," or "Lester, he." I couldn't say "I" even though I was being corrected. Why? I was not this body. I could talk about this body, but it was so obvious and glaring that I was not this body that I couldn't say I was this thing, any more than you could say you were your car. Because you are carrying yourself around in a car, would you call yourself the car? In the same way you'll look at this body. (This body is a car-case, a carcass.)

I say you're silly to not take the All.

Q: I think there's a stronger word than silly.

Lester: Yes, it's really stupid. He led me to say it. It's so stupid not to go through life with everything you want; with nothing but extreme joy, peace and loveliness every moment; when that is your inherent state. It takes no effort to be what you are. It does take extreme effort to be what you are not: a body with trouble, sicknesses and needing this and needing that. It takes effort to be what you're not, but to be what you are takes as much effort as you women would need to be a female, and as much effort as you men would need to be a male. It takes no effort to be what you are. And yet you persist in using effort to be what you are not. It's really stupid!

Q: Well, I persist in using effort to try to be what you say I am. I keep working at this thing of being effortless. Does that make sense?

Lester: No, does it?

Q: Not to me.

Lester: Right. There's something wrong there.

Q: What did I say?

Lester: You're using effort in trying to make yourself effortless — that's impossible! It's a contradiction. You've got to stop using effort. You've got to let go and let be. That's what is meant by "Let go and let

God." You are it, you're the god; let go and let your Self be. However, it seems to take much effort because you are using tremendous effort to hold onto and maintain your non-self, your ego, and there is where your effort is. It takes no effort to be what you are — the Self.

Q: If I could arrive at the dreamer instead of the dream, then I'd have it made. And that's why I've been thinking, "This is a dream? Whose dream is this?"

Lester: Right! Discover the dreamer. To make it more intimate: I, the Infinite Being, am dreaming that I am a limited body.

While you are in a night dream and you think you are a limited body in that night dream, it persists so long as you don't wake up. It's the same thing with this waking state. We're dreaming we're limited bodies. We have to wake up to the fact that we are infinite. We have to stop thinking that we're limited bodies, that's all. Stop thinking. Let go. Let be. Surrender is the word. If we would surrender this moment, that would be it. Not I, but Thou. Not my will, but Thy will. This is surrender. We could do that right now and that would be it. But no, we've got to be a busy ego-body, doing something. We must be a doer.

Q: Several of the people were discussing robots. Actually, I guess we could consider the body a robot. We're using this physical body, and when we're through with it, we drop the physical body, but what we have is still there.

Lester: That's an excellent way to look upon the body.

All right, now I'll tell you something more. If you were really convinced of what I've said so far, you'd go home, you'd forget everything else, and you'd sit down until you saw this; because this would give you everything — just for the thought. If you were really convinced, you'd go home determined to sit until you saw this; and if you did that — you'd see it! Just like Buddha did, when he left his throne and sat under a tree, determined not to leave until he saw the answer; and he saw the answer.

Q: Well, I think one thing that may be bogging some of us down, and I know to a certain extent it has to me, is that I have felt for a long time that I had to take something piecemeal and get each thing out of my system. Now, I'm finally beginning to realize that if I get above it, then none of it makes any difference.

Lester: Yes. We all start that way by undoing single things at first. It begins to show us our mastership. Then we master our tendencies or predispositions. This undoes all the numerous multitudes of thoughts that made up that tendency or predisposition. You should not keep undoing these single things piecemeal. That was all right for the beginning; you don't need it anymore. Drop a tendency or predisposition and you drop the millions of subconscious thoughts underlying it.

Q: When you first started to tell us that there's nobody out there but you, some of us just couldn't understand that, me included. I have discovered why there's nobody out there but me: because it is I who creates that out there, and it is in me.

Lester: Yes, that's true!

Q: So I really know, I had a realization that was as clear as crystal.

Lester: OK, why not clean up that "out there" until you do not waiver from seeing it all as in you?

Q: That's what I'm doing now.

Lester: You don't take enough time at it.

Q: That's true.

Lester: It should be all the time, regardless of what you're doing. While you're driving, talking to people, you can remain with it, and you would if you wanted it that much. If you really get with it, the joy of doing it is so great that you won't let go until you go all the way. It becomes the only thing you want. You begin to see the light and then nothing in this world can interest you more than it. You just stay with it, and you ride it all the way. Misery starts you in the direction, gets you to reverse your wrong direction. Then the desire for the wonderfulness of it takes you all the way to the top.

Q: Then you know you can play any game you want, because that mind is under your control.

Lester: Yes. However, the game played after reaching the top is usually the same game for everyone, although it will express differ ently; it's the game of helping others, which is really a great game.

Q: It becomes an interesting game.

Lester: It's the nicest game there is; it's the most rewarding game there is.

Q: What you are teaching me is really helping me.

Lester: That which I'm offering you is more than a million dollars. What I'm offering is the whole universe. If you wanted gold, you could pile it up by the tons. Of course, when you can create unlimited tons of gold, do you want to pile it up? No, you take only that which you can use.

Q: Of all the different ways that you've offered, it seems like there ought to be one that I could be successful with.

Lester: Take any one of many of those sayings in The Eternal Verities and if you carry it out until the end, that would be it. Take the good one mentioned before: get to the place where no one and no thing can disturb you. Every time you are disturbed, look for the ego motivation wherein you wanted it to be other than it was. On recognizing it say, "Oh, I see," and let go of your ego motivation of wanting it to be the way you want it to be. Every reaction or tendency is based on a selfish thing. We wanted it to be the way we wanted it to be. Keep dropping these reactive tendencies. Every time a reaction comes, look at it; see the selfish ego motivation and drop it. You'll soon reach a place where there is no more and you're there — all the way.

Q: Every time you feel offended, jealous, angry, hurt or anything like that, that's your ego and that's your mind?

Lester: Right. Rid yourself of all your feelings and you will go all the way. So, have we gained anything new?

Q: You have presented us with more of a challenge to understand what you're saying; you make it sound so darn easy and it affronts me to think that anything that easy could elude me.

Lester: When you do it, it is easy. When you don't do it, it's impossible. That's the way it really is. When you do it, it's easy. When you don't do it, it's impossible.

335

Q: Oh, Lord, wait a minute. When you do it, it's easy. When you don't do it, it's impossible.

Lester: It takes no effort to be what you really are: Infinite. It takes tremendous effort to be extremely limited as you now choose to be.

I feel as though I've given what I could on going all the way. If there's any further question, I'll be happy to do what I can to answer it. If not, this is it.

Q: I keep looking at you and I see that there's hope. If you've made it, somebody has. It isn't impossible, and I can do it.

Lester: Yes, do it. Go all the way. Everyone was moving rapidly upward and then leveled off; some came down just a little bit and leveled of there.

If you don't use what you've seen, you'll lose it. You have got to keep using it, otherwise the remaining subconscious habits will overwhelm you and you will lose your direction.

Q: When we go all the way, we still go on doing the same things; we still go on laughing; we still go to the ballet; do all these things There's nothing denied.

Lester: Yes. The only difference is that you're free to do or not to do whatever you want; you're no more compelled in any direction whatsoever.

I strongly recommend taking time out for thinking on these things every day, twice a day. In the morning before going to work, and a night before going to bed. Never should a day go by without doing this. Get with it, totally, in a quiet spot until it sucks you in more and more until you let go of the world pull. Getting quiet enough, the infinite parts of you just take over and you go all the way. You reach a place where you feel helpless because it's effortless. Keep that up and you'll effortlessly be sucked right into your Infinity.

Q: Well, I know sometimes it seems that I'm getting so tall.

Lester: There's a sense of surrender in that.

Q: There's that famous statement of yours: Let go and let God. finally struck me that it means let go of your mind and let God.

Lester: Yes, another way to say that is, "Surrender." Even if you surrender to a mountain, you will get it, because surrender is "Not my will."

Q: Ego, mind and will are all the same thing. So if you let go, that means let go of your mind, ego and all the other things.
Lester: Yes.

Q: Sometimes when something happens I can be very irritated but then I catch myself giggling to myself while I'm doing it. It really isn't affecting me.
Lester: Yes, get free and then you may act irritated.

Q: So you can act any part? And you're aware of the fact that you're an actor?
Lester: Right. Go all the way and there is only fun.

Q: You can even keep your humor too?
Lester: Right. But the motivation for the humor is to make others happy, not for ego approval. That's the difference.

When I say you leveled off and are on a plateau, it's not exactly correct. You leveled off into a slow, gradual, upward direction. It could be much faster, even immediate, rather than a slow, gradual, upward trend. Go all the way — life from that point on is just a ball. You don't have to work. If you want to you can. You can always be successful; or you can even choose to be unsuccessful, just to make a game out of it. If you can succeed in failing, you can also succeed in succeeding.

Q: Would helping others really be a fast way?
Lester: No so if your purpose is ego motivated. However, when you live only for others, it's a very fast way. Paradoxically, the most selfish thing you can do is to be totally selfless. When we are totally selfless, we have the All, the Infinity. It's a seeming paradox.

337

Q: That's it. You offer me the All!

Lester: Yes. We've all had glimpses of it. The thing to do is to establish that permanently, for all time.

So, again I say, take time out every day and effect it. Go all the way. You've got infinite power behind you; there's nothing to stop you but you. Make it part of your every day life and stay with it until it's established for all time. You can do it!

* * *

*"There is something far more beautiful
than nature — it is the Source of nature —
the ultimate beauty — God."*

Lester Levenson

Session 35

THE SELF, YOUR SELF

The Self, which is only your Self, is the real "I" of you. Knowing this you know all there is to know. Here are some thoughts which may help you to come to know this. Reflect on them.

* * *

Knowing your Self is being your Self.

* * *

The ultimate goal of every being in the universe is total freedom; and that is when you are only your Self.

* * *

The only reason why you are not aware of your Self is simply because you want to be a single body in the world.

* * *

Everyone will someday wake up to the fact that he is the Self.

* * *

To see your Self, you have to quiet the mind enough. When the mind is being stimulated by the thousands of thoughts in the subconscious, there's little chance of seeing your Self. The thousands of thoughts culminate in tendencies. Drop a tendency and you eliminate the thousands of thoughts under it.

* * *

The only things preventing you from being your Self are your mental habits called tendencies or predispositions. Will them out!

If you discover that the source of the tendencies or pre-dispositions is the Self, your Self, you drop them then and there.

* * *

When the mind gets free enough, then the Self of you takes over and you are from then on Self-propelled.

* * *

To be the non-Self requires much effort, and is the effort we feel in life.

* * *

It requires no effort to be your Self!

* * *

The effort that you think you use to try to be your Self is the effort you use in trying to resist being the non-Self ego.

* * *

Your wishes to be the ego and, at the same time, to not be it, doubles the effort.

* * *

All the effort you're involved in is effort to be an ego, or to resist being an ego. Do you see what the problem is? It is your constant effort. You must become effortless.

* * *

There is only one real killing and that's the killing of the Self. Kill the Self and you've got ego and troubles. So everyone is a murderer of the Self who thinks he is an ego.

The only reason why anyone isn't aware of the Self is because he wants other than that.

* * *

If one wanted the Self as much as he wanted the world, he would soon have it.

* * *

When you find more joy within yourself than in anything else, then you're really moving in the right direction. If you find any joy in life, you're in the wrong direction. Enjoying anything is wrong. Seek joy within. Be joy. There's nothing needed to enjoy if you are all-joyous.

If we are enjoying anything, we are in duality. If I enjoy this, there's "I" and "this." If there's God (Self) alone, there can't be any "I" and "this."

The basic Truth is that you are all joy. Enjoying something will impose an extreme limitation upon your natural state of all-joy. To enjoy something, you're recognizing something other than you. So, I repeat, we should never enjoy anything. Seek joy only within and then the natural state of infinite joy is discovered.

* * *

There is really only one happiness; it is being our very own Self. The happier we are, the more we are dwelling in our Self.

* * *

Every time you're high you're only being your Self, and it feels terrific.

* * *

Living in your Self is living in ecstacies. Living in worldly desires is living in miseries.

* * *

Everyone every moment is experiencing his Self and every moment saying otherwise.

* * *

It's only without thought that you can be the Self.

* * *

Discovering and being your Self is either easy — or impossible.

* * *

Finding the Self is the easiest thing in the universe when you do it. When you don't do it, when you continuously keep looking away from It, you can never see It. And then it is the most difficult thing in the universe.

* * *

Being your Self is easy. Being an ego is difficult.

* * *

When you realize what you are, it's the dropping of what you are not that is the growth. Each time you see what you are, you should drop that which you are not.

* * *

Everyone is seeking the Self, calling It by different names.

* * *

Anyone who's seeking happiness is seeking the Self. There are two kinds of people in the world: those who are consciously seeking God, happiness, the Self, and those who are unconsciously seeking them.

In the consciousness of materiality (mammon) there is no God (Self).

* * *

You cannot see God in the world until you see God in yourself.

* * *

God is All and God is Perfect. Therefore, anything that we see as imperfect is in us.

* * *

If you see separation you see not the Self.

* * *

When the world is real it is heavy. When the Self is real the world is light.

* * *

When our false identity as a body-mind disappears, our real identity as Self appears.

* * *

We are the Self now. All that we have to do is to let go of the concept that we are not.

* * *

The Self is God. The ego is the devil.

* * *

God (your Self) is infinitely individual and individually infinite.

The most beautiful is God.

* * *

There is something far more beautiful than nature — it is the Source of nature, the ultimate beauty — God.

* * *

No matter how much trouble man can get himself into, God is more resourceful in getting him out of it.

* * *

When we behave like God, we have God-like powers.

* * *

God (Self) can materialize anything instantly.

* * *

The All that is God is not every little thing; it is the singular same Essence behind all the little things.

* * *

God and good are sometimes used synonymously. Because everyone wants good, they make God good. God is above good and bad. However, good leads us to God.

* * *

If God is All, that leaves no room for the devil.

In Reality there is only God (your Self).

* * *

It's better to think of Self rather than God, because you generally think of God as other than you and you generally think of Self as you.

* * *

There's no such thing as an external called God. There is a God, but It is the internal beingness of each one.

* * *

Everything that is, is the Self, has its isness, its beingness, in your Self, God.

* * *

God is this World, the way this World is, and not the apparency that we see.

* * *

God, Truth, the Self is changeless. If God knew change, He wouldn't be changeless. There is no action in God. God knows nothing of this World as we see it. God is only the changeless beingness behind the World.

* * *

Everyone experiences his Self every moment of his life.

* * *

My Self is the nearest of the near and the dearest of the dear.

* * *

Look to the Self for everything!

* * *

If you want to get more comforts, know thy Self.

* * *

The only answer to all problems is knowing your Self.

* * *

We will never be completely satisfied until we are completely being the Self.

* * *

To discover your Self is the reason why you came into this world.

* * *

Everyone is seeking his Self in his every act.

* * *

The ultimate happiness is the Self. Any other happiness is only a bit of the Self.

* * *

When you know that the only joy there is, is of the Self, you take it directly and in its fullness rather than meagerly, as you formerly took it.

* * *

The only one needed to know your Self is yourself.

* * *

This feeling of needing someone else to be your Self is ridiculous. It limits your being your Self.

* * *

Everyone is actually the Self expressing the Self as extreme limitation, identifying as a limited body-mind. When you say "I" and add nothing to it, that's It.

* * *

When you are not identifying with the ego, you are the Self.

* * *

The only direct knowledge is of the Self. All other knowledge, needing something external to ourselves, is indirect.

* * *

If, at this moment, you identify with your Self, you are infinite.

* * *

That part of you that really is, your beingness, is eternal. It's the I that you really are.

* * *

The little self, the ego, is nothing but the innate infinite Self assuming that It is limited. There are no two selves, one higher, the other lover, no two "I's." There is only one Self. It is perfect and always will be perfect, even though you make the false assumption that It is imperfect and limited. You are now, always were, and always will be your Self.

* * *

Although one always experiences his Self, he usually needs to be directed to It before he becomes aware of It.

* * *

It is the Self that is the source of the ego, the source of everything.

* * *

You are every moment the unlimited Self, every moment saying, "I am limited." When you drop into the Self you stop saying, "I am a limited body-mind."

* * *

Look only at the Self; then the ego is eliminated.

* * *

When you dwell in your Self you have no desire to be liberated. It is only when you are in the ego that you desire liberation.

* * *

The Self is not aware of the ego, and the ego is not aware of the Self.

* * *

When I, the infinite Being, feel like a body, it's the infinite Being imagining it is feeling like a body.

* * *

When the Self is real, the body is not real, and vice versa.

* * *

Identify with your body and the extreme limitations of a body are yours. Identify with your Self and you are all things, all knowledge and power, with no limits.

* * *

There isn't anyone who couldn't materialize anything right now, if he or she would just let go of identifying as the limited body.

* * *

If you will discover your Self, you'll see that the body and mind are servant to you.

* * *

Obtain and maintain direct experience of the Self. It is easier to obtain than to maintain direct experience.

* * *

Every time you say "I" it's everything, all the power in the universe. Every time you add something to It, you pull It down into limitation.

* * *

When you see the Perfection, you see the other one as the other one really is, which is the real thing — the perfect Self.

* * *

There's not a higher Self and a lower Self. There's only you identifying with your limitless Being or identifying with your limited being.

* * *

You're never satisfied until you go all the way.

* * *

There's only one thing that satisfies fully and eternally and that's total awareness of your Self.

Everyone is aware of a selfhood. It is the Self, being wrongly identified as only a body.

* * *

If you would just be aware only, you would be your Self. If you would <u>be</u> only, you would be your Self.

* * *

This infinite glorious Being that we are, being absolutely perfect, can never change. It's always there.

* * *

The greatest of all teachers is your Self.

* * *

Look to your Self until you see It completely.

* * *

All Beingness is God, your Self.

* * *

In the Self there is no haver, having or thing had. There is no doer, doing or thing done. There's no knower, knowing or thing known. There, there's only Being, being all Beingness.

* * *

When man seeks and discovers the seeker, he discovers that:

In the Self:
God is not being something, God is beingness.
God is not conscious of anything, God is consciousness.
God does not enjoy anything, God is joy.
God does not love anything or anyone, God is love.

In man:
His beingness is God.
His consciousness is God.
His joy is God.
His love is God.

* * *

Act as though you are the Self. This will lead you to seeing It.

* * *

The Reality of you (Self) is perfect, all joyous, all glorious, all happy.

* * *

The higher you go, the more you realize your Self and the more you treat others as your own Self.

* * *

Being the Self is being selfless. In that state you are interested only serving others, serving them as your Self.

* * *

The Self is absolute, profound, indescribable peace.

* * *

The only requisite for the realization of the Self, your Self, is stillness.

* * *

When one realizes his Self, all his actions and possessions are not perceived as his. He has given up "me" and "mine." Everything is the Self.

* * *

When you experience the Self, you can't tell about It. Anything you can tell something about isn't It. It's the state of only being. There's no action there; there's no form there. It's Isness, and that's all that It is. You can't use It, you can't know It — you can only be It. When you're there, there's only One — You, and that's all there is.

* * *

Anything but the Self is wholly imagination. The ego is only an apparent actor in the imaginary story script you wrote. Thou are That, here and now. Do not delude yourself. Drop your illusory limitation.

* * *

The Self is Quiescence, perfect Awareness with perfect Stillness.

> He who seeks God will not find God in duality.
> There is no human, God being All.
> There is no time, no becoming.
> There is no creating in total perfection.
> Only God beholds God, there being nothing else.
> Only God loves God, God being All.
> Be still and know that you are God!

* * *

There is only God, nothing else. If there is only God, then I am That. At the end of the road we discover that there is only "I", all alone.

* * *

You are the Self saying otherwise — but that doesn't make it so. No matter how much you say otherwise, you are that infinite Being right now.

* * *

You can't become your Self — you are It!

* * *

Every time you say "I" that's the Self — if you would only stop there!

* * *

The word "I" with nothing added to it, is your Self. When you just say "I" that feeling of "I" is the Self. But when you say "I am something," that isn't It. But just pure "I" and only "I" is It. When that is all you see and all you know — that's God, your Self. That's why God is closer than flesh! Just hold on to the work "I" only, "I, I, I, I," Try it when you are alone. Just "I, I" and not "I am a body," but "I, I, I, I," that feeling of being. Hold That; experience It; be It! It is your Godhead — your Self!

* * *

"Look away from the body. Look away from the mind. Look toward the beingness that you are and never stop until you fully discover that Thou Art That!"

Lester Levenson

Session 36

THOU ART THAT

THE RIDDLE

At some level, everyone is aware of the infinite being that he is. Are you aware of the "I" that you are? The word "I," — that's it. That's the beingness part of you, but it is only the beingness part. If you experience "I am," — that's it. That part of you is infinite. And you are experiencing it all the time. There's no time when you are not experiencing it — otherwise you'd go out of existence.

However, you override it and hide it from yourself by saying "I am a body." And what you are doing is that you are saying "I, the infinite being, am this body." So, if you use the word "I" you are talking about the infinite being that you are. Every time you say "I am something," you are saying "I, the infinite being, am a limited something." And being Infinite, It allows you to assume limitation, as much as you want. That is why you can do such a good job of limiting yourself. Does that make sense?

QUESTIONS AND ANSWERS

Q: Yes.

Lester: We can drive ourselves into such extreme limitation that we think we are victims of our environment and subject to it. And it is an infinite being doing that!

Q: Why do we not realize that we are unlimited beings?

Lester: We have the conviction that we can't do it. If we were not convinced that we couldn't do it, we could do it quickly, even in a moment. How long should it take one with all knowledge, all power to recognize that he is all knowledge, all power? No time! And each one of us is that — all powerful, all knowing. It seems so hard, almost impossible, only because we won't do it. That's why it's so difficult— we won't do it!

We hold the concept that we are a body, rather than an infinite, unlimited being. As long as we hold to that concept, we are stuck with it. We don't look at the other, the opposite side of us which is unlimited.

356

Q: Well then, could you say that the only thing between us and realization is a thought?

Lester: Yes. It is a thought which is the culmination of a lot of thoughts.

For example, if you just examine how your thoughts flow after I tell you that you are unlimited, you will discover that immediately after hearing me you dive right into the thoughts of being a limited body. When I say that each one of us is infinite, unlimited, right now — at that moment you get a feel of it. Are you aware of the feel that you get as I say it? Right now, everyone here is infinite, unlimited omnipotent, omniscient, omnipresent. When I say that to you, for that instant you feel it, but the next moment you think you are the body, and immediately take your full attention off what you really are and put it on the concept of being only the body with all its affiliations.

All right, now that you have heard this, why don't you stop doing this to yourselves.

You have an example right now of what I've been talking about. Can you see what just happened? If what I said had been held on to, you would not have been distracted. But we're so interested in bodies that we immediately gravitate toward them. This is the problem — our persistence in being bodies. Every moment we hold that we are limited bodies. What you need to do is stop doing just that. Will you do it? If you do, you will see the infinite being that you are.

It's really simple, but I know it seems extremely difficult. Not only difficult but may even seem impossible. But this is only because we just don't do it, and that makes it impossible. We've heard these things again and again and again. But what use is it listening to this — if we don't do it? And, as I said, being infinite, there isn't anyone here who couldn't be the infinite being he is right here and now — if only he would do it. So, what you need to do is to get with yourself, look at yourself, and do it. And it's that simple.

How many of you women go about every day trying to discover that you're a female? None. Who of you men go about every day trying to discover that you are a male? Why don't you? Because you accept it without any doubt whatsoever. But you do not accept that you are infinite. Why not? Why play the game of limitation and be miserable? Why? I'm asking you the questions now instead of you asking me.

357

Why don't you be what you are, instead of this limited body? After all the body is a very cramped thing to be, and it hurts, lifetime in and lifetime out. Why insist on being so cramped and incapacitated. Compared to what one really is — infinite, unlimited and totally free. It is ridiculous, isn't it?

Maybe someone might want to answer the question, "Why don't you be what you are — infinite?"

Q: What does it feel like to be infinite?

Lester: Absolutely no limitation in any direction what so ever. No limitations, total freedom from everything — needing no food, no oxygen, no job. Instantly materializing anything you want. Being anywhere in the universe. Being as tall as you want, or the size of an atom. Being at perfect peace and contentment. Being in the most delightful state possible.

Q: What happens to this body when that happens?

Lester: To really know that you should experience what you are. Otherwise the reality on the body can't be understood. When you see what you are, only then do you know what the body is. It turns out to be a thought. A thought just like in a night dream when you dreamt about being a body in a situation. And when you awoke you said, "Oh, my gosh, that was all in my mind." The same thing happens to this body when you wake up from this dream called the waking state. You see the body, but you know it to be the dream nature that it is.

Do you see how much you're concerned about the body? And this point I make: Be as concerned about your infinite being as you are about your body, and, if you are, you will discover that you are infinite.

Q: What I really meant was, when you are away doing these things, how does this body function?

Lester: Automatically. The difference between how you are functioning now however, and how you can function is that when you focus, you can't be away from the "I" that you are. You're right where your "I" is. When you say "I," that's where you are. The individuality never leaves you, you never leave it. The "I" that you are always is — it's eternal. That's the real being that you are.

And if you will be that "I," and only that "I," then everything will turn out to be like a dream. And when you see it fully, this state you call reality turns into a dream that never really was. It's the same as when you wake up from a nightmare. As long as you remain in it, it's very real. It only becomes unreal to you after you awaken. Right? The exact same thing happens to this waking state dream when we wake up from it. We first say, "Oh, my gosh, it was all a dream," and then we add, "that never really was." And that's what happens to your body. You then see it as a dream body.

Your body will change but you never will. You don't disappear; you don't lose anything; you just take on more and more until you see yourself first, as every being, as every body, then as every atom in the universe. There's no reason to fear losing your body, or losing anything. You gain more and more until you become infinite. Yet, most of us are fearful lest we're going to lose our body and be nothing. That's a serious error. You could be a hundred bodies!

Q: If you think of the body in terms of beingness...

Lester: If you do, you're committing a gross crime against the word "beingness." Beingness is the infinity that you are. Your beingness is infinite. Your being a body is an extreme limitation in your beingness.

Q: We think of body in terms of limitation; that's the ordinary concept of body.

Lester: Right, which means we have to let go of the concept that the body is I. As long as we hold that, we are holding the concept: I am extreme limitation — a physical body.

Any slight maladjustment in the body and it dies. And everyone knows that. We know that sooner or later the body dies. It's a very disposable thing and everyone knows that sooner or later we will dispose of it, right? So if we hold on to this limitation and keep ourselves in extreme confinement it follows that we will always be afraid of the loss of the body. It is analogous to identifying with our car. To leave it, to trade it in or sell it would seem to us a terrible loss. And yet most of us do not think this way about our cars. They are temporary means of transportation . They are not us. Or viewed another way. We are like birds in a cage. The door opens but we refuse to fly out — free!

Q: Well, this sense of beingness, infinite beingness, is far more concrete than our present sense of body, is it not?

Lester: It should be. This is what, in effect, I am trying to say. If you just hold on to your sense of beingness, and only that, and not add "this body is I," — just hold on to your beingness only, and hold it, and hold it — you'll be letting go of the feeling that the body is I. And you'll get an insight into this beingness. And then you will remain in it. Then your beingness is very concrete to you and your body is like a dream body.

When you are only beingness you recognize that your beingness is all beingness. I say that everyone is, right now, that infinite beingness. And the infinite part of you is the "I," the beingness of the "I," the "I am." And that if you would hold that, that would become real and concrete to you, and all the limitation, misery, and trouble of the body would automatically be gone.

Q: I've had a few glimpses of that but holding it is a different thing.

Lester: The reason you don't hold it is because you are holding on to the belief that the body is you.

Q: The thing is that this beingness cannot be conceived of with the mind, can it?

Lester: Right. However, you don't have to conceive of it if you are it. Do you have to conceive of being a man or a woman? Just be it and be it only. Be it completely every moment.

Q: But this metamorphosis, this change that must take place within the individual, requires some intellectualization at first?

Lester: The intellect directs you toward looking away from what you are not, and looking at what you are. In that sense, you're right. We ask, "What am I?" and that's intellectual. However, the answer is an experience.

Q: Now this is what I was getting at. When does this intellectualization of the infinite stop and the experience begin?

Lester: When your thinking quiets enough. Then you see what you are and it becomes real to you.

Q: But you're not conscious of that transition?

Lester: You're conscious of letting go of the concepts of limitation. Discovering the infinite Being that you are is no transition, because you are that now; you always have been and always will be That. So there can't be any transition there. It's the letting go of the thoughts of limitation that is a transition.

Q: Isn't it difficult for one to think of his inner being experiencing it?

Lester: It's impossible only in your thinking. You must experience it.

Q: And yet it's real; you do come into it; there's no doubt about it?

Lester: Yes, sooner or later. When you get so fed up with torturing yourself, you then let go of all the nonsense of limitation and separation, and you become what you really are — infinite. Now, most people on earth will take millions of years to do this, and after what we've talked about you can see why.

When we take into account all people on earth you're very advanced; and yet look at how much you are holding on to being only that body! Your questions and talk relate mostly to the body, its transition, and what happens to the body.

Still I'm hoping to provoke you into letting go of identifying with the body, by telling you it's impossible to be infinite as long as you insist upon being the body. As long as you persist in being the body, it is impossible. You're stuck. You could remain stuck for millions of years.

I ask you, have you ever accepted the concept that you have no limitations?

Q: I've accepted the idea intellectually, but obviously not in practice.

Lester: That is true and because you believe you are finite it is impossible to be infinite. These bodies are very frail things, and they don't last very long. And yet we insist and persist in being the body. Now any time anyone decides, really decides, not to be it — then he will allow himself to see his infinite beingness.

What do we do twenty-four hours a day? We cater to the body;

we think we are it! We wake it up in the morning, we wash it, we dress it, we beautify it; we send it off to work so it can earn some money, so that we can put some other life (food) into it so it can digest & process that life inside so that it can persist. And then we go home and we park it for the evening. It is such a wonderful life that we have to escape from it; every night we have to go unconscious, that is, sleep. And this we repeat day in and day out, life in and life out — until we decide that we are not the body, that we are more than the body, that we are infinite beingness.

It is really simple. And I know I am repeating myself, but the repetition is necessary. The difficulty is the holding on to wanting to be the body. In doing so, we are constantly saying, "I am the body; I am not infinite." And, of course as a result, we can't feel the unlimited joy or happiness that we're seeking.

Q: What do you mean when you say we have such a wonderful life that we have to go unconscious?

Lester: This life, that we think is so great, we cannot take twenty-four hours a day; for about eight hours every day we have to escape it through the unconscious state of being asleep.

Q: While asleep, where am I? Why can't I remember?

Lester: Because you believe you can't. The reason is that you don't want to, because, unless you relate to the physical body and world, you believe you are a void. However, notice the fact that, although you drop the physical body and world in sleep, you still exist, don't you?

Sleep is an escape from this world of ours. As we go up into higher states of beingness, we all reach a place where we don't sleep any more. When we do not dislike the world, or state in which we exist, there's no need to go to sleep.

How wonderful is this world, this current state of awareness if we have to escape from it every night? Experiment with what I am saying — let go of it and be what you are. Be infinite. Stop looking at the world and look at the "I that I am." Keep your attention on the "I that I am" until you see it fully, and you'll drop being only a physical body with all the limitation associated with it.

Q: We keep imagining that this little limited life brings us happiness, and that helps keep us bound, doesn't it?

Lester: Yes, so why do it? Everyone is seeking the infinite being that he is. You call it happiness, happiness with no sorrow. It is your Self, your beingness. Why not just be it? Why don't you do it?

Q: Well, I guess we don't want it badly enough; we're afraid to go all out.

Lester: That's it — you don't want it enough. For whatever reason, you want to be the limited body with all its adjuncts of limitation — sickness, trouble, and finally death. Ridiculous, isn't it?

So what you are saying is that if this were the most important thing in your life, it wouldn't take long to become free and infinite. But instead we all have our side tracks which keep up going in all directions.

That's it. I'm saying we really don't want this knowledge of our unlimited state enough. Therefore our attention is in the other directions.

Q: Do you think we have resistance because we do not know exactly what is there for us?

Lester: Yes and no. We know we're infinite and we're seeking it. In our every act every day we're seeking this infinite being that we are. We call it happiness. If we would trace happiness down to its source, we would discover that there is no happiness in external things or people. Happiness is something we experience within. And it's there all the time if we just don't cut it off by making it dependent on someone liking us, or getting gold. Once we say, "In order for my inner happiness to be, I must have gold," we cut off that happiness unless we get gold. So we're cutting off that unlimited happiness and saying it's in the world, in tiny bits, while all the time it's unlimited right within us, not out there in the world. But, as you said, we're so convinced that it's in the world that our attention is in direction other than on the infinite Being that we are. If we really wanted to see this infinite Being that we are, our attention would be there all the time.

Q: And we could be That right at that moment!

Lester: Yes. At this moment, or soon, or at the very best in a month or two. And yet instead, we condemn ourselves to millions of years of misery by persisting in being the body.

Q: If one experiences very intense misery where everything seems to be cut off — an awakening can come out of this sometimes, can't it?

Lester: Yes. That's the way it usually happens. When we are in the direction of limitation we keep making ourselves more and more limited, until we go to extremes and think we are in danger of becoming incapacitated with something severe; with sickness or death. Then, with our determination, which everyone has, we say, "To hell with this!" and we go in the right direction. However, we could and should go in the right direction out of a sense of joy and discovery. We could go in the right direction because freedom is so wonderful.

Q: I think the tendency often is to try to contact the infinite and then use it to make this finite life more comfortable, pleasant, prosperous and things like that.

Lester: That's true. We try to contact our unlimited power and the use it to make a better body and world. We can make the body and world better, but we cannot achieve sustained happiness, because being subject to this body and world is being subject to limitation and non-freedom.

Q: Still, getting rid of your body isn't going to help much though, is it?

Lester: I'm not suggesting you do that. Until you consciously leave your body, if you forcibly got rid of your body, you would just come back again through the womb and wait twenty or so years while growing up, before starting again to learn that you're not the body. So forcibly dropping the body would be a very wrong thing to do. But to show you how much you think you are the body, just ask yourself how close you could come to throwing your body out on the highway and letting cars run over it. This will show you how convinced you are that your body is you.

Q: Is it our unconscious mind that prevents us from being infinite?

Lester: It's you, making your thoughts unconscious. I say it's you; it's not your mind. Or, if you want to argue it, show me this mind you are talking about. Where is it? And how is it holding you back? Does it have life other than you? Is it other than you? What is this thing?

You're preventing yourself, whether via the mind, via the body, or via anything. You are doing it. It's important that you take full responsibility because, if you don't, you will never get out of this trap.

Q: I understand that it is something that we have created ourselves, but it has reached such a proportion!

Lester: Not it, it is you who have reached such a proportion. So long as you blame something else, you'll never get out of it. You're doing it. Can't you see that you cannot undo your limitation as long as you'll not take responsibility for it? No matter what you call it, whether you call it mind, or body, you are doing it.

Q: I am taking responsibility for it, because I'm trying to do something about it.

Lester: OK. As long as you say, "I'm taking responsibility," that's all right. But when you say, "It is the mind," you are not taking responsibility for it; then the mind is responsible, not you. Do you see that?

Q: Well, I'm responsible for it; it's my creation.

Lester: Right. Whose mind is it? It's yours.

Q: But still, it has become a sort of Frankenstein that's gotten out of hand. And isn't that what stands in the way?

Lester: No. You do. As long as you think it's something other than you, you have no chance. As you speak, you are convinced that the mind is doing it, and not you.

Q: So we make the mistake that the mind is going to see, and the mind will never see It.

Lester: Right!

Q: And we're so conditioned to function as mind, that it seems to be the only tool that we know we have, and so we're using the wrong tool.

Lester: Right.

Q: So, what we need to do is just throw the tool out.

365

Lester: Right. Then what's left over is the infinite you. Throw the tool out. It takes no tools to be what you are!

Q: That's the mistake; we keep trying to do it with the mind, because that's the only thing we're familiar with.

Lester: It's not the only thing you're familiar with; you are also familiar with the "I" that you are. Just focus on the word "I." You are not your mind. You have a mind, but you are always experiencing this infinite being that you are, and it's the "I." You lose sight of this infinite "I" by identifying with the mind and body. Let go of identifying with your body and mind and what is right there in the pure "I," is an infinite being — you. Simple enough?

Q: You say the "I" has been for billions of years. Is the "I" always the same?

Lester: The "I" that you are is always the same changeless, eternal and perfect.

Q: It has always been the way it is, and the way it will be?

Lester: It has always been that way: perfect; changeless; immortal. And that's why we have the tendency to think of the body that way. We try to make it perfect and immortal, even though we know we can't.

Q: Does the body serve a purpose?

Lester: Yes, it is a vehicle that you occupy for this stage of the journey toward realization. But it hurts; it confines and this serves to redirect you back to seeing that you are infinite. The purpose of having the body is to help you learn that you have no limitation. So you conjured up the extreme limitation called the physical body, in order to learn that you have no limitation. That body is going to hurt more and more as you think that you are it, until someday you say, "The heck with it!" Then with full determination to see what you really are, you suddenly awaken to what has always been, that you are infinite.

Q: Has the "I" always used the body?

Lester: No, the "I" never used the body. The "I" is changeless and perfect. The "I" imagined, dreamed it used the body. It's an illusion;

it's a dream, but while you're in the dream it seems real. Wake up out of this dream. See what you are. That is the thing to do.

Notice how much you ask me questions about the body? Are you aware of that?

Q: In order, I guess, to define it.

Lester: No, you are trying to express your infinity in terms of this extreme limitation. This is why you're stuck. Reverse it. Let go of the body. Put all your attention on the infinite "I" that you are, and only then do you have a possibility of seeing the infinite "I" that you are. You must let go of the concept of that body being you.

Q: Pain is a great awakener then, isn't it?

Lester: Yes. However, we're not aware of how much pain there is, because we have accustomed ourselves to it and made ourselves immune to the real amount. Because we're infinite beings and we're trying to be this limited body — it's very painful. And when you awaken from this dream, you'll see how much pain there was. It's almost infinite pain compared to what you really are — infinite joy.

I'm emphasizing that you should be not the body; you should be not the mind—just be.

Q: In meditation, doesn't one use the mind to a certain extent?

Lester: Yes, however meditation is used for quieting the mind. You use the mind to quiet the mind. When the mind is quiet enough this infinite being that you are becomes obvious. That is the whole purpose of meditation. If anyone gets his mind quiet enough, he cannot help but see this infinite being that he is because it's only the thoughts that cover It. And the mind is nothing but thoughts. So, meditation is used to get the mind quieter, until you get it so quiet that you see your Self, your real Self.

Q: Would directing the thought toward the infinite be a step to getting there?

Lester: Yes. However, it is another thought.

Q: It's another thought, but some thoughts are more God-revealing than others, are they not?

Lester: No thought can reveal God. Every thought hides or covers God, your Self. Every thought is a chain; nice thoughts are golden chains. A golden chain will keep you imprisoned just as much as an iron chain. You must undo all thinking. Get the mind quiet; quiet enough so the infinite being that you are is self-obvious. It's there all the time. The thoughts are the noise that's covering it. However, if you must have thoughts, a thought in the direction of God is much better than a thought in other directions, as it points you toward God.

Q: But if the infinite is non-mind, how can you speak of it as infinite, because infinite is a mental concept.

Lester: No. No mental thought can be infinite. Every thought is a limitation.

Q: Then how can you know that you are infinite? How can you vocalize it?

Lester: You cannot mentally conceive of infinity nor can you vocalize it. That is impossible. It's impossible to conceive of unlimitedness.

Q: Well, it's an experience.

Lester: Right, it's not a thought; it's an experience, the experience of being infinite. The mind can allude to it but cannot describe it. Any description is necessarily a limitation.

Q: Where does the mind begin and where does the mind end? And where does God begin and where does God end? And where does the infinite begin and where does the infinite end?

Lester: God, the Infinite, the Self, has no beginning and has no end. The mind has a beginning when you create it. It has an end when you let it go.

Q: It is a painful struggle to let it go.

Lester: The pain comes because you're holding on to it while trying to let go of it. The holding on to it is the pain. Why don't you just be what you are? Why question me on the opposite side — on the struggle? Why do you talk about it? Because you're interested in it and you would like me to relate the infinite to it.

Q: Well then, if when you think, you just know who is thinking, that takes care of it?

Lester: Right! Discover who the thinker is and you'll have the answer. When you discover who the one is that has the mind and has the body and does the thinking, you discover the real you — an infinite being. So look away from the body! Look away from the mind! Look toward the beingness that you are and never stop until you fully discover that Thou Art That!

"If you could stop thinking for one moment, you would discover what you are."

Lester Levenson

Session 37

RELEASE YOUR LOVING NATURE

Thank you, Greetings and Love to each and every one of you. I think the biggest surprise tonight was to me. I didn't know I was going to talk until about 10 minutes before eight this evening, when I was told I was going to be the surprise.

So I began thinking, "What am I going to talk about? Talk about you, talk about me?" Then I realized, "What's the difference? We are all in the very same boat called life." We're all doing, in my eyes, the exact same thing that I did. We are all looking for the summom bonnom. The highest good is the ultimate place. It is happiness, and we are without it all the time. Struggling for it, looking for it, wondering where is it?

Back in 1952, I claimed I found the place. It is right where I am. It is right where you are, and all this looking for it everywhere, every day year in and year out, is such a waste of time — when it is right where you are. We're all here in this classroom called earth, trying to discover something, the ultimate. And we are all looking for it externally where it isn't. If we would only turn our direction back upon ourselves, we would discover it is right here, right where I am, right where you are, right in your very own being.

I say are you, you say yes. I say that's it. Do nothing else but that, and you will be in the ultimate state of happiness. So why don't you do it? You are so habituated in looking for it over there, over there in him, in her, in this job — and it is never there. So we are all going through the same trip of trying to discover what is this all about, where is my happiness, and when we stop chasing after it out there and we turn inward, we discover that all these hard negative, terrible feelings are only a feeling. And that it is possible to get rid of these feelings by releasing them. All these feelings are subconscious programs — every bit of them put in as pro survival — it's not only fear, but survival. All our feelings have been programmed in to automatically keep us surviving. They keep looking out there, trying to survive, keeping our minds active subconsciously 24 hours a day, so never do we stop to think and discover what we are. If you could stop your thinking for one moment, you would go through the most tremendous experience that there is. That you are the totality of this universe in your beingness, that when you mind goes quiet, you will automatically see that — I am the most terrific being in this universe. I am whole, complete, and perfect. I always was, I am now and I always be.

So what is it that is keeping us from being in the most delectable state that there is? Simply the accumulated programs called feelings. All these negative feelings have us constantly struggling to survive, having us constantly looking away from this tremendous thing that we are, and all we need to do is quiet that mind and become self-obvious to ourselves of this tremendous being that we are.

How do we do it? I say it's simple. The Release® Technique. It happens to be the fastest, the most effective way there is to achieve this high state of being. When we are in total control of our universe, where every moment is a wonderful, wonderful moment, it is impossible to be unhappy. And I say that is our natural state when these negative feelings are released.

Some day you are going to do it. You are in the same boat where you are struggling, and you're doing everything to achieve that happiness, and some day you are going to get it because you will never stop until you get there. But if you want to do it faster, do it our way. I promise you will be very pleasantly surprised. Everything you are looking for is right where you are. All you need to do is to take off the blinders. Your vision is very blurred. You're looking through these subconscious programs — when you release them, your vision becomes clear and you discover you are the greatest. You're whole, you're complete, you're eternal. All your fear of dying disappears. And life is so comfortable after that, and there is no struggle, no struggle whatsoever, when you get these negative feelings up and out.

So I urge you to learn this technique. It's a tool, and in one week's time, there will be a big change in you for the better, and from there on, you will continue to get better and better, lighter and lighter, happier and happier.

This thing called love is your basic nature. All the love in the universe is in your basic nature. You will discover that happiness — your happiness — equates to your capacity to love, and conversely all your miseries equate to your need to be loved. Just love, love, love and you will be so happy and healthy and prosperous. But again, you need to lift out the non-love feelings. So again I urge you to try our way. I promise that you will be very satisfied. Try it, you will like it. Thank you so much for coming.

* * *

A few more words from

Lester Levenson......

A MESSAGE FROM LESTER

So we have had a chance to talk heart to heart. I hope this has helped you. And I want you to know there is much more help available. I have talked to you in a manner that is designed to provoke thinking that leads you to a new realization. I have talked to you in a way that attempts to reach the part of you that inherently and intuitively understands more than your intellect. All this leads you to wisdom. Wisdom that is higher than intellectual knowledge.

If you have found these conversations of value, I suggest you go on and explore the do-it-yourself method I have developed that will show you how to increase your understanding every day. It is called the Release® Technique. It will give you keys to self-growth and allow you to keep it going from here on. The Release Technique is based on the premise that each one of us has no limits except those that we hold onto subconsciously, and when we let go of our subconscious limitations, we discover that our potential is unlimited. Unlimited in the direction of health, happiness, affluence and materiality. The Release Technique will help you achieve the kind of life you want and even more importantly, it will assist you in achieving self-realization.

The Release Technique is a kind of post-graduate course to this book. Practice it and achieve the ultimate state.

* * *

Appendix A
About The Release® Technique

About the Release® Technique

As a result of his experience, Lester Levenson helped those who came to him for guidance in the manner that you were guided through in this book from 1952-1974. Then in 1974, he distilled that teaching into a powerful, do-it-yourself, system which he later named the Release® Technique.

In short, what Lester realized was that anyone could learn to let go of the primary roots of their limitations and restrictions. As they used the Release Technique, they uncovered more of their "Unlimited Beingness." The results were immediate, powerful and long-lasting.

Being a scientist, Lester tested out his system with people from all walks of life, ages, and educational backgrounds, and he found that anyone who applied themselves to its use created very profound changes in their lives. These initial results have since been verified by thousands of people, over almost 20 years, who have been creating dramatic changes in their lives.

Today, the Release Technique is available in the United States, Canada and Europe to individuals and corporations through live seminars, and on both video and audio tapes. This work is presented by the Sedona Institute, the non-profit organization Lester founded in 1981.

A Special Report

Hale Dwoskin, Director of Training

The following material is being made available for the first time outside of our live and video seminars. It's designed to give you some practical first steps you can take to help you incorporate releasing into your life. It is also designed to introduce you to what you can expect from our programs. I want to stress, however, that this is meant as an introduction to the concepts behind the Release Technique, not as a substitute. If you like this report, you'll love the fun-filled and powerful direct experience of it in our seminars.

The Suppression/Expression Cycle

We handle the feelings that stop us from achieving our goals the same as how we handle feelings in general — most of the time we don't. We usually let our feelings handle us. They push us around... they dictate what we can or cannot do... In short, a lot of the time they run the show and color even our most "objective" decisions.

So we often pretend we do not have feelings. We push them down and try to pursue our aspirations. As a result, we create an exhausting tug of war.

This kind of "suppression" **runs** a large part of our lives. Disappointments, frustrations, hassles, delays and petty annoyances all take their toll. In fact, we've all gotten so good at suppressing our feelings that it's going on all the time without our even being aware of it.

For example, when we've had a particularly rotten day, we often try to escape! We'll have a drink... or several drinks; we'll watch T.V.; we'll exercise compulsively; withdraw into anger, or in more extreme uses, succumb to serious addictions... We often live our lives **running** from our uncomfortable feelings!

In some ways, suppressing is like trying to move forward with your foot on both the accelerator and the brakes at the same time! It feels like carrying around the weight of the world on your shoulders. Not only does it stop you from attaining full realization, it also causes tremendous psychological and health problems as well!

Most of us suppress and suppress and suppress until we can't take it anymore. Then we EXPRESS. Under such conditions, the smallest thing will send us into a rage. A bad day at the office might result in a burst of anger toward our spouse or children. Tears will come to our eyes over a minor frustration. We'll say and do things that we later regret. Even people on a spiritual path who have gotten so good at suppressing, don't realize they are doing it until it's already taken its toll.

So in many ways, we're like walking pressure cookers pushing more down and WAITING to explode! Of course, expressing does let off some of the steam. But it's only temporary and it doesn't put out the fire. Sometimes it feels a little better to express and it is a little healthier, **but what about the person you just expressed to?** And what about the effects you have to deal with as a result of their reactions?

What about *their* feelings? And what about your feelings about what you have just done? Even the expressing we do in therapeutic situations, although it can be very beneficial, does not effectively undo the inner cause of our pain and suffering. So, we go about trying to suppress again. We're still caught in the cycle!

It's a mess! And I know it sounds exaggerated, but we live in a society based on denial of this whole problem, and sometimes exaggeration is needed to get our attention. Now that I have, let's look at the alternative to the Suppression -Expression Cycle.

THE WAY OUT

What is it? It's simple. Releasing — letting go of the negative feelings and emotions instead of suppressing or expressing them. Letting go of our stressful emotions is a natural ability that we all have, but seldom, if ever use. Imagine how good your life will be as you start using this ability to instantly dissolve even long-standing problems. The benefits reported from releasing by thousands of our graduates over the past 19 years has been nothing short of **miraculous.**

If you've ever watched a young child, you know they have the ability to let go of their emotions — at will. Of course they don't realize what they are doing. It just comes naturally to them. The sad thing is that as a society, we are *unknowingly training them out of this remarkable, natural ability.* "Big boys don't cry..." "It's not polite to get angry..." "Stop being a brat..." "Because I'm the mommy, that's why..." "I said no and that's it..." As we get older, we learn to suppress more and more until we forget that we ever knew how to let go.

But we *do* know how! In fact, it's easy. Can you remember the last time you had a really good belly laugh? Not an artificial titter but a real guffaw that came from deep within you! Can you remember how good that felt? Well, that's what it feels like to let go. Genuine laughter is an external manifestation of releasing. No, I'm not suggesting that you go around laughing all day, although it's not such a bad idea. But sometimes it's not practical, and could prove quite embarrassing. But once you learn how to tap your natural ability to let go, you'll discover a quiet, internal experience that produces the same wonderful sense of ease and joy and release as laughter.

Imagine how good you will feel and how effective you will become as you learn or re-remember how to use your natural ability to let go of your stressful emotions.

You can, with practice, learn to Release in any situation... without anyone else ever needing to know.

Releasing is the key to power and freedom

How could letting go give you this wonderful sense of power and freedom? It's simple. Make a fist and grip it as tightly as you can. Now grip it even tighter. How does it feel? Does it hurt? Are you knuckles getting white? Do you notice how the tension is spreading to the rest of your body? Don't let go yet. What can you do with your fist? Punch someone? If you did, you would probably break some bones in your hand. Keep squeezing until you can't hold it any more. Now, on the count of three, *throw* your hand open. One... Two... **Three!** How did that feel to let it go? It feels a lot better, doesn't it?

That closed, painful fist is a metaphor for what we do all the time with our feelings. We hold back, shut down and in the process, waste a lot of energy which could be used for a lot more productive purposes.

As you practice that letting go of your feelings, you'll discover new strength, more power and increased effectiveness in the world.

Learning how to Release

The following are some practical steps you can take to start incorporating Releasing into your life. These exercises are simple and they work. If you apply yourself to using them, you'll find that you will not only start to achieve your goals, but you'll feel lighter, happier and freer.

> A. <u>Exercise</u>
> Pick up a pen, a pencil, or some small object that you would be willing to drop without giving it a second thought.

> Now, hold it out in front of you and really grip it *tightly*...

pretend this is one of your feelings. First, notice that you're the one holding onto it. This is true with your feelings, too. We hold onto our feelings and forget that we are holding onto them. We often feel that they are holding onto us. This is not true... we are always in control, but don't know it. Now, let it go. What happened? You let go of the object — and it dropped to the floor. Was that hard? Of course not. That's what we mean when we say let go. You can do the same thing with *any feeling*.

B. Technique
Next time you're having an uncomfortable feeling, really allow yourself to feel it, then ask yourself, "Could I let it go?" I know it sounds too simple, but practice this and you'll see that you'll start letting go of your unwanted feelings. Remember, *it's a natural ability that you already have* — you're just working on remembering how to use it. The more you practice, the easier it gets.

C. Technique
As you focus on your goals, and feelings come up, ask yourself, "Would I rather have this feeling, or would I rather have this goal?" You'll find by just asking yourself that question, you will have a tendency to let go.

D. It's only a feeling
Simple statement, but so important. Often, we blow our emotional reactions to things **way out of proportion**. If you're trying to let go of a feeling and you're not letting yourself let go of it, just remember it's only a feeling... and you'll find yourself easily letting it go.

E. The Course
Take the Sedona Method Basic Course. One of the main focuses of our live and video trainings is to show you how to master your natural ability to let go.

You may be wondering why we focus only on the feelings... It's simple. Every time we have a thought, it's coming from an underlying feeling. Each feeling is made up of thousands and thousands of thoughts. As you let go of your negative feelings, you'll see that you automatically start to think more positively. You'll find this is a lot easier than trying to think positively on top of your negative feeling. Don't take our word for it — try it out for yourself and see what happens.

Here's what you can achieve

Letting go of your stressful emotions has many applications and benefits. Use the following list to give you an idea of how you can start changing your life for the better as you Release.

The Sedona Institute has been teaching people how to tap this natural ability since the early 70's. I've taken the liberty of interspersing testimonials from our students in this section so you can see how people just like you have applied Releasing to their lives.

Gain full realization

As you let go of your limiting feelings, your mind gets more and more quiet until you become self-obvious to yourself of this wonderful, glorious being that you are right now.

"This is the most enlightening course I've ever experienced. With continued use I can see how we can easily say 'Yes' to life, health, abundance, happiness, love and peace. I find myself 'letting go' instead of thinking I am and just stuffing my feelings. I feel more focused... and at ease."

Carolyn Schaefer,
San Francisco, CA

"I am able now to feel a great peace in my life, just like when I was a little boy, when I used to feel that life just flowed like a river."

Anonymous

"This has been a very freeing experience for me. It helped me very much to move forward in realizing my purpose for being here, and in the achievement of my goals and peace of mind."

John Adams, Mesa, AZ

Have financial security

Have you ever noticed that two people with the same background and training, in the same field, often perform very differently? Why? Their **attitude**. Our emotions create our thoughts, and our thoughts either put us into action or prevent us from acting. As you use your natural ability to Release, you'll create a solid, positive mental attitude which will help you succeed where others might fail, even in today's difficult economic times.

"For a long time, I felt like I was worth a lot more than what I was being paid for my work, but when I actually released on it — and my worthiness — I got a raise of $6,000 a year. Hooray!"

Penny Braun
Phoenix, AZ

"I increased my real estate commissions to well over $100,000."

Kay O'Connor
New York

Improve your relationships

Every feeling except love is a non-love feeling, and is therefore preventing us from loving those we care most about. As you Release your non-love feelings, you'll rediscover the magic that brought you together in the first place. It's like falling in love all over again.

"My wife and I are getting along for the first time in years! We can finally communicate."

Gary Simpson
New York

Take charge of your life

Most of us have long lists of things we have been trying to get ourselves to do or to stop doing. It's only our emotions that stop us from pursuing what's right for us. As you access your natural ability to let go, you'll start to check off items on both lists. Your life will get back on track and stay there. You can be in better control of your life.

"Releasing has enabled me to be more decisive — the final decisions come quicker and clearer. My energy level has dramatically increased! The daily chores are being done quicker and more cheerfully. Enthusiasm is returning into my attitudes in leaps and bounds."

Pamela Barber
Scottsdale, AZ

Find your perfect mate

Have you ever noticed that when you're in a relationship or in love, there doesn't seem to be a scarcity of men or women who are attracted to you? When you are not in need of a partner, they're all over the place. It's your longing for your perfect mate that keeps them away. As you let go of the longing, you'll become more loving and you'll start attracting potential partners like bees to honey. So you can find that person that makes your heart sing.

"Since learning how to release, I am feeling an amazing love toward people I know or have just met — whether or not I agree with their actions or speech."

Fred Hohne
Stony Brook, NY

Gain the competitive edge

Our fears and doubts make us defensive. When we're are defensive, we are holding in mind what we don't want and that's what we get. As you release your defensiveness, you see solutions, not problems. You naturally hold in mind what you want and you'll know how to take the offensive and win every time.

"Releasing continues to play a major role in this success. All of the key people in my company have taken your course. Not only has there been a dramatic (over 200%) increase in sales, but the best part is that we enjoy working together in harmony, watching our dreams unfold. As a company, releasing gives us a major advantage over our competitors!"

Rick Solomon
President
CPA NETWORK

"Releasing is an invaluable tool in helping to focus my mind on the real problems in my business and removing the hindrances to effective action."

H.S. Keefe, President
TALBOT, BIRD & CO.,
INC.

Be calm when it counts

You don't have to be in the middle of a natural disaster to see that crises and emergencies can happen anywhere, anytime. You will be prepared and you release. So no matter what life throws at you, you'll be able to handle it with **calmness** and **clarity**.

"I've noticed that I'm feeling very relaxed, objective and much more effective at work. Meetings that in the pre-Releasing days would have been very high tension are now very objective and enjoyable."

Greg Worsley, President
G.M. WORSLEY, INC.

Eliminate stress

There are many techniques and courses which purport to show you how to manage, cope with or handle your stress. Wouldn't you rather just eliminate it so that even the situations in your life right now that are causing you the most stress become completely stress-free? By applying your ability to release, you can do just that.

"The Releasing has given me tremendous assistance in handling stress. I have highly recommended learning how to release to many of my colleagues and they have been very pleased."

Dr. Albert M. Golly,
D.C.
Colorado Springs, CO

"Without doubt the simplest and most effective means of stress alleviation that I have read about or experienced."

J.B. Lambert, President
T-BAR INCORPORATED

"I was feeling very stressed by having too much that I 'had to do.' When I let go of my feelings about my time and my feelings about myself, I immediately felt all the stress go."

Marian Humberson,
Albany, NY

Boost your performance

The Mutual of New York Corporation used this ability to boost the sales of their field underwriters **33%** over the six-month period after they learned how to release. The second three months were even better than the first. Their results continued to increase over time. Couldn't you or your company use an increase in performance?

"I achieved my yearly quota in 6 months and for the full year, my sales were 201% of sales quota. I attribute my success in selling to my use of the Sedona Method. It has reduced the feeling of pressure and increased my confidence level. I find that I am far more able to quickly see alternate ways of solving problems."

Norma De Sofi,
San Francisco

Be a better parent

Many times we know what we should be doing with our children, but we find ourselves doing things again and again that we know we should never do. This is avoidable whenever you access your natural ability to release. You can respond appropriately in the moment, have the **quality** time you have so longed for, and uncover and express the true love you have for them in your heart.

*"My daughter and I had a dysfunctional relationship and had lost touch. After learning how to release, I began looking for her again, and we have now reconnected. We not only have resolved our differences, but my daughter is now releasing, too! We communicate better now than we have in **years**!"*

Carole Dunham,
Miami, FL

Kick those nasty habits

Have you ever noticed when you reach for a cigarette or an extra piece of pie, it's when an emotion is pushing up that you don't want to feel? As you tap your ability to release you'll let go of whatever it is that is causing you to smoke, overeat, or hold onto any habit that you are now trying to get rid of.

> *"I am happy to tell you that I have made the biggest gain so far. At last, I have finally **quit** smoking — something that I felt only a **miracle** would accomplish."*
>
> Royetta Monroe,
> Los Angeles, CA

> *"I have no more craving of alcohol and drugs, which for the last 15 years have run my life."*
>
> Richard Preston,
> Boston, MA

Have boundless energy

Sometimes you'll work hard all day and come home exhilarated or do nothing and be totally exhausted? Suppressing all day long is exhausting. As you release throughout your day, you will have all the energy you need to accomplish all you choose. Plus, you'll be able to easily release whatever is robbing you of a **good night's sleep**.

> *"I can get much less sleep and feel energetic, stress-free and be productive during the day."*
>
> James Heller,
> New York, NY

> *"I'm able to have a good night's sleep after many years of having difficulty sleeping all night. It feels great!"*
>
> Rosella Schroeder,
> Dubuque, IA

"I use my ability to release when I have trouble sleeping and find that I can release to relax, stop worrying and sleep. If I wake during the night, I can release to again relax and go back to sleep."

R. Duane Clay,
Phoenix, AZ

Have more radiant health

Medical science now agrees that stress and suppressed emotions are a major contributing factor to the majority of all illnesses. Our graduates have reported back to us over the past 19 years many... some even miraculous... improvements in health as they used their ability to release, even though we have never attempted to treat, diagnose or cure anything.

"I have lost 90 pounds within the past year and a half."

Sandy Gabin,
New York

"When I started Sedona in January, I was taking Elavil and Valium for severe depression. It is no longer necessary to take any medication. I feel better than I have for many years."

Cynthia Mollod,
Great Neck, NY

"The most beautiful gain of all, and this one I can hardly write. It brings my so much joy — I feel I am finally free of the cervical cancer that threatened my ability to choose whether to have children or not. Learning how to release helped me discover the reason I was holding on to it, and gently let it go."

L. B., Los Angeles, CA

You CAN have it all

By applying what you learned in this report and mastering your natural ability to let go, you'll be well on the way to having, being and doing *whatever you will and desire.*

These challenging times demand new and dynamic solutions. They also require a high degree of readiness to adapt to change. Releasing is the key.

I know from my own personal experience, and from watching thousands of people use these concepts to live happier, healthier, prosperous and stress-free lives, that you can too.

You have what it takes. Just do it! We at Sedona Institute **expect** your success. Thank you for taking the time to read this report.

Accelerate your progress

We have a special video and live seminar training program for you and/or your company, designed to quickly and experientially show you how to master the materials contained in this report **and much more.**

What you will learn

The following is a partial list of what the course covers.

The Release Technique — Level One

Learn how to master your natural ability to let go of the stressful emotions that hold you back from abundance, success, happiness and inner peace.

    1. Learn how to easily identify what's stopping you from making more money, improving your relationships and having radiant health and experiencing bliss — and how that relates to what you are feeling *in the moment.*

    2. Learn how all the feelings relate and *how to stop them from holding you back,* from having all that you choose.

    3. Learn why you get stuck in lifelong habits and

patterns... and *how to break them...* Use this information to stop smoking, lose weight...

4. *Learn how to use releasing to make every part of your life better,* including your financial freedom, relationships and your health and well-being.

5. Master the process of achieving your goals with ease.

The Release Technique — Level Two

Learn how to identify the root cause of all limitation and how to let go of the basic programs that cause all pain and trouble. Turbo charge your releasing.

1. Learn how to *be in control all the time.*

2. Find the love and happiness *you have always been seeking.*

3. Learn how to let go of even your deepest insecurities and feel calm and safe *no matter what is going on around you.*

4. Unlock your power to create all that you choose.

5. Learn a unique, powerful process for solving problems and making decisions. End procrastination *for good.*

6. Learn how to safeguard what you have already achieved and produce increasing results from now on.

7. Learn the six steps to solidly building a new and exciting life.

A gift for a lifetime

The results you get from the Release Technique are cumulative — the more you use it, the more you will receive. As you practice this new ability, it gets easier and easier... until it becomes second nature. Our graduates have reported steadily increasing benefits over many years.

Two great ways to learn the Release Technique

Since 1976, thousands of people have learned the Release Technique in a relaxed and informal classroom type setting. It is presented in 20 hours over four days, designed to gently guide you into rediscovering your natural ability to release and mastering its application in all areas of your life — **without** the need to share anything of a personal nature.

Now you can also learn the Release Technique in the comfort and privacy of your own home or office with the Sedona Method Home Study Video Course.

The Home Study Course is presented through eight video tapes: It has all the advantages of the live course, as well as the added benefit of being able to review any part of the course *as many times as you would like.* It's like having your own personal instructor at your beck and call, any time you choose.

Both the Home Study Course and the live class come with your own complete set of course materials and workbooks, including the three Special Areas of Interest workbooks, entitled "Your Financial Freedom", "Your Relationships" and "Your Appearance, Health and Well-Being."

For information on ordering your video course or reserving a spot in a live class in your area, call us today at (800) 875-2256, or use the attached postcard for more information. You'll be glad you did. You have nothing to lose but stress and unhappiness... and everything to gain! Start living a happier, healthier, stress-free life **today**. Your goals are waiting for you now, including the ultimate goal of total freedom.

Sedona Institute

P.O. Box 32685

Phoenix, AZ 85064-2685

or

(800) 875-2256